lonely planet

NATIONAL PARKS *of* AMERICA

Contents

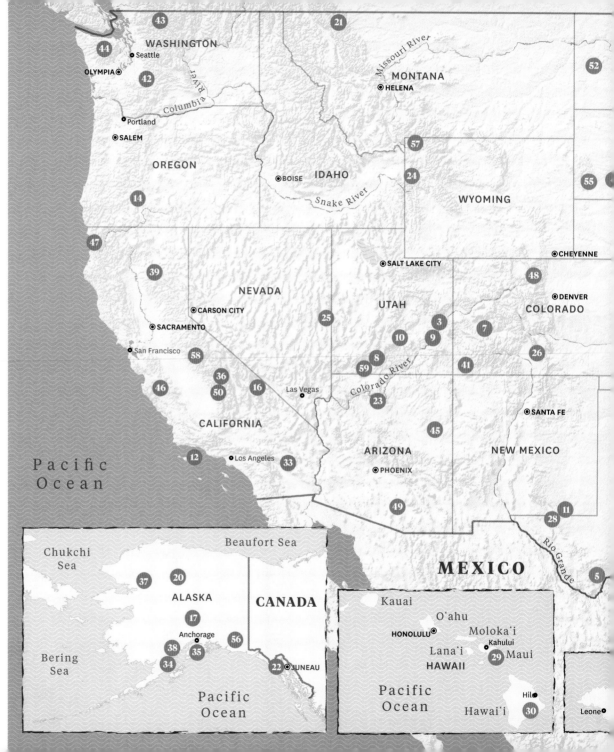

Introduction

I got lucky the first time that I visited an American national park. I was in Utah and with a few days free before my flight out of the state, and a pair of hiking boots in my luggage, I headed for the closest national park, not knowing what I'd find. That park was Bryce Canyon (see p46). It was October and there had already been some flurries of snow. When I arrived at a viewpoint overlooking a vast bowl – that I later discovered was called 'Silent City' – snow remained in the sun's shadow, highlighting every ridge and feature. But glowing red, yellow and orange under the blue sky were row upon row of Bryce Canyon's extraordinary hoodoos, narrow spires of rock formed as fins created by water erode into columns. It was an epiphany.

America's national parks are full of such marvels: the world's largest trees in Sequoia; its most spectacular geothermal site in Yellowstone; the grandest canyon. It's around these world-famous places that the story of the National Park Service is woven. President Woodrow Wilson created the National Park Service (NPS) on August 25, 1916, but the drive to protect some of America's most remarkable wild spaces, to be 'used and preserved for the benefit of mankind', began in the 1860s.

Perhaps the movement's most eloquent advocate was Scottish-born writer John Muir. He had worked in the Yosemite Valley in the 1860s and later, in 1903, camped there under the stars with President Theodore Roosevelt, who created five national parks during his administration. 'Thousands of tired, nerve-shaken, over-civilized people,' Muir wrote in *Our National Parks*, 'are beginning to find out that going to the mountains is going home; that wildness is a necessity...'

This book is intended to be a practical introduction to each of America's 59 national parks, distilled by Lonely Planet's expert authors. We highlight the best activities and trails, explain how to get there and where to stay, show you the wildlife to watch out for, and suggest ideal itineraries. Whether you're lucky enough to have a park on your doorstep or need to travel further, we hope that the following pages inspire you to explore what Stephen Mather, the first director of the NPS, described as America's 'national properties.'

Getty Images | Chris Murray

01

Acadia National Park

See New England at its most glorious from the seaside cliffs of Acadia, at the easternmost tip of the United States.

You're sitting on a smooth granite outcropping, the dark ocean pounding some 1530ft (466m) below. Finally, you see it: a blood-red finger of sunlight piercing the horizon. Slowly, the dark clouds go rosy pink, the ocean becoming an ever-lightening purple. This is sunrise on Cadillac Mountain in Acadia National Park, the first place the sun shows its face in the United States.

Much like New England itself, Acadia pings between utterly civilized and utterly wild. There's high tea on the lawn and there's harsh, crashing gray surf along rocky beaches. There are horse-drawn carriage rides and hikes through leg-slashing thorn bushes. There's lobster ravioli in thyme butter at the elegant bistros of Bar Harbor and there's roasting hot dogs over an open fire at the park's primitive campgrounds.

Painters and other artists 'discovered' the Acadia area in the mid-1800s, spending summers boarding with local fisherman and painting the stunning scenery. These 'rusticators' grew in number so quickly there were soon several dozen hotels catering to their needs. By the 1890s, Gilded Era captains of industry were arriving to summer in enormous 'cottages' on the island. But the Great Depression, WWII and, finally, a huge wildfire in 1947 destroyed this lavish lifestyle, along with most of the cottages.

In the early 1900s, George Dorr, heir to a New England textile fortune, began working to preserve the area from the onslaught of tourism and industry. The land that he and others donated to the federal government became Lafayette National Park in 1919, the first national park east of the Mississippi; its

name was changed to Acadia in 1929. Today, Acadia and the nearby town of Bar Harbor still attract moneyed Eastern elites who sail, hold charity balls and dine in the area's many fine restaurants. But like all national parks, Acadia is a democratic place, welcoming everyone.

↑ Catch the sunset at Bass Harbor lighthouse, which is now a private residence.
→ Try cross-country skiing in winter. Previous page: Jordan Pond.

Toolbox

When to go
The park gets the usual July/August rush, but it's just as pretty (if a bit colder) in May, June and September. In October, when the leaves burst into flaming reds and golds, it's positively heavenly.

Getting there
Acadia is on the coast of Maine, near the town of Bar Harbor. Most of the park is on Mt Desert (pronounced 'dessert,' as in cake) Island. The nearest sizeable airport is in Bangor, about an hour's drive from the park.

Park in numbers

74
Area covered (sq miles)

1530
Highest point: Cadillac Mountain (ft)

40
Miles of shoreline

→ Hold onto the handrails if you hike the steep and exposed Precipice Trail.

Stay here...

🏕 Blackwoods Campground
The only one of Acadia's three campgrounds open year-round, Blackwoods has tent sites set in shady forest. Roll out of your tent and onto the trail to Cadillac Mountain and other popular hikes. In summer, facilities such as a store and shower are available; in winter it's primitive all the way. The shuttle stops outside.

🏠 Holland Inn
Since there are no accommodations other than campgrounds within the national park, most visitors stay in nearby Bar Harbor. This white wooden inn has an austere Yankee charm, with friendly innkeepers. It's on a quiet side street just a few minutes' walk from the cafes and boutiques of Bar Harbor village.

🏠 Saltair Inn
Built in 1887 as a summer 'cottage' for a New York businessman and his wife, this Victorian mansion is now a charming B&B. Guests watch the light play over Frenchman Bay from the deck. Owners earn kudos for their advice about local sights and activities.

Do this!

🥾 Mountain summiting
The gem in Acadia's crown, Cadillac Mountain rises 1530ft (466m) above the crashing surf. The highest point on the North Atlantic seaboard, it's the first place to see the sun rise in America for much of the year. You can hike Cadillac but the easiest way to get here is to drive the 3.5-mile (5.6km) road to the top. Come at dawn bundled in your woolliest sweater to watch light break over Frenchman Bay.

🐎 Carriage riding
Acadia has some 45 miles (72km) of carriage roads, built by philanthropist John D Rockefeller Jr, who wanted to be able to get into the park without using a car. The hand-hewn stone roads and bridges are made of locally quarried granite – and are extremely photogenic. Explore them with a horse-drawn carriage ride at a leisurely pace.

☕ Having high tea
In summer everyone flocks to the rolling green lawns of Jordan Pond House to sit in wooden chairs, sip tea and munch warm popovers with jam. It's one of the park's most charming traditions, dating back to the 1890s. After filling your belly, head down the hill to stroll around the pond itself. This is a particularly family-friendly walk, with wood and gravel paths circling the clear water.

What to spot...

Encompassing roiling ocean, rocky beaches, dense forests, boggy marshes and granite peaks, Acadia has a dramatic diversity of flora and fauna. While you won't see many large mammals here, there's a wealth of amphibians, reptiles, birds and smaller mammals. Bar Harbor is a jumping-off point for whale-watching tours, while colorful starfish, crustaceans and sponges can be found on Acadia's shoreline. Much of the park is blanketed in spruce-fir forest; unique scrub oak and pitch pine woodlands can be found as well.

SPOTTED SALAMANDER These inky black amphibians with mustard-yellow spots typically burrow under moist leaves on the forest floor. In early spring, they head to ponds to breed.

PEREGRINE FALCON Acadia has been integral in boosting the population of these magnificent, light-brown birds of prey, who nest in the park in spring.

RACCOON Recognizable by their distinctive black 'eye masks,' these medium-sized mammals are considered pests in most of the US for their garbage-eating habits. (Store your trash properly when camping.)

Hike this...

01 Cadillac Mountain South Ridge Trail

The park's longest hike, this 7.4-mile (11.9km) round-trip climb gives killer views over the crashing gray Atlantic on the way to the top of the North Atlantic's highest peak.

02 Ocean Path

Explore tide pools along this 4-mile (6.4km) round-trip walk, which runs from Sand Beach to Otter Cliffs, passing the roaring Thunder Hole along the way.

03 Acadia Mountain Trail

Puff your way up the park's namesake mountain, taking in views of the deep blue waters of Somes Sound, the East Coast's only fjord. It's 2.5 miles (4km).

⬆ Winter brings storms to the coast, and snow and ice to inland areas for activities such as ice-climbing.

Itineraries

Be the first person in America to watch the sun rise, hike along pink granite cliffs or eat buttery lobster by the Atlantic. Whale spotting? That too.

➡ Cycle along the traffic-free carriage roads beside Jordan Pond and Eagle Lake.

01
A day

Get the best of the park in the least amount of time by hitting the major sights on Park Loop Rd, a 27-mile (43.5km) scenic drive around the east side of the park. The roads starts at the Hull Cove Visitor Center (stop for a map), then ascends Paradise Hill for dramatic views over Frenchman Bay, with Bar Harbor glimmering in the distance. Continue on to Sand Beach, the island's only proper sandy beach. (We must warn you, however, that the gray ocean water rarely rises above 55°F (13°C) – even in mid-summer – so unless you're a polar bear you'll probably just want to dip your toes.) A mile (1.6km) south is one of Acadia's icons, the Thunder Hole. When large swells hit this small, underground cave in just the right way, it produces a terrifying roar. Take in the 100ft-high (30.5m) Otter Cliffs before heading for tea and popovers at Jordan Pond House (summer only). Cap off the day with a drive up Cadillac Mountain to watch the late afternoon sun play on the waters more than 1500ft (457m) below.

02
Two days

On your first day, hit Park Loop Rd. At Sand Beach, walk the 4-mile (6.4km) round-trip Ocean Path to Otter Cliffs, taking time to explore the short spur trails leading along the pink granite cliffs to tide pools full of quirky sea creatures. If the tide's coming in the right way (ask at the visitor center), stop at Thunder Hole. Otherwise continue on to Jordan Pond House for lunch. Though famous for its afternoon tea, it also serves New England–inflected mains, such as lobster quiche and seafood chowder. Work off lunch with a stroll around Jordan Pond, whose picture-pretty waters seem like they could be home to fairies or other mystical creatures. Head back to Bar Harbor for an evening of exploring the town's boutiques and cafes. The next morning, get up in the pre-dawn darkness and drive up Cadillac Mountain to be among the first people in America to see the sun rise. Then head to the park's west side to spend the day paddling the waters of Long Pond, with dozens of hidden coves perfect for exploring.

03
Four days

On day one, do the Park Loop Rd as per the one-day itinerary, bringing a picnic lunch to eat at Sand Beach while you wiggle your toes in the chilly sand. On day two, hike the Cadillac Mountain South Ridge Trail, which traverses rocky outcrops and cool maritime forest to finish with jaw-dropping views over the wild gray Atlantic. On clear days you can imagine seeing straight to England. Reward yourself with a fat red lobster drenched in butter at the Trenton Bridge Lobster Pound, along the causeway connecting Mt Desert Island with the mainland. On day three explore the park's 45 miles (72.4km) of hand-hewn stone carriage roads by bike. The 8.3-mile (13.4km) Jordan Pond–Bubble Pond loop is popular for its shady forest and pond views; end at Jordan Pond House for afternoon tea and popovers on the neatly trimmed lawn. On day four, take a whale-watching tour from Bar Harbor. From summer to fall you stand to spot humpback, finback and minke whales breaching the blue-gray waters.

02

AS

American Samoa National Park

America's only south-of-the-equator national park occupies an island cluster offering beautiful beaches, remote reefs, magical mountains and extraordinary cultural encounters.

Scattered across 10 volcanic islands and two coral atolls in the deep blue immensity of the Pacific Ocean, 2600 miles (4184km) southwest of Hawaii, American Samoa hosts the US's southernmost national park. It features unique wildlife, towering topography and reef-fringed beaches. Immerse yourself in the 3000-year-old traditions of Polynesia's oldest surviving culture, discover 950 species of fish while exploring 450 aquatic acres (1.8 sq km) of coral reef, and trek through cloud forests to volcanic peaks.

Samoan history isn't recorded in written form – instead, beliefs, traditions and creation myths are kept alive through storytelling. The account of how a US national park came to be created in this far-flung land is an intriguing addition to the canon. It began with a 19th-century squabble between the US and Germany. Both nations used Samoa as a whaling base; the deepwater harbor of Pago Pago was perfect for refuelling their steam-driven ships. In 1889, an altercation threatened to flare into all-out warfare, until nature intervened and a typhoon sank all six battleships. Subsequently, the two powers agreed to split the islands between them.

A century later, US Congress authorized the creation of the country's 50th national park on the islands. Samoa means 'sacred earth,' and it wasn't until 1993 that the Samoan chiefs, guardians of the islands for three millennia, agreed to sign a 50-year lease allowing the National Park Service (NPS) to manage an area of rainforest, coast and coral reef on the three islands of Tutuila, Ofu, and Ta'ū. In 2002, the park was expanded to include Olosega and Ofu islands. Samoans retain a role as custodians, with villages offering visitor facilities in a traditional setting, adding a cultural layer to an already unique experience.

Toolbox

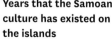

When to go
Located 14° south of the equator, the park has a tropical climate and is warm and wet year-round. June to September is the dry season, which is the most comfortable. There are several interesting carnivals in October, including the Moso'oi Festival, which features boat racing.

Getting there
Fly to the main island of Tutuila from LA (14 hours total) via Honolulu, Hawaii. Take a light aircraft between Tutuila and Ta'ū, from where you can hitch a lift on a local boat to Ofu.

Park in numbers

21.1
Area in sq miles – about one third of which is underwater

3170
Height in ft of Mt Lata (Ta'ū Island)

3000
Years that the Samoan culture has existed on the islands

◄ Looking towards Sunuitao Peak and Mt Piumafua on Ofu island.
► Red plumeria blossoms.

Stay here...

🏠 Tisa's Barefoot Bar
Camping isn't permitted anywhere in the park, but accommodations are available on all of the islands except Olosega. There are standard hotels in central Pago Pago, but a more memorable option is to stay in a beach-facing *fale* (Samoan house), such as those available at Tisa's Barefoot Bar on Tutuila.

🏠 Mauga's Homestay
To make the most of your visit, stay with a local family and learn about traditional Samoan culture and homelife. Several homestays are available around the park – including Mauga's on Ta'ū Island – where you can stay in the community, sleep in a *fale* and join in with activities.

🏠 Vaoto Lodge
Family-owned and -run lodges, such as Vaoto Lodge on Ofu Island, also offer accommodations with a distinct Polynesian flavor; the communal meals are often cooked around the barbecue pit and served 'family style' around a large table, while its position, a short stroll from a beautiful beach, can't be beat.

Do this!

🤿 Snorkeling
About a third of this 21.1 sq mile park is covered by coral reef and ocean, home to thousands of fish and 250 kinds of coral – the snorkeling and diving are world-class. Ultra-remote Ofu Beach is particularly special. Bring your own good-quality mask and snorkel. For cultural reasons, avoid revealing swimwear.

🏉 Connecting with locals
Community life is vibrant across the islands, and there are numerous opportunities for meeting the super-friendly locals, from taking public buses to going along to watch village dances and sports. Rugby is massively popular here, but Samoa's favourite game is *kirikiti*, a local version of cricket. Look out for longboat racing competitions too.

🪧 Guided touring
Numerous tours are available, including around the marine sanctuary, to millennia-old archaeological sites or through the park's forests, where a local expert explains how native plants were used in traditional Samoan medicines.

Hike this...

01 Mt Alava Trail
Trek the 7-mile (11.3km) round-trip through plantations and tropical rainforests to the top of Tutuila. Enjoy stunning vistas across the island, looking out for bats and birds en route.

02 Mt Healy Overlook Trail
Walk through the coastal forest of Ta'ū, past the sacred site of Saua (considered the birthplace of the Polynesian people) to the southeastern tip of the island; it's a 5.7 mile (9.2km) round-trip.

03 Trailless Hiking
Follow rainforest trails to Ofu's highest point (1621 ft/494m) and Leolo Ridge for breathtaking views of all three of the Manu'a islands and the national park's coral lagoons; 5.5 miles (8.9km) round-trip.

What to spot...

Thanks to their heartbreakingly lonely location, these remote islands are cloaked in endemic vegetation. Native mammals are scarce, and most birdlife is migratory. Tree life, particularly on Tutuila and Ta'ū, is rich, with all five distinct rainforest communities present – lowland, montane, coast, ridge, and cloud (the only place on US territory where this happens). Sea life here is exceptionally diverse, with hundreds of species of fish, plus whales and turtles.

SAMOA FLYING FOX These bats, American Samoa's only native mammals, play a crucial role in pollinating the islands' plants. This endemic species is a day-dweller and a lone ranger.

ORNATE BUTTERFLYFISH An intricately coloured but fragile species of tropical fish, which occurs only in coral-rich areas – commonly encountered in lagoons and on reefs around American Samoa.

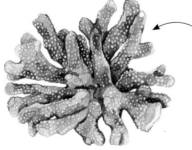

ANTLER CORAL This stony coral, part of the park's sub-aquatic decor, owes its colors to millions of single-celled marine plants, called zooxanthellae, that live embedded in its flesh.

Itineraries

Laze under coconut palm trees, snorkel in a coral paradise or hike some of the highest sea cliffs in the world, your only dilemma is: which island?

◀ Vatia Bay on Tutuila Island, showing tiny Pola Island.
▶ Beaches fringe Tutuila Island.

01
A long weekend

This is a long way to come for a few days, but if your time is limited it's possible to get a taste of American Samoa by exploring the main island of Tutuila and the parkland around Pago Pago. Rainmaker Mountain stabs 1716ft (523m) into the sky above this old deepwater port, where whalers and merchants once stopped off to get supplies and enjoy some R&R. Home to most of the population, this is American Samoa's closest claim to a city, but it's chilled-out and friendly.

Leaving town behind, join welcoming locals on the colorful buses that chug along the forest-fringed roads, zig-zagging through mountainous switchbacks and wending their way around the curvaceous coastline. Hop off at the various sandy coves that punctuate the rocky foreshore to enjoy picnics under palm trees, or to plunge into the ocean with a snorkel and mask. Save some energy, though, for a hike along the high-summit trail above the harbor, which joins several peaks, and rewards with wonderful views across the ocean.

02
Five days

Leave the main island behind aboard the twin-prop light aircraft bound for Ta'ū, 70 miles (112.7km) west of Tutuila, before touching down in the village of Fiti'uta, arrival point for American Samoa's Manu'a island group – Ofu, Olosega and Ta'ū. While the pace of life here is somnambulant, the scenery is anything but, with cloud-piercing peaks forming a serrated skyline and some of the highest sea cliffs in the world erupting right out of the ocean.

Ta'ū is home to American Samoa's highest peak, the 3170ft (966m) Lata Mountain, as well as the culturally significant site of Saua, popularly believed to be the birthplace of the Polynesian people. From the airport, you can find yourself in the national park within 30 minutes' walk, but there's no rush. With accommodations available on the island you can split your time between bumming on the beautiful beaches with a book and exploring the cloud forests skirting the volcanic cones that form the roof of the island.

03
A week or more

Going the extra distance to the remote island of Ofu is an experience reserved for true explorers. To reach the sensational shores of this little paradisiacal Pacific Ocean isle, you must first get yourself aboard a local fishing boat from Ta'ū.

This isn't a place for clockwatchers or those on a tight schedule – time is an abstract concept in American Samoa at the best of times. And once you do arrive, worries about how you might get back will likely evaporate, since you won't want to leave.

Ofu is all about the ocean.

Here, coconut palm–framed beaches lead snorkelers out into a warm aquatic universe, where thousands of fish scoot around cathedrals of coral in a kaleidoscope of color and activity.

You'll spend nights in a seaside *fale*, being lulled to sleep by the lapping of the water on the sand. And when you've had enough of idyllic indolence, there is plenty of walking to do, along ridgelines up in the hills and even across a narrow landbridge to the rainforest–cloaked neighboring island of Olosega.

03

UT

Arches National Park

Delicate Arch (right) poses on its sandstone catwalk like a runway boss: graceful, vibrant, flirty. And oh-so-patient with the photo-snapping masses.

Getty Images | Don Smith

R ed rock formations rise from the desert in strange and hypnotic clusters, holding your gaze as their colors and shapes transform on your approach. But it's the up-close views of the sandstone monoliths that will surprise you most, as you realize just how fragile it all is. Hoodoos crumble before your eyes. Balanced Rock seems to teeter on its stem. And Landscape Arch? This golden span looks hardly more solid than a whisper. An 18-mile (29km) scenic drive rolls through this wonderland of rocks, with spur trails providing the closer look. Today, there are more than 2000 arches in this high-desert park.

About 65 million years ago, dry seabeds covered the sandstone here. Geological forces squeezed the rock into folds, which eventually fractured. After a massive uplift punched the region skyward, the sandstone expanded and cracked all over again. Erosion revealed the sandstone to the elements, and water sculpted the fantastical shapes travelers see today. Rock formations in the park highlight the stages of this geologic progression. The Fiery Furnace and its fins emerged when ice fractured immense blocks of sandstone; arches formed when rocks broke away from the fins. Waterways carved the lofty bridges. And hoodoos? Eroding fins left these skinny pinnacles in their wake.

Hunter-gatherers roamed the region 10,000 years ago. Ancestral Puebloans followed, living in villages and cultivating crops across the Four Corners region, where Arizona, New Mexico, Colorado, and Utah collide. Ute and Paiute tribes arrived next, followed by Europeans, explorers, trappers and settlers. The most famous inhabitant was author Edward Abbey, a park ranger at Arches National Monument in the 1950s; his classic book *Desert Solitaire: A Season in*

the Wilderness criticized industrial tourism while encouraging preservation. He also urged visitors to ditch their cars and explore the sandstone wilderness with intensity – an intensity that should cause you, he said, to bleed. Practically speaking, a few blisters here should suffice.

⬅ Double Arch.
⬆ Petroglyphs drawn by Ute tribespeople on the sandstone.
Previous page: Delicate Arch.

Getty Images | Alacatr; Leanne Walker

Toolbox

⚙ **When to go**
With daytime temperatures between 60°F (16°C) and 80°F (27°C), the park is most inviting in April and May and from mid-September through October. Summer temperatures are typically in the 90s F (30s C), but regularly top 100°F (38°C). Traffic is thick March through October, with the heaviest crowds on weekends and holidays.

🧭 **Getting there**
Arches is located in southeastern Utah. The park entrance is 27 miles (43.5km) south of I-70. Salt Lake City, Utah, is 236 miles (380km) northwest; Grand Junction, Colorado, is 110 miles (177km) northeast.

Park in numbers

119.8
Area (sq miles)

8 – 10
Annual rainfall (in)

3600
Weight of Balanced Rock (tons)

Stay here...

Devils Garden Campground
What exactly does the Devil grow? In this striking garden, located 18 miles (29km) north of the park entrance, tents and RVs sprout beside prickly pear cacti, yucca and stands of juniper and piñon pines. Massive crimson fins double as the garden wall.

Cali Cochitta
An oasis of cozy style in the heart of Moab, this lovely B&B will relax you in a heartbeat with hammocks, porch chairs and a backyard hot tub. The smartly decorated rooms are tucked inside brick cottages that surround a well-manicured yard. Tall tales from yesterday's hike are made for sharing at the communal outdoor breakfast table.

Red Cliffs Lodge
Ruggedly stylish cabins and suites – set on a working ranch – overlook the Colorado River and Castle Creek. Horseback riding tours and a Western film museum keep things cowboy cool. The on-site winery offers a nod to more civilized enjoyments.

Do this!

Hiking
Southern Utah is often called an outdoor playground. That label proves true on the ranger-led Fiery Furnace Hike, a three-hour adventure through a maze of red rocks in the heart of the park. You'll scramble over boulders, squeeze through narrows and navigate ledges, with geologic wonders around every bend.

Photographing

Morning and sunset are the best times to shoot in red rock country, with the warmest blues at sunset. When photographing sandstone, a warming filter added to an SLR lens can enhance the color of the rocks; on a digital camera adjust the setting to 'cloudy.' Shadows can add depth.

White-water rafting
Whomp. Splash. Oww! Ah yes, the poetic sounds of a paddle fight on the Colorado River, which tracks the southern border of the park. Wildlife viewing is a highlight on the stretch between Dewey Campground and Hittle Bottom, northeast of the park. Class I and II water closer to Moab keeps the ride lively but family-friendly.

➤ Utah's iconic rock formations are the result of millions of years of erosion.

What to spot...

Arches National Park sweeps across the high desert, where the climate is marked by very hot summers, cold winters and sparse rainfall. Habitats include mixed grasslands, dry washes and riparian areas, with lots of slickrock in between. Larger mammals like foxes and bobcats, as well as most rodents, are nocturnal, saving their hunting and scavenging for cooler nights. As for amphibians, calls from a chorus of male toads may fill a canyon after a spring or summer rainstorm.

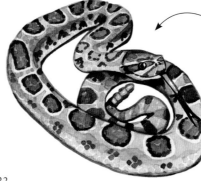

DATURA FLOWER This enigmatic plant is easily identified by its white, trumpet-shaped flowers, which bloom at night. Look, but don't taste – the datura is quite poisonous. The plant is also called Angel's Trumpet, moonflower and jimson weed.

WHITE-THROATED SWIFT Like tiny, feathered rocket ships, these chattering birds zip between rocky cliffs. Marked by white throats splashed against black wings and bodies, these fast fliers spend most of their time in the air, where they mate in a tumbling whirl.

MIDGET-FADED RATTLESNAKE The pattern on the back of this rattler looks like faded drops of blood. It's known for its highly toxic venom – fortunately, it keeps a low daytime profile.

Hike this...

O1 Delicate Arch

Hustle up the slickrock, navigate a ledge, then unpack your fancy camera for the park's marquee attraction: a freestanding arch gracefully framing the La Sal Mountains. The hike is 3 miles (4.8km) round-trip.

O2 Devils Garden Trail

This 7.2-mile (11.6km) round-trip hike passes eight arches; it's a 1.6-mile (2.6km) round-trip from the trailhead to Landscape Arch. Stretching more than 290ft (88.4m), it's the largest natural rock arch in the world.

O3 Windows Trail

This easy, 1-mile (1.6km) hike passes round windows, a double arch and one formation that looms like a turreted fortress.

Getty Images | David Wall Photo; Philip Lee Harvey; Whit Richardson

◀ Hiking Devils Garden Trail.
⬇ Arches National Park is a popular destination for winter sun-seeking RV drivers.

Itineraries

Watch the sun set stone arches and fins aglow as you hike these sandstone formations. Or take to two knobbly wheels to see this widescreen landscape by mountain bike.

➡ Mountain bike trails around Moab, flowing over grippy slickrock, are world famous.

01

A half-day

Courthouse Towers and Balanced Rock are red rock showoffs, begging for attention on your morning drive to the Wolfe Ranch parking area. From here it's a 1.5-mile (2.4km) hike with a slickrock climb and a final spin on a wall-hugging ledge. Your reward? A highly photogenic view of Delicate Arch – an already familiar sight if you've seen the Utah license plate. The colors of the arch change hypnotically as the sun climbs. Check out petroglyphs carved into the rocks near the footbridge on your return hike, then continue to Wolfe Ranch, a well-preserved pioneer cabin built in the early 1900s.

Next up? Five magnificent arches on a 1-mile (1.6km) loop. North Window opens onto canyon views, followed by South Window and the castle-like Turret Arch. Across the way, a short walk ends at the joined Double Arches. For lunch, unpack your cooler at the picnic area across from Balanced Rock.

02

A day

Parking at Arches can be challenging, so start early. Buy picnic sandwiches at City Market in Moab, then stop at the park visitor center to pick up your permits for a ranger-led hiking tour of the Fiery Furnace – this half-day adventure twists through all sorts of wondrous sandstone formations.

Worked up an appetite? Drive north to Devils Garden for a picnic near an impressive grove of colorful fins and arches. From here, hikers can drive to the short trails at Window Rock and Balanced Rock, both close to the main road. Fun fact: Balanced Rock is the weight of three school buses.

If education is your jam, join a ranger walk or drive to the Wolfe Ranch parking area to view Native American petroglyphs and an early-1900s cabin. End the day with a late-afternoon hike to Delicate Arch. You won't be alone as the sun drops, but crowds don't detract from the fragile beauty of this iconic arch.

03

Two days

Grab a burrito and coffee at Love Muffin in Moab, then drive north to the park's visitor center, to check the daily program schedule. From here, it's a Technicolor trip on the 18-mile (29km) scenic road to Devils Garden Campground, where you'll pitch your tent. Follow the Devils Garden Trail to soaring Landscape Arch, the largest natural arch in the world; if you hike to the end of the trail, you'll pass seven more.

In the afternoon, walk to Window Rock, then stroll around the base of Balanced Rock, a formation that defines the word 'precarious.' Join a ranger talk, then hike to Delicate Arch for sunset. Hungry? Savor smoked elk at the Desert Bistro, followed by local brews at Moab Brewery.

In the morning, pick up your Fiery Furnace permit, then join a ranger for a three-hour hike through red rock wilds. In the afternoon, splash down the Colorado River on a raft or cycle the family-friendly Bar M Loop. Moab is mountain bike central; ask at the bike rental shop about other good rides. Celebrate the day with a burger at Milt's, a Moab favorite.

04

SD

Badlands National Park

People tend to go rather quiet when they first approach the Badlands. The otherworldly landscape defies clever commentary or summing-up.

French trappers called it 'bad lands to travel across'; before them, the Lakota held much the same opinion. It's eerie, this rocky desert moonscape, with its weird, crinkly shapes and seeming absence of vegetation. But the longer you stay, the more you see.

For starters, these seemingly barren rocks are actually full of life – and the evidence of life. The Badlands hold one of the most plentiful concentrations of fossils in the world. The study of fossils here has thrived since 1846, when paleontologist Hiram Prout dug up and described a titanothere

mandible (the jawbone of an extinct hoofed mammal related to horses and rhinos).

The other thing you might begin to notice is that the Badlands aren't finished. The rocky formations consist of distinct layers. These are the result of the accumulation of different kinds of sediment over different periods. Some of it is volcanic; some is mud left over from the floors of long-vanished rivers and seas. It took ages – literally – to build the landscape you see here, but for the past 500,000 years or so erosion has been un-building it: the Badlands erode at a rate of about an inch a year.

In addition to the secrets held within the Badlands themselves, the park also encompasses two kinds of prairie grasslands in the surrounding area. These are teeming with activity – animal, vegetable and meteorological. A huge variety of birds and other wildlife can be seen here, including about 400 plant species, from shrubs and flowers to, unsurprisingly, grass. Often, though, the main attraction is the weather: sudden, violent rain and hailstorms all through spring and summer, blizzards in winter, and extreme temperature variations mean visitors should be prepared for atmospheric drama.

Toolbox

When to go
Summers are hot, with frequent sudden hail or rainstorms; June sees the most rain. Winters are snowbound and cold. The park and the Ben Reifel Visitor Center are open year-round (except for Thanksgiving, Christmas and New Year's Day). The visitor center at the south entrance is open in summer only.

Getting there
The Badlands are located in southwestern South Dakota, 75 miles (120.7km) east of Rapid City. There's no public transportation to the park, so your best option is to visit by car.

Park in numbers

381
Area covered (sq miles)

1
Annual landscape erosion (in)

3247
Highest point (ft)

Stay here...

Cedar Pass Lodge
There's been a lodge here since 1928, when local businessman Ben Millard and his sister, Clara, first opened a service camp for trendsetting tourists; back then there was even a dance hall where traveling bands would perform for guests. These days you can recreate that same atmosphere, waking up in a cabin that looks just like one of the originals, but with the extra pleasure that comes from having a TV, hairdryer and the knowledge that your rustic digs are LEED-certified. Closed October to April.

Badlands Inn
Rooms in this family-friendly motel are basic, but each one has an unobstructed view of the park – ideal for the Badlands' famous sunsets and sunrises – and it's a stone's throw from the Ben Reifel Visitor Center.

Sage Creek Campground
Bypass the popular Cedar Pass Campground and seek out this primitive area, where camping is free. Set in the park's North Unit, it's so remote that wildlife often strolls through. Located off the unpaved Sage Creek Rim Rd, access may be restricted in severe weather.

Do this!

Scenic driving
The scenic, 38-mile (61km) Badlands Loop Rd (Hwy 240) roams a winding, U-shaped path between the towns of Cactus Flat and Wall and it's easily worth taking the time to drive. From it you can see most of the park's characteristic features, especially if you stop at the various information points and scenic overlooks.

Stargazing
Big open skies and the lack of light pollution means you can get an unparalleled look at the stars from the Cedar Pass campground area, either with the naked eye or through telescopes staffed by rangers, who will point out interesting features. Seeing the Milky Way Galaxy with this level of clarity is an unforgettable experience.

Learning
The working paleontology lab (open May through September in the Ben Reifel Visitor Center) allows visitors of all ages to learn more about the importance of the fossil studies that go on in the park.

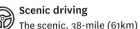 South Dakota's roads draw motorcycle riders, especially for the annual Sturgis Motorcycle Rally in August.

Hike this...

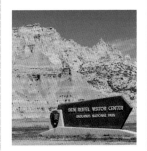

01 Fossil Exhibit Trail
This 0.25-mile (0.4km), wheelchair-accessible boardwalk trail is dotted with fossil replicas and displays about the evidence of extinct creatures discovered in the park.

02 Notch Trail
Starting from the Door and Window parking area, this 1.5-mile (2.4km) round-trip trail includes scaling a ladder up to a high ledge with dizzying views over the White River Valley.

03 Sage Creek
Backcountry hikes in the Badlands require no permits; enquire at the visitor center first for detailed info and topographical maps. A two-day hike along Sage Creek provides a taste.

Getty Images | Ed Freeman; Mark Newman

What to spot...

The Badlands, as well as the grassland areas that surround them, are home to a huge variety of plants and wildlife. Hundreds of kinds of birds inhabit the area, along with grasses and wildflowers, hardy shrubs, butterflies, snakes and lizards, and a wide variety of mammals, from prairie dogs to bison. Wildlife photographers can have a field day here, capturing these creatures against the glamorous backdrop of the rock formations and wide-open sky.

BISON These 2000lb (907kg) creatures are often spotted in the western part of the North Unit, along Sage Creek Rim Rd.

ROCKY MOUNTAIN BIGHORN SHEEP Look for these camouflaged climbers near the Pinnacles or Cedar Pass. The impressive horns and sturdy skulls of bighorn males are built to withstand the impact of annual pre-mating-season headbutt battles for dominance.

TURKEY VULTURE With the face of a puppet-movie villain, this large bird, also called a buzzard, has an unusually well developed sense of smell for sniffing out fresh carrion.

Itineraries

Loop the Loop Rd for iconic photo pitstops, camp under the stars, or just hike this park's backcountry for middle-of-nowhere solitude.

◄ Bighorn sheep battle.

▲ The eerie landscape of the Badlands National Park.

01

A day

The Badlands Loop Rd (Hwy 240), one of the nation's most beautiful drives, covers 38 miles (61km) in a rough 'U' shape south of I-90; it can be driven in either direction. If you're traveling east to west, you'll enter the park at the Northeast Entrance Station. Be sure to stop and look around at the Big Badlands Overlook inside the entrance; in fact, you should plan on stopping as often as you like at the many overlooks and information points along the drive. Before long you'll arrive at the Fossil Exhibit trailhead – hop out here and take the short, easy stroll along the boardwalk path, which is lined with displays about fossil collecting and the history of paleontology in the area. Continue along the Loop Rd, but stop again at the Window Trail parking lot to snap a photo against the iconic background. Don't miss a stop at Yellow Mounds Overlook and the Pinnacles as well, before leaving the park and returning to I-90 at the town of Wall. This little town is a good spot for refreshments – it's almost mandatory to stop in at the vast and corny Wall Drug.

02

A weekend

Enter the park at the Northeast Entrance Station and follow the Loop Rd after viewing the Big Badlands Overlook. Further along, stop at the Notch trailhead and hike the 1.5 miles (2.4km) to a point overlooking the river valley. Back on the road, pause at the Ben Reifel Visitor Center for a schedule of the evening's events. Set up camp at the Cedar Pass Campground or check into an eco-friendly cabin at the Cedar Pass Lodge before dinner. Finish up in time for the ranger-led Night Sky presentation, after which you can stargaze solo. Next day, check out the fossil laboratory in the visitor center. Having restocked your supplies – especially water – continue along the loop road. After the Pinnacles Overlook, you'll come to the turnoff for the gravel Sage Creek Rim Rd (a good place to break out a fat-tire bike). Follow this road to the Sage Creek Campground, a good base for hikes into the backcountry or a campout in as close to the middle of nowhere as you'll find.

Getty Images | Danita Delimont

05

Big Bend National Park

A vast and sunbaked wilderness, Big Bend has long captivated those who make the journey to this remote corner of Texas.

In the heart of the Chihuahuan Desert, where summer temperatures often surpass 100°F (38°C), Big Bend may appear at first glance like a barren wasteland. But, in fact, amid its steep-walled canyons, fertile river corridor, desert scrubland and forested ridges, you'll find varied microclimates that support abundant wildlife – including more recorded bird species than any other national park in America.

The area has a complicated geological history, with a mix of 500-million-year-old rocks and sand dunes still being shaped by today's desert winds. Walking this parched landscape, it's difficult to imagine that Big Bend once lay beneath an ancient tropical sea, which later evaporated and disappeared beneath clay and limestone sediments. Deposits found here reveal an incredible record of life from this time. Among the fossilized treasures is the skull of a three-horned chasmosaurus, a 50ft-long (15m) crocodile and a flying reptile with a wingspan of 36ft (11m).

Home to a long stretch of the Rio Grande, a life-giving river system in these inhospitable lands, Big Bend has a deep connection to human history in the region. Artifacts from Paleo-Indians that lived in the region date back 10,000 years. Later groups include the Chisos tribe, followed by Comanches, who led raiding parties into the interior of Mexico. The Spanish also had a presence here, with explorers crossing the Rio Grande in search of gold and silver. Following the Mexican-American War, Big Bend saw a succession of ranchers, miners, revolutionaries, outlaws and intrepid homesteaders.

The creation of the national park is largely credited to Everett Townsend, a Texan-born deputy marshal who first ventured into the Chisos Mountains while tracking a pack of stolen mules back in 1894. Inspired by the natural beauty around him, Townsend vowed to preserve this landscape, a promise he later fulfilled while serving on the state legislature. Big Bend officially became a national park in 1944, and Townsend – then in his 70s – became its first commissioner. He is remembered today as 'the father of Big Bend National Park.'

⬆ Canoeing on the Rio Grande in Big Bend National Park.
➡ Santa Elena Canyon at sunset.
Previous page: road riding.

Toolbox

When to go
The most pleasant time to visit is between October and April. In the summer, temperatures regularly soar above 100°F (38°C) – sometimes even reaching 110°F (43°C) – making long hikes unbearable. Spring (March to mid-May) is a great time to see migrating birds.

Getting there
Big Bend lies in a southwestern corner of Texas. The closest airports are in Midland, 195 miles (314km) north (a three-hour drive); and El Paso, 290 miles (467km) northwest (a 4½-hour drive). Rental cars are available at either airport.

Park in numbers

1252
Area covered (sq miles)

7832
Highest point (ft)

1200
Number of plant species

Stay here...

 Chisos Mountain Lodging Aside from camping, this is the only in-park accommodations. It offers a range of options for all budgets, all with scenic views and an ideal location just a few steps from hiking trails in the Chisos Mountains. Book well ahead for one of the five Roosevelt Cottages, with stone floors, wood-beamed ceilings, and porches with peaceful views of the mountains.

Chisos Basin Campground Surrounded by mountains, this scenic campground earns rave reviews for its location. It's great for sunsets and the nightly spectacle of stargazing, and it's a short walk to the trailheads and a decent restaurant. Back in the 1930s, this site was used as barracks for the Civilian Conservation Corps, the young men who blazed trails and built access roads and park lodging.

Posada Milagro Built among the ruins of an historic ghost town in Terlingua (a half-hour drive from the park entrance), the adobe-style cottages at this guesthouse, set with west-Texas decor, blend in with the surroundings. Sit on the pleasant patio after a day's hiking and enjoy the cool evenings.

Do this!

Rafting You can go for a scenic paddle along the Rio Grande, taking in the dramatic beauty of Elena Canyon and Big Bend's towering cliffs. There's even challenging class IV white water at certain times of the year. Outfitters located in nearby Terlingua provide guided trips.

Stargazing Far from city lights, this remote park is an outstanding site for taking in the night sky. You'll be able to see over 2000 stars on a clear night. It's well worth camping a few nights here – or else just gazing up at the sky while soaking in the hot springs.

Bird-watching One of the great birding hot spots in North America, Big Bend has over 450 documented bird species, and you'll find unique ones among the park's diverse habitats. The Rio Grande Village offers some of the best year-round bird-watching, where you can see herons, ducks, kingfishers, white-tailed doves, vermilion flycatchers and Cooper's hawks.

Soak sore legs in the mineral salts of the geothermal Hot Springs pool, a short stroll from the trailhead.

What to spot...

At first glance, Big Bend seems like a barren and unforgiving desert landscape. But delve deeper and you'll encounter a wondrous variety of plant and animal life. In fact, among its three different habitats – desert badlands, river valley and forested mountains – Big Bend harbors over 1200 plant species and more species of birds, bats and cacti than any other park in America.

TEXAS BROWN TARANTULA Covered in hair and nearly as large as a mouse, the Texas brown tarantula looks frightening, but is actually quite docile and not dangerous to humans. These spiders live in burrows, in front of which they place lines of webbing to detect passing prey.

GIANT SWALLOWTAIL BUTTERFLY Found throughout the southern and eastern United States, the yellow and dark brown giant swallowtail is the largest butterfly species in North America, with a wingspan of 10–16cm (3.9–6.3in).

COYOTE One of 75 mammal species in Big Bend, coyotes have gray or reddish gray fur, stand 2 ft (61cm) high at the shoulder and weigh 30–70lbs (14–32kg). They mate for life and have a home range of 40 to 100 miles (64 to 100km).

Hike this...

O1 Hot Springs Trail

An easy 1-mile (1.6km) round-trip walk from the parking lot takes you out to the hot springs, which run at 105°F (41°C) – worthy of a dip on cool winter days.

O2 Lost Mine Trail

This moderate 4.8-mile (7.7km) round-trip hike is an excellent introduction to the natural riches of the Chisos Mountains. You'll pass through forests of pine, juniper and oak before reaching a ridge with views out to the Sierra del Carmen in Mexico.

O3 Emory Peak

Emory Peak, a strenuous 10.5-mile (17km) round-trip hike winds up to Big Bend's highest point – offering spectacular views over the desert landscape from its summit in the Chisos Mountains.

Itineraries

Hike up Emory Peak for the best Big Bend views, raft down the Rio Grande, cross the border to Mexico or just watch wildlife under the starry sky.

← Prickly pear purple cactus; the Teepee Rest Area on River Rd.
→ Beware of black bear mothers with cubs.

01

A weekend

On a weekend visit, spend the first day making one of the iconic hikes up into the Chisos Mountains: the 10.5-mile (16.9km) round-trip ascent up Emory Peak offers some of the finest views in Big Bend. You'll pass through valleys of wildflowers, taking in cactus blooms with Mexican jays flittering overhead. The views get more inspiring the higher you go, with chiselled peaks and the desert below. Keep an eye out for white-tailed deer that graze near the trail. Treat yourself to a first-rate meal, with views to match, at the Chisos Mountain Lodge.

On day two, take the 30-mile (48.3km) Ross Maxwell Scenic Drive. You can make a day of it, looking for desert wildlife at the Sam Nail ranch, taking in fine views over the desert floor at the Sotol Vista Overlook, then pulling off on a side road to the colorful cliffs of Burro Mesa. Wander through the Castolon Historic District to find remnants of an early 20th-century cavalry camp, and end the day at 1500ft (457m) Santa Elena Canyon. Take the 1.7-mile (2.7km) trail that follows the river along one of the park's most picturesque chasms.

02

Four days

After doing an all-day hike and a scenic drive on days one and two, spend your third day rafting down the Rio Grande. For a leisurely paddle, head to the Hot Springs Canyon, where you'll have superb views of the Sierra del Carmen in Mexico. You'll have the opportunity to soak at hot springs and discover Native American pictographs along the way. That evening, stay up to watch Big Bend's dark skies fill with stars. The park has the least light pollution of any national park in the lower 48 states. Today, park managers are trying to keep it that way by reducing unnecessary lighting in the park.

On the fourth day, head to the Rio Grande Village, where wildlife-watching opportunities abound, particularly for avian species in this birding hot spot. In the early evening, head west to the Chisos Basin and make the short hike along the Window View Trail, one of the best places in Big Bend to watch the sun set.

03

A week

Do the four-day itinerary, then spend a fifth day exploring the tiny Mexican village of Boquillas – the border at this laid-back crossing reopened in 2014. A boatman will row you across the river; from there you can take a truck or donkey, or walk the 1 mile (1.6km) to Boquillas. Once there, snack in a local eatery and shop for souvenirs, before returning in the afternoon. (Don't forget your passport!)

On day six, explore the old ghost town of Terlingua, just outside the park. You can visit ruins and a cemetery, then dine at the Starlight Theater, a former roofless cinema turned Western-themed restaurant. On your last day in Big Bend hike the Lost Mine Trail, a 4.8-mile (7.7km) trail that offers grand views from a promontory overlooking Juniper Canyon.

If time allows, squeeze in a scenic drive outside the park. Drive west of Terlingua to Lajitas on one of Texas' most spectacular highways. With the Rio Grande (and a barren stretch of Mexico) on your left and looming mountains to your right, desolate, winding Rte 170 offers astounding scenery at every rise.

06

Biscayne National Park

Haunted by shipwrecks, populated by turtles and manatees – Biscayne is an ex-pirate's paradise rescued from the claws of developers to become the Atlantis of America's parks.

East of the Everglades, just off Miami, lies a drowned dreamland that nurtured human life 10,000 years ago – and has since hosted indigenous tribes, Spanish conquistadors, plundering privateers and partying presidents. Biscayne thrills modern adventurers who camp on the keys, kayak around atolls and snorkel in a seascape that comprises 95% of the national park, home to 200 species of fish and marine mammals.

But it could have been very different.

Wandering Spaniard Juan Ponce de León 'discovered' Florida in 1513, delivering disease and destruction to the Tequesta people; subsequently, several Spanish ships, some laden with treasure, came to grief on the reef here. Later, Elliot Key was home to Black Caesar, an 18th-century African pirate. Biscayne continued to see eyebrow-raising activity well into the 20th century. During Prohibition the raised-shacks community of Stiltsville hosted drinking and gambling shindigs, and the CIA used the area as a training ground for Cuban exiles ahead of the Bay of Pigs invasion.

Israel Jones, one of America's first black millionaires, made a fortune from growing pineapples and limes here. His sons offered guided fishing tours; their clients included John F Kennedy, Lyndon Johnson, Richard Nixon and – crucially – vacuum-cleaner magnate Herbert W Hoover Jr and his family.

As Florida flourished, developers announced plans to dredge the bay and gouge a 40ft (12m) channel through the reef to create a new city and port. People protested, calling for the area to be protected, and they gained support from the *Miami Herald* and Hoover himself, who flew legislators down to see the area he'd loved as a child.

As momentum for the park grew, landowners attempted to despoil the area by bulldozing a strip across Elliot Key, ostensibly to build a road. It became known as 'Spite Highway' since it led nowhere. In 1968, congress approved the creation of Biscayne National Monument, which became a national park in 1980. Today, Spite Highway has greened over to become a hiking trail.

Toolbox

When to go

The park is open year-round, but camping is more comfortable during the winter months, when mosquitoes and no-see-ums (little biting flies) are less of a nuisance. The snorkeling, however, is better during summer and fall.

Getting there

The park is accessed via the Dante Fascell Visitor Center at Convoy Point, 7 miles (11km) east of the city of Homestead (an hour's drive from South Beach, south along the Florida Turnpike), where there's a museum, and boat launching facilities. Arrange tours at the visitor center.

Park in numbers

270.3

Area covered (sq miles)

44

Number of documented wrecks within the park's boundaries

10,000

Years that humans have been active in the park area

Stay here...

This is a place for explorers, not the pampered. There are no hotels, motels, lodges or cabins – it's camp or go home. (The nearest accommodations to the park's entrance are in Homestead or Florida City.) Camping can be uncomfortable during summer, when mosquitoes and no-see-ums are a problem. Campers should be completely self-sufficient, packing in all food and water.

Boca Chita Key Campsite

A waterside site on the park's most visited island, next to the harbor and opposite the Pavilion.

There's a grassy area, picnic tables and toilets, but no shower.

Elliott Key Campsite

There are waterside and forested camping areas here, plus a seasonally staffed ranger station, picnic tables and grills. You'll also find toilets and even a cold-water shower.

Stiltsville

Currently shut to the public, this historic cluster of over-water stilted shacks in Biscayne Bay (used in the 1930s for gambling and drinking soirées) falls within the park. Development plans are in the air.

Do this!

Snorkeling & diving

Biscayne is 95% underwater and the only way to really explore it is by donning snorkel, mask and fins (and a scuba tank if you're dive-qualified). Besides the astonishing variety of fish (over 200 species), there are 44 wrecks to discover – including one, the Mandalay, in shallow water. Snorkeling is possible from the shore in places, but the reef proper is further out and you'll need to arrange a boat.

Canoeing & kayaking

A paddle-powered adventure around Biscayne's islands is an excellent experience. Explore shallow channels, creeks and lagoons that are off-limits for larger craft, and spot turtles, dolphins and manatees as you glide across turquoise water. Guided trips can be arranged, but confident paddlers can reach the park independently.

Fishing & lobstering

Responsible fishing is permitted within Biscayne, and the park even offers a free Fisheries Awareness Class so you can make sure you're using sustainable practices.

◀ Casting for catch-and-release bonefish on the saltwater flats.
▶ The Great Land Crab is a slower-moving adversary.

Hike this...

01 Spite Trail

The park's only hiking trail has a great backstory. In the 1960s, when the fight between developers and conservationists got nasty, an ugly gash was bulldozed right across Elliot Key. Originally nicknamed Spite Highway, this scar has healed into a beautiful trail, tunnelling through 7 miles (11.3km) of tropical hardwood forest.

02 Maritime Heritage Trail

Submerged hikers (divers) can follow this unique underwater archaeological trail – complete with informative site cards – which links a series of shipwrecks, including the Arratoon Apcar (sank 1878), Erl King (1891), Alicia (1905), Lugano (1913) and Mandalay (1966).

What to spot...

Biscayne boasts four different ecosystems – mangrove swamp, lagoon, island key and offshore-reef habitats – and its biodiversity is extraordinary. More than 50 kinds of crustacean, hundreds of species of fish and 27 types of mammal live here. Among the more interesting locals are American crocodiles, giant blue land crabs, rattlesnakes and Caribbean reef octopuses. A couple of ecozones crash into each other in South Florida too, attracting some species of birds that aren't seen anywhere else in the country.

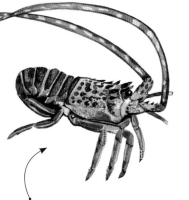

SPINY LOBSTER Like 'true' lobsters but minus the claws. When threatened, these Biscayne buskers make a screeching noise by rubbing a 'plectrum' on their antennae against their exoskeleton.

FLORIDA MANATEE
These eccentric-looking animals – related to elephants and likely the inspiration for mermaid myths – are star residents. During their evolutionary journey they lost rear legs but kept front fingernails (handy for eating shellfish).

YELLOW-CROWNED NIGHT HERON Sometimes known as the American night heron or squawk, this small heron is a nocturnal stealth hunter, terrorizing amphibians along the water's edge. They were once eaten in Cajun cuisine.

Itineraries

Anchors away, whether you day-trip on a glass-bottomed boat, rent a canoe or plan a significant kayak journey, the diving and snorkeling are excellent here.

 Red mangroves at Rubicon Key in Biscayne National Park.
➡ The Least Tern is North America's smallest tern.

01
A half-day

Biscayne is unique within the NPS system, since you need to board a boat in order to see any of the park – making some degree of organization and planning required for any trip here. But people who are simply passing by (or committed landlubbers) can still get a taste of Biscayne by exploring the Dante Fascell Visitor Center at the entrance to the park. Found 50 miles (80.5km) south of Miami, and 9 miles (14.5km) east of Homestead, the museum uses multimedia magic to transport you through the four ecosystems of the park without getting a drop of water on you. Several educational films are screened, explaining the biodiversity that exists beneath the waves, and both big and little kids can enjoy the touch-and-play display of bones, feathers, sponges, corals and other items from the park. You can also walk the short Jetty Trail and enjoy a picnic overlooking the water leading out to the park. Let's be honest – this dry run is only going to whet your appetite for a proper exploration, so get planning.

02
A day

OK, so you don't have your own boat (yet), but you're dying to dive into Biscayne to see what all the fuss is about. No problem – there are plenty of options. People who prefer to stay dry and see the park as a passenger can hop on one of the glass-bottomed boats that depart the visitor center each morning for a three-hour reef-viewing experience. Besides an abundance of colorful corals and tropical fish, you may be lucky enough to meet a manatee or spot a dolphin. Seeking a more immersive experience? Take a three-hour snorkeling tour (which will get you about 90 minutes in the water) for face-to-face encounters with the finned community of the keys. Canoes can be rented by the hour, and guided half- and full-day canoe and kayak trips can be arranged in winter (late November to April). Qualified divers can arrange trips with local operators. If you're flush with cash and want a boutique boat experience, charter a private vessel and get a tour of the whole park.

03
Five days

Paddling away from the visitor center, it feels as though you're embarking on the ultimate aquatic adventure. The kayak is sitting deeper in the water than normal, but you've got several days' food on board and a tent in the sealed storage compartment. First stop is the campground at the north of the park, Boca Chita Key, to bag a good pitch and stash your gear. There are two camping sites in the park – here and at Elliot Key – and you've arranged two nights in each.

You plan to spend a couple of days paddling around, exploring such parts of the park as Jones Lagoon (a good spot to see sharks, rays and upside-down jellyfish), Hurricane Creek (where there's excellent snorkeling among the mangroves), and the shallow lagoons and channels south of Caesar Creek – named after a pirate who once had a base here. One day you'll dedicate to hiking the length of the Spite Highway across Elliot Key, but the thing you're most looking forward to is diving the Maritime Heritage Trail.

07

CO

Black Canyon of the Gunnison National Park

Deeper than the Grand Canyon, the yawning, dark chasm of the Black Canyon of the Gunnison is nature stripped to its most elemental.

This craggy canyon has been two million years in the making. The Gunnison River carved a vertical wilderness with fast-moving water, carrying rock and debris. 'Narrow' is an understatement – only direct overhead light filters down to the canyon floor. A peek over the edge inspires trembling awe, and probably some vertigo. No other canyon in America competes with the sheer and dizzying depths of this 2000ft (610m) chasm.

Experts feed on the challenge of scaling these walls and kayaking the river's Class V whitewater. They grab these extreme photo ops so you don't have to. Most visitors will be more than content to browse the scenic vistas, hike the steep canyon or horseback ride along the rim. Fly-fishers should pack their waders. The clear jade waters of the Gunnison River offers some of the best fishing in Colorado and even the US. It has been designated as Gold Medal Water and Wild Trout Water, an exclusive status few rivers can boast.

Historically, this massive canyon has presented a formidable barrier. Utes settled the rim, but there's no evidence of human habitation within the chasm itself. Surveyor John W Gunnison sought a railroad crossing here, but he was massacred in Utah after bypassing the canyon in 1853. In 1901, two lucky adventurers floated through the canyon on rubber mattresses, traveling 33 hard-won miles (53km) in nine days.

Park status came only in 1999. Today, in addition to being one of the smallest US National Parks, the Black Canyon of the Gunnison happens to be the least-visited of the four that are in Colorado. Maybe that is because it is far from the interstate and major cities. But it does occupy Colorado's sweet spot, a region that has become infamous for its powder skiing and mountain biking.

Toolbox

When to go
All park roads are open from mid-April to mid-November. In wintertime the park is covered in snow and the South Rim Rd opens to cross-country skiing and snowshoeing. Fly-fishing is best during the spring hatch and early fall.

Getting there
The park is 262 miles (422km) from Denver International Airport. The closest accommodations and services are in Montrose and Gunnison. A bit further afield, the winter and summer resort of Crested Butte has ample visitor services.

Park in numbers

47

Area covered (sq miles)

8775

Highest point (ft)

14°F/88°F

Average low/high temperature (-10°c–31°c)

Stay here...

East Portal Campground
For water access, camp at the riverside East Portal in the adjacent Curecanti National Recreation Area. It's shaded by lovely box elders: a big bonus in the summertime heat. It's near the historic Gunnison River Diversion Tunnel, a 1909 engineering marvel that diverted canyon water to irrigate early farm settlements.

Vintage Inn
This adorable cottage home oozes Western ease and charm. Grab one of the loaner bikes to explore the side streets of Gunnison's leafy residential district, put your feet up in the lush garden or take a spin to the local brewery to try a chilled ale. You've found home.

Ruby of Crested Butte
Ski town Crested Butte is a hub of outdoor fun all year round; plus, there's something to be said for its incongruent fine-dining-and-cowboy style. The pampering continues if you bed down at Ruby's. It's thoughtfully outfitted, down to the bowls of jellybeans and pet beds.

Do this!

Fly-fishing
Come for the spring hatch and snag a few of the plentiful stock of rainbow trout in these gold-medal waters. Strict regulations are enforced to maintain this status. A Colorado fishing license is required and bait fishing is not allowed – only lures and flies. River access points may require permits.

Scenery-gazing
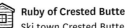
Colorado's highest cliff face is the 2300ft-high (701m), marble-striped Painted Wall. You might spot climbers ascending one of its vertiginous climbs, though some routes face seasonal closures to protect nesting raptors – it is a national park, after all. Also stop at Chasm View, which is nearly as wide as it is high.

Horseback riding
Coloradans love a good bluff: match them by not blinking first. So when you find out that the only horse trail at the park is called Deadhorse Trail, well, we say saddle up. The park's only route for horses, the 5-mile (8km) trail travels moderate terrain to the spectacular North Rim.

◄ The Black Canyon itself.
➡ Wild perennial lupins flourish beside trails in the national park.

Hike this...

01 Rim Rock Nature Trail
This easy 1-mile (1.6km) walk to the canyon rim is lined with sagebrush, Gambel oaks and Utah juniper.

02 Chasm View Nature Trail
This short, 0.3-mile (0.5km) spur drinks in the dramatic North Chasm View, Painted Wall and Serpent Point. Watch for swifts, swallows and raptors.

03 S.O.B. Draw
Hiking the North Rim Inner Canyon is no picnic, hence its name. Reserved for experienced hikers, the steepest trails feature chutes and handrails. This one drops a steep 2 miles (3.2km) in two hours – but then the solitude's all yours.

What to spot...

High on the Colorado Plateau, the Black Canyon of the Gunnison is home to a unique vertical wilderness composed of diverse elements. On the plateau, pygmy forest and oak flats once provided edible pine nuts and firewood to early inhabitants. Precipitous cliffs provide shelter for bighorn sheep and raptors. On the canyon floor, trophy trout, beavers and chokecherry thrive in river and wetlands. Bring the binoculars – bird-watching here is excellent, especially in spring and early summer.

MULE DEER Named for their long ears, these elegant deer are ubiquitous in the park. Look for their spotted fawns early in summer.

GREAT HORNED OWL With a 5ft (1.5m) wingspan, this is the Americas' largest native owl. It hunts over the canyon rim in sweeping night patrols.

MOUNTAIN BLUEBIRDS Foraging on insects and berries, bluebirds inhabit the canyon in spring and early summer to raise their young. Only the males are signature blue.

Itineraries

One of the smallest parks but challenges abound: rollercoaster drives, steep hikes and wild camping for the adventurous.

◄ Anglers lure trout in the Gunnison River; rainbows are catch-and-release only.

⬆ A coyote and fall colors in the park.

01

A day

In the US West the landscapes come oversized and unwieldy. Not so with Black Canyon of the Gunnison National Park, a compact treasure by local standards. A visit to this haunting chasm offers appreciation for the visual diversity of Colorado.

Take the scenic drive along the paved South Rim route, stopping at the Visitor Center for the exhibits on resident wildlife. A little preparation is conducive to potential sightings, best at dawn or dusk.

The South Rim has a dozen scenic overlooks. Black Canyon's metamorphic rock was likely volcanic debris built up on the floor of an ancient sea billions of years ago. It's worth examining the canyon from all angles, since the steep, south-facing wall contrasts with the more eroded north wall, thick with vegetation.

Take a walk along the Rim Rock Nature Trail. Stop to admire the Painted Wall, the state's tallest cliff. Look down below for rock climbers at the beguiling Chasm View. This is the canyon at its narrowest, with a rim-to-rim distance of 1100ft (335m).

02

A weekend

Follow the day-trip itinerary for the first day of your visit. Set up camp at the riverside East Portal Campground. It's accessed via a rollercoaster drive to the canyon floor, where the howls of coyotes punctuate summer nights.

Day two is for adventure. Plan your trip in advance and you will have a shot at the park's most coveted permit: to hike Red Rock Canyon to the Gunnison River. The most gradual descent to the canyon floor at 3.4 miles (5.5km) one-way, it boasts fly-fishing and wild-camping. A lottery system held in early spring issues permits for this partially private route. Come prepared. The stream crossings require careful navigation and poison ivy lines the way.

Another option is to tour the North Rim by car via gravel road. Views from the North Rim are the most vertical and most impressive. Make a brief stop to hike the short Chasm View Trail. Arrange to go horseback riding on Deadhorse Trail or take on the challenging S.O.B. Draw and hike to the canyon floor.

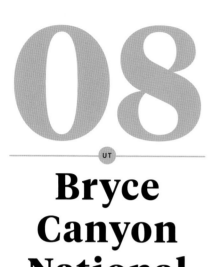

08

UT

Bryce Canyon National Park

Salvador Dalí would have felt right at home wandering this utterly surreal collection of rock spires, slot canyons, arches and castle-like mesas.

Getty Images | Ed Freeman

The landscape of Bryce stirs your imagination – hoodoos (tall, thin towers of rock) become totem poles carved with strange faces, mesas turn into ships sailing on pink seas, cliff walls look like pulled taffy, buttes become ancient fortresses. The wonderful bizarreness goes beyond the geological formations. Bryce is home to living trees that were saplings around the fall of the Roman Empire. It shelters the delicate, fuchsia Bryce Canyon Paintbrush, a wildflower so rare it was only discovered in 1965. Bryce's skies are so clear you can see all the way to the Andromeda Galaxy, 2.2 million light years away. This is a place of magical extremes, among the finest and strangest sights the world has to offer.

Despite its name, Bryce is technically not a canyon, but a series of natural amphitheaters carved into Utah's Paunsaugunt Plateau, the largest of which is 12-mile (19.3km) Bryce Amphitheater. Limestone was carved by frost and rainwater into whimsical and extravagant shapes, turning the park into the top step of what's known as the Grand Staircase, the enormous geological terrace that includes the Grand Canyon.

Paleo-Indians hunted large mammals in Bryce during the last Ice Age. Later, the Ancestral Puebloans hunted its meadows, and Paiutes gathered pine nuts in the piñon groves. In the 1870s, Mormon settlers Ebenezer and Mary Bryce began cattle-ranching in what's now the park; when visitors marveled at the canyon's beauty, Ebenezer Bryce reportedly told them, 'It's a helluva place to lose a cow.' The canyon became locally known as 'Bryce's,' and the name eventually stuck.

Railroad companies began pushing

southern Utah as a destination in the early 1900s: 'Colorful – colossal – sublime,' reads a Union Pacific ad for Bryce from 1927. The park was established in 1928 and expanded in the 1930s. Today, it's one of the smaller national parks, often visited in conjunction with nearby Zion.

⬆ The Navajo Loop trail (and on previous page) passes Bryce Canyon's iconic hoodoos.

Toolbox

 When to go
Summer is crowded in Bryce, so spring and fall are good picks (though they can be chilly at this elevation). In winter, the park turns into an icicle-hung snowy wonderland, but many services are closed.

 Getting there
Bryce Canyon is in southwestern Utah. The nearest airports are Salt Lake City and Las Vegas, both about 270 miles (434.5km) away. There are smaller airports closer by in Cedar City and St George, Utah. There's a park shuttle, but you'll need a car to get here.

Park in numbers

56
Area covered (sq miles)

9105
Highest point: Rainbow Point (ft)

200
Number of Utah prairie dogs in the park

Getty Images | Philip Lee Harvey

Stay here...

Bryce Canyon Lodge
Built during the 1920s' railroad boom, this is Western 'parkitecture' at its finest, all stone and log and dark-green roof shingles. Guests cozy up to the big stone fireplace in the timbered lobby, relax in hickory rockers on the porch or dine on bison burgers. Accommodations range from small studios and hotel rooms to cabins with fireplaces.

North Campground
This enormous year-round campground has sites set within stands of shady pines. There's a full complement of amenities – showers, camp store, laundry, etc. Walk up a short hill for views across the canyon; at night, there's plenty of space for gazing at the shimmering Milky Way. Reservations are required in summer, while the rest of the year it's first-come, first-served.

Ruby's Inn
A mile (1.6km) north of the park entrance, this sprawling complex has been serving guests for a century. In addition to 400 motel rooms and a campground, there's a grocery store, two gas stations, a post office, laundry facilities, restaurants, and a pool. The Best Western–run facility can arrange any kind of tour you desire – ATV, horseback, plane, walking or sleigh.

Do this!

Horseback riding
Trot along like an 18th-century explorer on the 5.5-mile (8.9km) Peek-a-Boo Loop trail, which takes riders through stunningly varied terrain. Gawp at the Wall of Windows, a series of arches and hoodoos looking like the fortress wall of some ancient desert kingdom. Marvel at the slender spires of the Fairy Castle. Local stables offer both horses and mules for riding.

Photographing
The park's most famous viewpoint, Bryce Point offers boggling views across the Silent City, a forest of hoodoos like Martian skyscrapers. The point is a fenced-off outlook jutting over the canyon floor 1000ft (305m) below. In late afternoon, the sinking sun turns the hoodoos a deeper and more alien orange, and shadows play along their craggy edges.

Stargazing
Bryce's remoteness makes its night skies as dark as black velvet. You can see an average of 7500 stars here, compared with a mere 2500 in most parts of America. In high season, rangers lead multimedia night-sky programs, followed by stargazing with telescopes. In summer there's a four-day astronomy event: you've never seen the Milky Way so luminous or Venus as radiant as you will here.

What to spot...

Though Bryce's arid spires and crevices may seem inhospitable, the park is home to a variety of plants and animals perfectly adapted to the habitat. Prairie dogs guard their nests in the meadows on the north side of the park, golden-mantled ground squirrels scurry around the base of piñon trees, mountain lions prowl the snowy backcountry in winter, short-horned lizards blend in with trailside pebbles and Clark's nutcrackers perch in juniper trees.

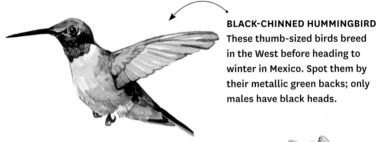

BLACK-CHINNED HUMMINGBIRD These thumb-sized birds breed in the West before heading to winter in Mexico. Spot them by their metallic green backs; only males have black heads.

PONDEROSA PINE Towering ponderosa pine trees dominate the West. Recognize them by their large scales of bark and bright-green needles. You'll find them throughout the park.

BRISTLECONE PINE These gnarled trees are among the oldest living things on earth – the oldest bristlecone is going on 5000 years old! Spot them on Fairyland Loop and Bristlecone Loop.

Hike this...

O1 Bristlecone Loop Trail

See the ancient, weathered bristlecone pine trees along this easy, 1-mile (1.6km) loop, which also takes in hoodoos and long vistas across the canyon.

O2 Navajo Loop Trail

The oddly shaped hoodoo called Thor's Hammer is the main draw for this 1.3-mile (2.1km) hike, along with the narrow canyon known as Wall Street.

O3 Queen's Garden Trail

Families with kids will enjoy this slow, 1.8-mile (2.9km) descent into the canyon, with stunning views over the amphitheater and a loop through the hoodoo wonderland of Queen's Garden.

Itineraries

See why Bryce Canyon Scenic Drive got its name, catch some unbelievable sunrises, then hit the rodeo and gorge on buffalo steak.

◄ Ground squirrels live among the rock formations of Bryce Canyon.
➔ Horse trekkers near the Queen's Garden Trail.

01

A day

Get the most bang for your buck in a short time by driving Bryce Canyon Scenic Dr. This 17-mile (27.4km) road starts at the visitor center and winds south along the rim as far as Rainbow Point. At the very beginning you'll hit three of the park's most iconic viewpoints in quick succession: Sunset Point, Sunrise Point and Inspiration Point. All offer mind-blowing views onto psychedelically shaped hoodoos and mesas glowing red and gold in the sunlight. A little further down, Bryce Point is a

don't-miss, with primo views across Silent City.

At Swamp Canyon, take a stroll through the towering pines for close-up views of the canyon's pink walls. Have lunch at the picnic area a few miles further on. Sandwiches taste that much better when eaten gazing over the yellow-and-white layer cake of Noon Canyon Butte. Don't miss the arch at Natural Bridge, which has been defying gravity for millennia. Take in the sunset over Rainbow Point, watching the color slowly drain from the mesas as the sun goes down in a ball of flame.

02

Two days

Begin day one at Fairyland Point; its slightly isolated location makes it quieter than nearby Sunset and Sunrise points. With your backpack loaded with food and water, descend down the 8-mile (12.9km) Fairyland Loop Trail, which circles the vastness of Boat Mesa, passing primeval bristlecone pines and wandering beneath the shadows of hoodoos like something out of a surrealist painting. Keep your eyes open for short-horned lizards and (very occasionally) rattlesnakes.

When you drag yourself, exhausted, back to the rim, treat yourself to a dinner of Wasatch Range buffalo steak or grilled Utah lamb at the dining room in Bryce Canyon Lodge. On day two, wake early to see the sunrise turn the canyon pink and yellow. Bryce Point is a choice spot for this purpose. Head south on the Bryce Canyon Scenic Dr, hitting the major viewpoints and stopping for a picnic lunch overlooking the mesa. Near the end of the road, take time for a hike along 1-mile (1.6km) Bristlecone Loop Trail.

03

Four days

On day one, get your bearings with a drive down Bryce Canyon Scenic Dr, stopping to gawk (and maybe take a selfie) at the world-class viewpoints. On day two, warm up your legs with a moderate hike along the Navajo Loop and Queen's Garden trails. You'll see Thor's Hammer, traverse the claustrophobic slot that is Wall Street and gaze over Silent City. On day three, book a horseback ride down the Peek-a-Boo Loop Trail. The steep drop-offs to the canyon's distant dusty floor add a

touch of thrill to this varied ride. Highlights include the otherworldly Fairy Castle and the mammoth Cathedral. Wake up early on day four for sunrise over Bryce Point, then cool off with a short walk to Mossy Cave, near the park's north end. In the winter, the cave is fringed with icicles like tinsel on a Christmas tree. If it's summer, treat yourself to a night at the rodeo, just outside the park at Ruby's Inn (Wednesday through Saturday only), along with a plate of ribeye at Ebenezer's Barn and Grill.

09

UT

Canyon-lands National Park

Mighty rivers carved this high desert plateau into an adventure-ready patchwork of soaring mesas, crumbling pinnacles, graceful arches and impenetrable red rock canyons.

Canyonlands makes you wonder about your place in the universe. With sheer cliffs dropping more than a thousand feet, rugged mesas stretching into the horizon and a vast night sky sharing clear views of the Milky Way, it's easy to feel unmoored. Which might explain the allure of Mesa Arch, a gold-and-crimson span stretching delicately across the rim of the park's central mesa. By directing your gaze and framing a handful of distant sandstone formations, Mesa Arch renders the landscape accessible, less terrifying. You feel as if you're admiring a landscape portrait in Mother's Nature's living room. Mesa Arch is especially beautiful at sunrise, when the fiery sun sets the rocks aglow.

The Colorado and the Green Rivers merge in the northern section of the park, forming a 'Y' that divides Canyonlands into three distinct districts. In the center is the Island in the Sky District, which sprawls across a flat-topped mesa with sweeping views over the Needles and the Maze. Island in the Sky sees the most visitors, luring travelers with unique geologic formations and overlooks perched atop sheer walls. The Needles District is a storybook wonderland of orange-and-white sandstone pinnacles. The Maze, packed tight with labyrinthine canyons and bad roads, is the most remote and inaccessible of the districts. (As the old maps might warn: 'There be dragons.')

The park lies within the Colorado Plateau, a 130,000-sq-mile (336,698 sq km) tableland of layered sedimentary rocks that began forming hundreds of millions of years ago. Ten million years ago geologic forces pushed this tableland skyward; water carved the spires, arches and bridges. A high desert park, Canyonlands experiences very cold winters and hot summers, and sees less than 10in (25cm) of rain per year. The park earned an International Dark Skies Park designation in 2015, meaning it's one of the best places in the world to stargaze, with minimal light pollution and vividly clear views of the cosmos.

Toolbox

When to go
For ideal temperatures, visit in April, May or from mid-September through October. Expect daytime highs between 60°F (16°C) and 80°F (27°C) degrees. The temperature drops 30 degrees F (17 degrees C) at night. Summer highs can top 100°F (38°C).

Getting there
The park is divided into three sections, which are not connected by roads within the park. Island in the Sky is 30 miles (48km) from Moab. The Needles is 75 miles (121km) south of Moab. Dirt roads link Hwy 24 and the Maze, a 3½-hour drive from Moab.

Park in numbers

527
Area covered (sq miles)

350
Number of bighorn sheep in the park

7120
Highest point: Cathedral Point, Needles District (ft)

Getty Images | David Epperson

Stay here...

Willow Flat
Ah, sweet solitude. There are only 12 campsites at this lonely campground, which sits atop the Island in the Sky mesa. Well-situated, the campground is a short distance from the Green River Overlook, Aztec Butte and Mesa Arch.

Squaw Flat
How would you like to pitch your tent beside toadstool red rocks in a campsite at the end of the map? This 26-site campground in the Needles District feels a thousand miles from the modern world, but camping here allows you to sleep-in before hitting nearby trails. (Those hikers staying in Moab? They've got a 90-minute drive to get here.)

Three Dogs & A Moose
Active travelers and fun-loving families, here's your basecamp. It's easy to unwind after a hard day on the trail in these lovely and low-key cottages in downtown Moab. Touches are playful-modern, with corrugated tin showers and recycled doors.

Do this!

Mountain biking
Ready to grunt, sweat and kick up some red dust? Built by uranium prospectors, the 100-mile (161km) dirt-road White Rim Trail loops around the base of Island in the Sky mesa. Steep and exposed switchbacks, dropping from the top of the mesa to the canyon floor, start the fun. The ride takes three or four days; campsites dot the trail.

Stargazing
Viewing the silky Milky Way from the top of the Island in the Sky district is breathtaking. In the spring and fall, rangers from Canyonlands and nearby Dead Horse State Park lead star talks, which are followed by stargazing and telescope-viewing. Canyonlands is an International Dark Skies Park.

Rafting
Class III rapids keep the ride wild in Cataract Canyon, just south of the confluence of the Colorado and Green Rivers. Local outfitters offer multiday trips. The wildest rides are in the late spring when the rivers run high with Class IV and V rapids.

Mountain bikers swoop around the switchbacks of the 100-mile (160km) White Rim Rd. Previous page: the Needles District.

What to spot...

In this scrubby high desert park, mammals, amphibians and reptiles have adapted to temperature extremes and the unforgiving landscape. Who survives? The quickest, the wariest, the nocturnal foragers and those that are masters of camouflage. Eleven species of cactus grow in the park, including the prickly pear. Cottonwood trees and willows thrive near rivers and streams. Look for wildflower blooms in April and May and again in early fall after heavy summer monsoons.

MOUNTAIN LION
These wide-ranging hunters prey on mule deer and other small mammals, which keeps populations in check. Quiet and elusive, mountain lions are rarely spotted by visitors.

KANGAROO RAT The kangaroo rat doesn't need to drink water – ever! That's right, this desert wunderkind gets all the water it needs from gnawing on plants. Expert long jumpers, these athletic rodents can jump up to 9ft (2.7m) in just one hop!

UTAH JUNIPER This stubborn desert tree seems to thrive on conditions that would destroy other plants. Extreme temps? High winds? No water? No problem. Often seen growing from barren rock outcrops, it's supported by a sprawling root system persistent in its search for water.

Hike this...

01 Mesa Arch & Grand View Point
Short trails lead to big views atop the Island in the Sky mesa. Mesa Arch Trail ends with inspiration; Grand View Trail ends with an exclamation – and a step back from the rim. Mesa Arch Trail is an 0.5-mile (0.8km) round-trip; Grand View Trail is a 2-mile (3.2km) round-trip.

02 Chesler Park/Joint Trail
Striped pinnacles, desert grasslands and slot canyons impress on this 11-mile (17.7km) loop in the Needles district.

03 Horseshoe Canyon
The millennia-old rock art in the Great Gallery is impressive. Horseshoe Canyon is west of the Island in the Sky District. The hike is a 7-mile (11.3km) round-trip.

Itineraries

It's all epic roadtrips in this Thelma and Louise setting. But mountain-biking, whitewater rafting and hiking fans won't be disappointed either.

← Hiking in the Needles District of Canyonlands National Park; Petroglyphs on Newspaper Rock.
→ Taking a 4WD safari.

01

A day

Got your camera? Water and lunch? And your hat? Then you're ready for the Island in the Sky District, which sits atop a mesa. On your way, detour to Dead Horse Point State Park. From its 2000ft-high (610m) perch you'll enjoy sweeping views of the Colorado River and the Canyonlands. Remember the movie *Thelma & Louise*? This is where the duo soared over the abyss.

At the Island in the Sky Visitor Center, check the daily schedule for ranger-led programs and hikes. Next up is a cruise on the scenic road, which is dotted with mesa-rim overlooks, short trails to big views and plenty of odd-shaped rocks. For the biggest wows, drive 12 miles (19.3km) to Grand View Point. The expansive views of the park from the overlook are stunning, but stunning jumps to epic at the end of the 1-mile hike (1.6km) to the point, which serves up a glimpse of a sheer drop down the mesa wall.

Savor your picnic at the Grand View Overlook, then head to a ranger talk. Feeling spry? Then hike 0.5 miles (0.8km) to the viewpoint at Upheaval Dome, a circular depression that may have been created by a meteor strike 60 million years ago. Stop by the Green River Overlook, and then it's time for the end-of-day showstopper: Mesa Arch. This slender arch stretches across the rim of the mesa, framing Washerwoman Arch, Monster Tower and the La Sal Mountains. Mesa Arch is also popular at sunrise, when the span glows fiery red as the sun rises behind it. At the end of the day, burgers and microbrews beckon at Moab Brewery.

02

Two days

For sunrise views, secure a campsite at Squaw Flat Campground in the Needles District. Juniper trees and red rock cliffs provide shade for many sites on side A of the ground. After breakfast, drive north to explore Dead Horse Point State Park and the Island in the Sky District.

On day two, stop by the Needles Visitor Center to watch the short movie *Wilderness of Rock*. Then explore the family-friendly sites and short trails along the scenic road. The 0.6-mile (1km) Cave Spring Loop climbs ladders and traverses slickrock on the way to an abandoned cowboy camp. (Don't miss the handprint pictographs in the last cave!)

Other sights along the road include arches, petroglyphs and an Ancestral Puebloan granary. The Pothole Trail passes sandstone basins filled with water and animal life. This is a nice trail for watching the sunset, which splashes light across the Needles District. Hard-core hikers may prefer spending the day on the Chesler Park/Joint Trail, which loops through desert grasslands and slot canyons.

03

Six days

Ease into your red rock neighborhood with a one-day jaunt across Island in the Sky mesa, taking a detour to Dead House Point State Park. Spend your second day among spires and canyons in the Needles. The last few days? Choose your own adventure. Take a four-day bike ride and camping trip on the 100-mile (161km) White Rim Trail around the base of Island in the Sky District – or if white water is your passion, join a multiday guided trip through Cataract Canyon, where the Green and Colorado Rivers collide.

10

UT

Capitol Reef National Park

Once called the Land of the Sleeping Rainbow by Native Americans, this is canyon country at its dazzling best.

Getty Images | Danita Delimont

I t hardly matters that you've never heard of it. Among Utah's many visual riches, this one, large but low-key, has many facets. A wonderland of improbable formations, Capitol Reef is made up of red arches, stone domes, cathedral monoliths and terracotta canyons. It's a geography so convoluted that Butch Cassidy once used it as a hideout.

Visitors explore its serpentine paths, raise dust on its rugged 4WD roads and admire its thousand-year-old rock art. The park has 150 miles (241km) of hiking trails, with the longest and most established routes in the northern and southern sectors. At Gooseneck overlook, gaze out over the Sulphur Creek twisting its way through red rock. Road tours showcase breathtaking scenery on rough roads. Though the pioneers rode them in wagons, you will be much better off with a high-clearance 4WD.

It is all part of the Waterpocket Fold, a 100-mile-long (161km) buckle in the earth's crust that served as a barrier for explorers' westward migration like a reef blocks a ship's passage. The rest of the name comes from the park's white domes, thought to resemble the US Capitol building. At Capitol Reef's heart grow the abundant orchards of Fruita, a Mormon settlement dating back to the 1870s.

Before them, the Fremont people occupied the fertile floodplain of the Fremont River, growing grains, squash and lentils until the 13th century, when their settlements were abandoned. Some of their granaries and intriguing petroglyph panels remain for visitors to peruse.

Yet history runs even deeper here. Scientists have discovered that this area is

part of the oldest megatracksite in North America, with trace fossils from sharks and reptiles that roamed the earth even before the dinosaurs. Capitol Reef has always been a land of transformation – and thus, enchantment – an ancient seabed that is now a majestic desert.

 Hiking the Grand Wash in Capitol Reef National Park. Previous page: cottonwood trees along Sulphur Creek.

Toolbox

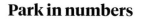 **When to go**
Most travelers prefer to visit in spring or fall, as summers bring intense heat and monsoon thunderstorms. Visit between June and October and pluck ripe fruit from the trees for a small fee.

Getting there
Capitol Reef is 3½ hours by car to Salt Lake City, the state capital (which has international flights). The best way to travel through Southern Utah is by car, or 4WD to explore the backroads. Accommodations and services are in nearby Torrey.

Park in numbers

390
Area covered (sq miles)

887
Plant species

2700
Fruit trees

Stay here...

Fruita Campground

Welcome to your desert oasis. Set under sturdy cottonwood trees along the Fremont River, this park campground is also surrounded by historic barns and orchards planted by Mormon settlers. It's no wonder it's so popular. It's also central to hiking trails.

Torrey Schoolhouse B&B

Black-and-white portraits of fidgety generations of schoolchildren line the hallways of this restored 1914 schoolhouse. With antiques and country elegance, it's solid brick on the outside and full nostalgia on the inside. For today's guests it's a sound sleep and a gourmet breakfast with travelers from around the world.

Lodge at Red River Ranch

Modeled after the great Western ranches, this immense timber lodge in Teasdale invokes an upscale cowboy sensibility. Guests enjoy country quilts, Navajo rugs and a sprawling great room. The red-rock surroundings are sublime, especially if you want to take in the constellations from the outdoor hot tub.

Do this!

Mountain biking & driving

The best of the desert lies along its backroads. Long-distance mountain bikers and 4WDers love the bumpy, roughshod 58-mile (93km) loop route through Cathedral Valley. It's the ideal way to explore the park's remote north, with its alien desert landscapes, pierced by giant sandstone monoliths eroded into fantastic shapes.

Fruit-picking

The first Mormon homesteaders arrived here in 1880; Fruita's final resident left in 1969. Among the historic buildings, the NPS maintains 2700 cherry, apricot, peach, pear and apple trees planted by early settlers. Pick fruit in season or enjoy a picnic surrounded by deer and songbirds – a desert rarity.

Exploring ancient culture

Rock-art carvings (called petroglyphs) can be found at roadside panels or deep into the dusty backcountry. From bighorn sheep to horned beings and spirals, these riddles, clues or remnants speak to the 2000-year-old culture of the Fremont people. You can find the most accessible petroglyphs along Hwy 24 just east of the Visitor Center.

What to spot...

A variety of habitats, such as piñon-juniper, perennial streams, dry washes and rock cliffs, offer microhabitats and niches that allow for diverse plant and animal life in the park. Even the fragile biological soil crusts play a major role in the ecosystem. More than 300 animal species live here, including a number of lizards, snakes and reptiles in addition to deer, coyote and small rodents.

YELLOW-BELLIED MARMOTS
This large squirrel or rock chuck abounds in the Fruita area; you'll find it active in spring through summer before it retreats to burrows for the winter.

MIDGET-FADED RATTLESNAKE
Common in the West, these 2ft (61cm) poisonous snakes subdue their prey with an anesthetic venom injection via their hollow fangs.

GOLDEN EAGLE
Brown with golden neck plumage, this eagle is among the most respected birds in falconry. Agile and quick, it swoops down from the cliffs to claim rabbits and marmot as its prey.

Hike this...

O1 Grand Wash Trail

This 2.2-mile (3.5km) walk through the narrows grows dramatic as the canyon walls reach 80 stories high – and only a car's width apart.

O2 Navajo Knobs

For superb views of the park and beyond, follow a high slickrock ledge for 9 miles (14.5km) to these twin knobs perched on the edge of the Waterpocket Fold.

O3 Lower Muley Twist Canyon

A lovely, twisting 15-mile (24km) trail follows a deep and narrow canyon through an old Mormon wagon route. An overnight hike with ample opportunity for side trips and exploration.

Itineraries

Whether you drive or hike, Capitol Reef's red rock art is a must-see. Combine it with some backcountry 4WD odysseys, fortified by Fruita's fruit pies.

 The hedgehog-like claret cup cactus; on the road in Capitol Reef.
➡ Fruita schoolhouse.

01
A day

In the heart of Utah's canyon country, Capitol Reef sits between Canyonlands and Bryce Canyon National Parks along Utah Hwy 24. Many visitors do a pass-through. Do it justice by spending the day.

In the desert, first light is the coveted hour to hike. Much of the hiking here is shadeless, and sandy paths absorb and radiate heat. By high noon, you want to be snoozing under a cottonwood or wading into the cool Fremont River. Start at Hickman Bridge trail, a 1 mile (1.6km) stroll though wildflowers to a canyon with a natural bridge. Break for lunch in the shade of Fruita's orchards.

Along Hwy 24, visit the petroglyphs. There's also a historic schoolhouse and the one-room 1882 Behunin Cabin, once home to a family of ten. The park's scenic drive was actually the main highway until 1962. This skinny, zig-zagging road gets you up close with the buckling Waterpocket Fold. Its final miles are the most stunning, passing Capitol Dome and the Golden Throne as it reaches deep passages of the gorge.

02
A weekend

Follow the one-day itinerary. Pitch your tent at Fruita Campground and pick up dessert from the small store next door – the fruit pies sell out daily. Catch the evening ranger program for insights on local culture or ecology. The next morning, hit the trail early.

How ambitious are you? If the answer is very, take Cohab Canyon and the Frying Pan link over the top of the Waterfold to reach Cassidy Arch – you'll find canyons within canyons, fragrant juniper forest and undulating slickrock criss-crossed by lizards. The Cassidy Arch is approached from above; walk it like a pirate-ship plank if you dare. It's 7 miles (11km) one-way, but easiest if you make it one-way and shuttle a car to the end at the Grand Wash parking area.

Finish the trip with a drive along 58-mile (93km) Cathedral Valley loop in a 4WD vehicle. Late in the day is the golden hour for a photo safari: long shadows add to the drama of the many monoliths of Cathedral Valley and its hills banded with rainbow hues.

03
Four days

Nothing says adventure like the twisting watercourses and squiggly lines of a topographic map. If you have the right set and know how to use it, backcountry hiking is awesome here. Think solitary trails, sculpted landscapes and dark nights lit with constellations.

Spend days one and two seeing Capitol Reef and Cassidy Arch, then visit with rangers to work out backcountry permits. Head north to the Cathedral district for roadless expanses marked by stunning monoliths with names like Temples of the Sun and Moon. Or journey to the southern Waterpocket district to explore landscapes of slot canyons, arches and slickrock. There are lots of options, but all require supplies of drinking water, and some a 4WD vehicle.

If you have time, drive Loop the Fold, a scenic 124-mile (199km) trip. Part paved, part 4WD trail, it circles the Waterpocket by several iconic routes, including the burly Notom-Bullfrog Rd, an odyssey through curious formations and kaleidoscope colors with views of the eponymous fold.

11

NM

Carlsbad Caverns National Park

Hidden beneath the cactus-covered ridges of the Guadalupe Mountains lies a sprawling, subterranean wonderland of soaring chambers and otherworldly features.

Elaborately carved by the slow hand of time, the magnificent underground rooms and glittering passageways of Carlsbad Caverns feel like a portal into another realm. It's hard to imagine a more dramatic transition than to leave the desert air behind and step through the cool, utterly silent tunnels, with every twist and turn revealing a wondrous collection of artfully wrought formations.

The magic and mystery of Carlsbad becomes all the more apparent when you realize the extraordinary processes that created these sparkling chambers. It all began some 250 million years ago, when a large but shallow inland sea covered this area, along with a horseshoe-shaped reef that stretched for 400 miles (644km). As the climate changed and the earth evolved, the reef was buried under deposits of salt and gypsum. A few million years ago, uplift caused the ancient reef to rise some 2 miles (3.2km) skyward, creating large cracks and fissures. Over the following millennia, rainwater seeped into the cracks, fresh water mixing with saltwater to create sulfuric acid, its corrosive power slowly shaping the massive underground chambers. The birth of the cave as a magnificent work of nature began about one million years ago, as rainwater, drip by drip, seeped through the layers of the earth, each droplet depositing a tiny mineral load of calcite – thus creating the spectacular array of stalactites, stalagmites, soda straws, helictites, draperies and cave pearls.

Although little early human evidence has been found inside the caves, Native American tribes left their mark in the area, including a 1000-year-old pictograph near the main entrance. Carlsbad's fame, however, really began with Jim White, a 16-year-old cowhand who entered the caves in 1898 – a discovery that would change his life. He became the first to explore the caves and named many of its rooms and major formations (the Big Room, King's Palace, Bottomless Pit, Witch's Finger). He was also the cave's biggest promoter, leading members of a scientific expedition and later serving as the chief ranger of the caves.

⬆ Stalactites and stalagmites in Carlsbad Caverns, deep in the Guadalupe Mountains.
➡ The Chandelier.

Toolbox

When to go

It's worth planning a trip around the nightly bat flights, which happen May through October. Specific caving tours are offered only certain times of the week; advanced reservations are recommended. To beat the crowds, avoid coming on busy holiday weekends.

Getting there
Carlsbad Caverns National Park is located in the southeastern corner of New Mexico. The closest airports are in El Paso, 140 miles (225km) southwest (a 2¼-hour drive), and Midland, 160 miles (258km) east (a three-hour drive). Rental cars are available at either airport.

Park in numbers

73
Area covered (sq miles)

830
Deepest point (in ft)

120
Number of known caves

Stay here...

The Trinity Hotel
Set against the big open skies of southeastern New Mexico, this historic 1892 building was once a bank; you can almost imagine the row of horses saddled up out front. Overnighting here amid big arched windows and corridors lined with antiques is a journey back to a bygone era, when the southwest was still a mysterious and little-known frontier.

Fiddler's Inn
You'll receive a warm welcome when you roll up to this tranquil B&B located a few blocks west of Lake Carlsbad. Julie and Tonk, who plays the fiddle (hence the inn's name), make you feel right at home, regaling you with stories of their own travels and sharing their favorite places in Carlsbad.

Camping on BLM Land
For a true back-to-nature experience, pitch your tent on a hillside a short drive from the turnoff to the caverns. Gazing out over the landscape with no human presence in sight is pure magic; by evening you can catch dramatic sunsets, then watch the Milky Way light up the sky.

Do this!

Bat-watching
From May to mid-October, hundreds of thousands of Brazilian free-tailed bats roost in the caves. The nightly exodus happens just after dusk; you can watch from an amphitheater built near the cave entrance. Around sunset, rangers give a short presentation describing these fascinating mammals, before the bats take to the Chihuahuan desert in search of food.

Stargazing
The night sky is exceptionally dark in this remote corner of New Mexico – seeing the Milky Way and hundreds of stars and constellations is not to be missed. The Caverns hosts periodic 'star parties,' where visitors can gaze through telescopes. Rangers also lead dark-sky wilderness walks to point out celestial wonders on short hikes into backcountry.

Hiking
Outside the caves, you'll find over 50 miles (80.5km) of hiking trails, from short, 0.5-mile (0.8km) desert trails to more challenging all-day treks. The Rattlesnake Canyon Trail follows a steep descent into a side canyon, past the ruins of a 1930s homestead on a 5-mile (8km) round-trip hike.

Explore this!

01 Kings Palace
This 90-minute, 1-mile (1.6km) ranger-led tour takes you through four underground chambers, including some of the deepest caverns open to the public.

02 Slaughter Canyon
For a look at the wilder side of Carlsbad, sign up for the moderately challenging 5½-hour guided trek. Among the highlights: the 89ft-high (27m) Monarch, one of the world's tallest limestone columns.

03 Lower Cave
Adventurers will enjoy this three-hour tour taking in an amazing array of formations, including cave pearls and the stalactite-filled 'Texas toothpick.' Descent is by 60ft (18.3m) of ladders and a knotted rope at the cave's entrance.

What to spot...

Set in the Guadalupe Mountains, and surrounded by the Chihuahuan Desert, Carlsbad Caverns has several distinct habitats, chief among them desert shrublands. Although this is a semi-arid environment, it is one of the wettest deserts in North America, with an average of 14.4in (around 37cm) of rain per year. This helps support a diverse ecosystem, including 67 mammal species, 357 bird species and more than 900 plant species.

BRAZILIAN FREETAIL BATS The mammalian star of Carlsbad Caverns is the Brazilian freetail bat, which has a wingspan of 11in (28cm) and weighs just 0.5oz (14g) – about as much as three nickels. More than 400,000 of these insectivores roost in the caves.

TULIP PRICKLY PEAR This striking desert plant is found all across the southwest. The flowers grow atop flattened green, spiky pads, and typically have yellow petals with reddish coloration toward the base.

GIANT DESERT CENTIPEDE These impressive-looking creatures can grow up to 8in (20cm) in length and are capable of delivering a nasty (though not life-threatening) sting. Swift and agile, they typically hunt at night.

Itineraries

Bat cave or spider cave? There's plenty of both creatures to observe here, along with stunning cavern formations. Or just hike the trails under sunset desert skies.

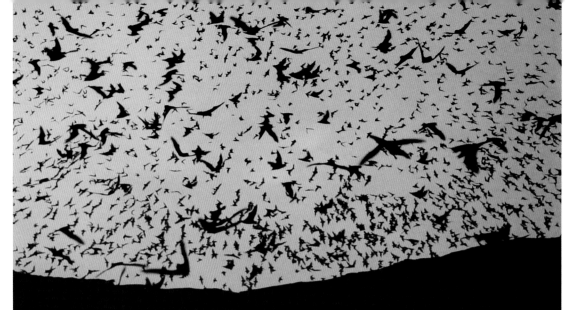

◄ Stalactites drip down, stalagmites grow up.
► Bats exit the caves every night to feed.

01

A day

Get an early start by arriving at the caverns around opening time, at 8am. In the early morning, the winding drive in to the park can be magical, with the desert landscape bathed in a golden light. If you're in good shape, skip the elevators and make the long descent to the cave entrance on foot, as it gives a fine perspective on just how deep underground – 750ft (229m), or about 79 stories – you're going. Once at the entrance, paths lead to the mesmerizing Great

Room – the largest single cave chamber in North America. It's a wonderland of glittering, sculpture-like formations of all shapes and sizes, from massive columns to elaborately carved stalactites and such curious depressions as the Bottomless Pit.

Once you finish the circuit, take the elevator back up to the surface and grab a bite to eat in the cafeteria. Then head out for a 9.5-mile (15.3km) scenic drive through the otherworldly landscape of the Chihuahuan Desert

along the Desert Loop Rd. Keep an eye out for mule deer and javelinas, a small mammal also known as a collared peccary but, despite pig-like appearances, is only very distantly related to wild boar).

Around dusk, return to the cave entrance to watch the bat flight program, when huge swarms of Brazilian free-tailed bats fly out of the cave in the fading light of day for their nightly feeding: a mesmerising end to the day and your cue to head on to Carlsbad.

02

A weekend

After the self-guided tour, scenic drive and bat-watching on day one, spend your second day delving deeper into the caverns.

Sign up for one of the private ranger-guided tours. For a real adventure, head into the Spider Cave: true to its name, this cave is full of (harmless!) spiders, which you may encounter on crawls through damp, narrow tunnels. You'll get dirty as you crawl, climb and clamber your way past stunning formations,

like the so-called Medusa Room with its intricate web of helictites. (A helmet with headlamp, along with kneepads and gloves are provided.)

Later that day, take a hike along the Rattlesnake Canyon Trail, one of Carlsbad's most scenic hikes. Few visitors make the trip out, so you'll largely have the trail to yourself. The 6-mile (9.7km) round-trip hike starts at the top of the mesa ridge and takes you down to a dusty creek bed, up a small incline

and then down into the bone-dry canyon, with dramatic views along the way. The rest of the hike winds its way along the canyon. You'll pass a wide array of desert flora, with blooming cacti in springtime. You might also hear the coo of a Bobwhite quail, stumble upon a few pronghorn, and spy a few spotted skunks slinking along the parched lowlands. End the day back at the visitor center, watching the desert turn an auburn glow at sunset.

Carlsbad Caverns

12

CA

Channel Islands National Park

Off SoCal's sunny coast, these islands – nicknamed 'California's Galapagos' – harbor abundant wildlife and memorable adventures by land and sea.

I f you've ever dreamed of sailing off the edge of the world, this may be as close as you'll ever get. It's hard to believe these utterly remote islands were once populated. But when you step off the boat onto these ancient rocks, you are following in the footsteps of indigenous people who arrived here more than 12,000 years ago. Chumash tribespeople paddled *tomols* (canoes carved out of redwood logs) across the channel and built villages here, followed much later by European explorers, seal and abalone hunters, livestock ranchers, shipwrecked sailors and smugglers.

Even more fascinating than the story of people in this place is the islands' remarkably varied wildlife. Many animals and plants that exist here are found nowhere else on the planet, making a vivid display of evolutionary biology. For other species endangered now or in the past, the islands have been a safe haven, including for such animals as northern elephant seals, northern fur seals (called 'sea bears' by 19th-century European explorers) and migratory gray whales, which pass by every winter. For visitors, the islands present an unequalled opportunity for wildlife spotting, whether you want to hike your way across windy bluffs or kayak around the coast.

Each of the park's five islands is unique. Anacapa, the island closest to the mainland, comprises three tiny islets totaling less than a square mile; in springtime thousands of nesting seabirds crowd every available inch of space here. Santa Cruz, the next island further west, is almost a hundred times larger, and features Diablo Peak, a 2450ft-high (747m) mountain, and one of the largest sea caves in the world, Painted Cave. Santa Rosa, the second-largest island, abounds with archaeological sites and fossil finds – try to imagine what it looked like during the Pleistocene epoch, when miniature mammoths roamed across the landscape.

Toolbox

When to go
Fair autumn weather brings calmer seas for water sports. Spring sees colorful wildflowers, but also fog and strong wind that may persist into summer. Late summer is hot and dry. Winter can be stormy, but it's spectacular for wildlife-watching.

Getting there
Most people arrive by boat, either on an organized tour or a ferry from Ventura, off Hwy 101 in Southern California, between Los Angeles and Santa Barbara. Flightseeing planes depart from Camarillo, closer to LA.

Park in numbers

390
Area covered (sq miles)

5
Number of islands

145
Species found nowhere else in the world

Stay here...

The only way to stay overnight on the Channel Islands is to camp. No matter which island you choose to visit, advance reservations are required – both for campsites and ferry transportation. Come prepared for a primitive wilderness experience, far from any of the creature comforts of civilization.

Scorpion Ranch Campground
The park's biggest campground is popular with families and groups. It's a flat, 0.5-mile (0.8km) walk from where boats dock on Santa Cruz Island. Hiking trails start nearby.

Santa Rosa Campground
On Santa Rosa Island, this mid-sized campground is tucked into a windy canyon, where campsites are partly sheltered by lean-tos and eucalyptus trees. It's a flat 1.5-mile (2.4km) walk from the ferry dock.

Anacapa Campground
From the ferry dock, it's a steep 0.5-mile (0.8km) walk that ascends over 150 stairs to reach these sunny, exposed campsites with unforgettable ocean views. Don't forget to pack in all the water you'll need.

Do this!

Kayaking
Paddle your own kayak beneath sea arches and towering cliffs, or explore marine caves from the inside out. Beginners can start with a shoreline float around Santa Cruz Island, putting in at Scorpion Beach for easy access to sparkling clear waters.

Diving & snorkeling
Don a mask and plunk your face down into the ocean to peer at schools of brightly colored fish darting around kelp forests. The orange garibaldi, California's state fish, is particularly easy to spot. These islands also offer some of the best scuba diving in the US. Divers might even encounter a giant black sea bass weighing a whopping 800lb (363kg) – wow!

Tidepooling
Set far from the crowded, overdeveloped mainland, the islands' tidepools are protected by Mother Nature. Around every island's shoreline, rocky pools harbor a spectacular array of rainbow-colored marine critters, including hungry sea stars, spiny urchins, clinging barnacles and mussels, and tiny periwinkle snails.

← A harbor seal plays in an underwater forest.
➜ Anacapa Island.

Hike this...

01 Inspiration Point
Soak up Anacapa Island's best views on this 1.5-mile (2.4km) trail, which passes Pinniped Point, where sea lions haul out to sunbathe.

02 Cavern Point & Potato Harbor
On Santa Cruz Island, climb a steep 5.5 miles (8.9km) for clifftop vistas and whale-watching, then hike atop the bluffs to a picturesque harbor.

03 Cherry Canyon
Traipse 3.5 miles (5.6km) through riparian wetlands on Santa Rosa Island, detouring to white-sand Water Canyon Beach or to summit Black Mountain.

Getty Images | Douglas Klug; Mint Images

What to spot...

California's Channel Islands were something of a primeval Garden of Eden before the arrival of humans. Their isolation spurred the evolution of marvelous biodiversity, just like what Darwin observed in the famous Galapagos Islands. After centuries of environmental abuse, such as rampant livestock grazing, accidental oil spills and military bombing practice, the islands are now on the road to recovery. In recent decades, ambitious conservation projects have restored lost habitat and protected rare wildlife.

CALIFORNIA SEA LION The most playful of the islands' pinnipeds like to bark, bask on the sand and splash around in the surf, then dive deep for squid.

NORTHERN ELEPHANT SEAL Once in danger of going extinct, these enormous beasts are thriving again on the islands, where they mate and give birth in winter.

CALIFORNIA BROWN PELICAN These pouch-billed birds were officially endangered until 2009. Today, the only known breeding colonies are on Anacapa and Santa Barbara Islands.

Itineraries

Spend a day on Anacapa Island or several on Santa Cruz or Santa Rosa. There's plenty of snorkeling and swimming on offer.

◄ Purple sea urchins populate the ocean floor.
➔ Divers will spy wildlife large and small.

01
A day

Have a light breakfast before boarding the ferry to Anacapa Island – the channel crossing can be a bit bumpy for landlubbers. Spy wild dolphins chasing your boat through the water as you sail toward Landing Cove, while iconic Arch Rock appears on the horizon. Arriving on the island, firmly grasp the metal ladder rungs and scramble up onto the wooden dock, then climb a steep stairway until you pop out atop the islet, where panoramic ocean views welcome you.

Drop by the island visitor center to watch a live scuba-diving broadcast or to join a ranger-guided program. When you're ready, 2 miles (3.2km) of hiking trails await outside. But there's no rush, because you can see it all in an afternoon – just don't miss the last boat back. Start hiking toward Inspiration Point, pausing at Pinniped Point to peer down at a noisy California sea lion colony. In spring, look for colorful wildflowers alongside the trail. On the return hike, detour to Cathedral Cove, another spectacular lookout over captivating rock formations.

02
Two days

See more than day-trippers ever do on an overnight camping trip to Santa Cruz Island. The morning ferry drops you off at curvy Scorpion Beach, where brightly colored kayaks are lined up on the sand. Heave-ho with your backpack for the 0.5-mile (0.8km) walk to the campground, where island foxes run around (note that you're not allowed to feed them). After setting up your tent and having a picnic lunch in the shade, head back to the beach for an afternoon of swimming and snorkeling when the ocean is calm.

Get up early the next day and step into your hiking boots. It's a huff-and-puff climb from the campground up to Cavern Point, but you'll be rewarded by stunning panoramas of cliffs and coves. Follow the rolling North Bluff Trail out to Potato Harbor. Passing through a eucalyptus grove, loop back to the campground and pack up your gear. Poke around the historic buildings of Scorpion Ranch on your way back to the beach to catch the last afternoon ferry.

03
Three days

After sailing 40 nautical miles (74 nautical km) off the California coast to Santa Rosa, you'll want to stay at least a night or two, especially with so many places to explore. The boat ride takes just over two hours – or you can pay more for a faster flight that touches down on the island's dirt airstrip.

Set up base camp at the sheltered canyon campground, then hoof it back to gorgeous, white-sand Water Canyon Beach. If it's not too windy, picnic tables fronting this 2-mile (3.2km) strand are a perfect spot for lunch before a bit of beachcombing. The next morning, pack a day-pack for a long hike through grassy Cherry Canyon and, if you're up for it, all the way to the top of Black Mountain.

On your third day, walk just as far as you feel like along the coastal road toward East Point, passing rare Torrey pine trees and hidden beaches. Pack up camp after lunch and go meet the afternoon boat to reluctantly return to civilization.

13

SC

Congaree National Park

Canoeing through the black waters of Congaree – Spanish moss dripping overhead, muffled bird-cries in the distance – is a journey into South Carolina's heart of darkness.

ongaree is 41 sq miles (106 sq km) of Southern Gothic landscapes. At the park's southern boundary, the wide, brown Congaree River snakes past forest and bluff, its waters alive with fish, turtles and snakes. The park's interior is the largest old-growth bottomland forest in the southeastern US. Here, you'll find a fairyland of floodplain trees – bulbous cypress with fluted trunks; towering swamp tupelo overgrown with emerald-hued lichen; water hickory with strips of peeling bark like wallpaper in an old mansion. These dark swamps hide a bestiary of reptiles, amphibians, insects and birds, as well as the occasional snorting feral pig – not to mention mosquitoes. (Bring your bug spray!)

The Congaree people who fished these waterways were largely killed off by smallpox introduced by European settlers around 1700. The new settlers tried their best to make the land farmable, but flooding washed away their efforts time and again. Eventually, in the early 1900s, logging operations bought up the land, cutting down the bald cypress and floating it down river. But logging, too, proved difficult, thanks to the bogginess of the land, and the loggers ultimately left the area to nature. Half a century later, high timber prices led private landowners to consider logging again. The Sierra Club, horrified at the thought of the pristine land being destroyed, led a campaign to have the land protected, and the Congaree Swamp National Monument

was established in 1976. In 2003, the monument became a national park.

A casual day-visitor will enjoy checking out the displays in Congaree's visitor center and ambling down the well-kept boardwalk trail nearby. But the swamp-lover who wants to take a deeper look can spend days paddling Congaree's shallow, vegetation-choked waterways, fishing in its still lakes and camping on its bluffs. At night, the hoots of owls and the guttural croak of frogs, pierced by the occasional coyote howl, makes civilization feel very far away indeed.

⬆ Butterweed blooms in the Frenchman's Gut area of Congaree National Park.

Toolbox

When to go
Congaree is open year-round, and the temperate climate makes it pleasant to visit any time. While it's rarely crowded, on weekends the campsites can play host to local scouting troops and college groups.

Getting there
Located in the state of South Carolina, Congaree is a 30-minute drive from the capital city of Columbia, home to a major airport. It's two hours from the popular vacation destination of Charleston. You'll need your own car.

Park in numbers

41.5
Area covered (sq miles)

167
Tallest tree (ft)

0
Park entrance fee ($)

Stay here...

Longleaf Campground
Congaree's accommodations are two primitive campgrounds; Longleaf has car access while Bluff does not. Get close to nature here, camping under the pines with no amenities (beyond a fire ring, picnic table and chemical toilet), waking to the hammering of woodpeckers. Water is available 24/7 at the visitor center. And even better: camping in Congaree is free!

1425 Inn
South Carolina's capital, Columbia, is the nearest non-camping place to stay when visiting Congaree.

This sweet Southern B&B is about as far as you can get from a swamp, with its poster beds, claw-foot tubs and rocking chair–graced porch. The innkeepers earn high marks for Southern hospitality.

Inn at USC
Adjacent to the University of South Carolina campus, this elegant brick hotel is a favorite with alums and parents (don't even think of trying to stay on graduation weekend). You'll be comfortable here, with pillowy beds, enormous bathrooms and a porch lined with rocking chairs. Breakfasts are highly rated.

Do this!

Canoeing
Paddling the dark waters of Congaree through primeval, old-growth forest is the number-one reason to visit the park. See otters, turtles, snakes and even (occasionally) gators as you pass beneath bald cypress trees dripping with Spanish moss. In the deliciously spooky heart of the swamp, it's almost possible to forget that civilization even exists.

Walking
Did you know that Spanish moss belongs to the same plant family as the pineapple? Learn fun facts like this on one of Congaree's 90-minute nature walks, led by volunteer naturalists every Saturday morning. Stroll the boardwalks as the guide points out air plants, wading birds and even the occasional snake while detailing what life is like in Congaree's 22 different plant communities.

Fishing
For a peaceful afternoon, paddle out into the middle of a wide brown Congaree waterway and drop a line. Fishing is allowed throughout the park (except for the Weston Lake overlook) with a South Carolina fishing license. Catches include largemouth bass and catfish – deep-water holes and undercut banks make the Congaree River good territory for the latter, which can grow as big as hogs.

Hike this...

01 Boardwalk Trail
You can't visit Congaree without strolling this 2.4-mile (4km) elevated boardwalk through the old-growth bottomland hardwood forest. Pass beneath cypress, tupelo and loblolly pine, keeping your eyes open for turtles and snakes.

02 Weston Lake Loop
Skirt Cedar Creek, looking out for otters and wading birds, on this 4.4-mile (7km) loop, with good views of a creepy, dried-up river full of cypress knees.

03 River Trail
Hike 10 miles (16km) through dense bottomland forest and into the pines on the way to the wide, coffee-colored Congaree River. Bring binoculars for the excellent bird-watching.

What to spot...

Knobby-kneed bald cypress and water tupelo fringed with Spanish moss abound throughout the floodplain, while higher elevations are shaded with tall pines. The swampy waters are home to turtles and salamanders; the river teems with bass, bowfin and catfish; and the trees host screech owls and a huge variety of warblers. Don't be surprised to see a cottonmouth or an alligator glide by your canoe. This is a swamp – OK, technically a 'floodplain' – after all.

BALD CYPRESS These tall swamp trees are easily identified by their bulbous bases and 'knees' – root structures that stick up around the trunk like bent legs.

SPANISH MOSS Technically a flowering plant rather than a true moss, it looks like a gray beard hanging off the branch of a tree.

EASTERN BOX TURTLE Identify these reptiles by their distinctive orange-and-black shells. Adults are usually around 6in (15cm) long; males have red eyes.

Itineraries

Canoe or kayak past alligators and armadillos or stroll through the cypresses on the Boardwalk Trail. It's misty, swampy serenity here.

◄ Boardwalk trails wind through stands of old-growth hardwood forest.

▲ Swallowtail butterflies and a timber rattlesnake.

01

A day

Hit the Boardwalk Trail through the eerie bottomland forest, where the cypresses grow so thick hardly a drop of sunlight reaches the ground in summer. The wooden walkway is only 2.4-miles (3.8km) long, but take your time to look for flocks of warblers flitting through the canopy, iridescent dragonflies landing amid the reeds, and red-bellied water snakes wriggling through the water. If it's Saturday morning, do the volunteer-led nature walk, which will point out the park's coolest and oddest features. After a picnic lunch (there's no food for sale in Congaree), drag your canoe or kayak to the Cedar Creek put-in. Paddle through the silent, tannin-dark waters beneath canopies of bald cypress bearded with Spanish moss. At Dawson's Lake, stop to fish or to spot river otters, who splash and play in the area. Paddle back the way you came, and camp beneath the pines at Longleaf Campground, waking early to see the mists rising over the swampland before heading back to civilization.

02

Two to three days

The 50-mile (80.5km) Congaree River Blue Trail is one of the South's great weekend paddles. Launch your canoe or kayak in the city of Columbia, under the bridge at the West Columbia Amphitheater. Pass the turn-of-the-century Granby Lock and Dam, crossing via the lock on the right side, and glide into the Congaree Creek Heritage Preserve, with its stands of rare Atlantic white cedar. From here you'll mostly be on your own, passing the occasional ramshackle river cabin as you paddle deeper into the wilderness. The river is wide and sandy, with numerous sandbars perfect for a snack and a leg-stretch. Spend a night camping on the banks, watching the sun sink over the longleaf pines as the river turns from brown to black. On the second day you'll pass oxbow lakes, forested bluffs and muddy creek-mouths, spotting deer, turtles, egrets, snakes, alligators and maybe even an armadillo or feral pig. Spend a second night camping before finishing the paddle at Bates Bridge Landing on the third day.

14

OR

Crater Lake National Park

No matter how many times you've seen it, the stunning blue jewel that is Oregon's Crater Lake never fails to take your breath away.

Born of astonishing geological violence, the lake today radiates tranquility, while serving as a reminder of the fierce power of the natural world. It was created by the eruption of Mt Mazama some 7700 years ago. Over the course of just a few days, the mountain blew its top and then collapsed into itself, scattering ash across hundreds of thousands of miles and forming a caldera with sheer, steep rock walls. The caldera gradually filled with snow and rainwater to form Crater Lake. At 1943ft (592m), it's the deepest lake in the United States, and famous for the clarity and color of its water.

The lake and its surrounding area became a national park on May 22, 1902. It's one of the few places on earth where you'll find a volcano within a volcano: Wizard Island is a cinder cone that pokes up out of the water on the western side of the lake. Daily shuttles ferry visitors across to the island for hikes and exploration, but if you miss the boat you can also get good views from several vantage points along the rim. Look out too for the Old Man of the Lake, a floating tree stump – improbably vertical – that has been bobbing around the lake wherever the breeze takes it since at least the 1890s. The park is also home to the Crater Lake Science and Learning Center, which offers lab space and various facilities to support the study of natural resources by scientists, artists, students and teachers.

Whether you gaze out at the lake from the top of Rim Dr road, study it from a hiking trail along the rim, or cruise past volcanic islands on a ranger-led boat tour, Crater Lake is an experience you won't soon forget.

Toolbox

When to go
The lake is gorgeous in all weather – a blanket of snow adds glamour in winter, but access is easier during summer. The park and main visitor center are open year-round; the Rim Visitor Center closes October to May, as do gas stations and most other facilities. During fire season (July to August), visibility may be hampered, as smoke from nearby forest fires drifts over the lake.

Getting there
Crater Lake is in southwest Oregon, about 65 miles (105km) from Medford, 45 miles (72km) north of Klamath Falls. It's best reached by car.

Park in numbers

286
Area covered (sq miles)

5
volume of water in the lake (in trillion gallons)

6600
years since most recent eruption

Stay here...

Crater Lake Lodge
Like many of its fellow lodges in national parks, this rustic 1915 beauty encourages lingering over a glass of wine at the fireplace in the Great Hall before retiring to one of its basic rooms. It's only a few steps from the caldera, so you can peer over the edge of the lake with minimal effort. Open from late May to early October.

Mazama Village Campground
Though it's huge, this campground near the park's south entrance is all nooks and crannies, arranged for privacy and surprisingly quiet. You'll wake up in what feels like remote wilderness, but you're only 7 miles (11km) from the rim of the lake, and as a bonus there are conveniently located services – gas station, grocery store, laundry, cafe – so you can gear up before venturing into the park.

Mazama Village Cabins
If you prefer comfy duvets, a hot shower and a roof over your head to sleeping in a tent, you're in luck: a bed and private bath await you in these cabins near the Mazama Village campsite. Best of all, from your hut you can poke your head out the door and smell the pine forest all around.

Do this!

Exploring
From the north side of Crater Lake, hike just over a mile (1.6km) along the steep Cleetwood Cove Trail down to the boat dock. A 45-minute shuttle ride takes you to Wizard Island, where you have three hours to hike around and explore on your own. The 75-minute round-trip includes rangers' explanations of the area's natural history. (The hike back up involves a 700ft (213m) elevation gain and can be strenuous.)

Cycling
The steep, narrow Rim Dr road circling the lake offers 33 miles (53km) of exciting bicycling. Start from park headquarters and make the loop clockwise to get the hardest part out of the way first. Elevation means the terrain can be challenging, and you may have to navigate traffic in busy periods.

Skiing & snowshoeing
In winter, nine trails of varying difficulty let skiers and snowshoers of all levels of experience and fitness explore the Crater Lake area. Ask for a map at the visitor center.

◄ Hiking Crater Lake; there are several trails with views of the lake, until winter weather appears in late fall when snowshoes may be required.

Hike this...

01 Discovery Point
An easy 1.1-mile (1.8km) hike that leads west from Rim Village to a dirt trail offering great views of Crater Lake.

02 Garfield Peak
A steep, 3.4-mile (5.5km) round-trip hike delivers spectacular views of the lake and its surroundings. The trail starts near Crater Lake Lodge and heads east along the rim before ascending the peak.

03 Pacific Crest Trail
This long-distance trail, made famous by the book and its subsequent movie adaptation *Wild*, cuts through the park heading north to south.

What to spot...

The high elevation of Crater Lake results in short summers and long, harsh winters, which means only the sturdiest of plants survive. Spring offers brief glimpses of early wildflowers, including Pasque flowers, lupine and Indian paintbrush. Animal life is plentiful and varied, but seldom seen: skittish deer, bear and pine martens inhabit the park's wild areas. Rainbow trout and Kokanee salmon live in the lake, introduced there by humans (no fish were native to the lake).

CLARK'S NUTCRACKER Not at all shy – and totally ignoring the 'Do Not Feed Birds' signs – these gray-and-black crows entertain visitors in hope of snacks.

SPOTTED OWL The lower-elevation conifer forests of the park are ideal for the spotted owl, a species made famous by its role at the center of debates between environmentalists and the timber industry in the 1990s.

MAZAMA NEWT Believed to be unique to Crater Lake, these rough-skinned amphibians have been threatened recently by the introduction of non-native crayfish to the lake.

Itineraries

Whether you cruise Crater Lake or hike into Sky Lakes Wilderness, the bird-watching and scenic views reward. S'mores by a campfire are a perfect finish.

◄ Wizard Island in Crater Lake.
► Crater Lake Lodge.

01

A day

From the southern entrance at Mazama Village, drive to park headquarters in the Steel Visitors Center for an introduction to what's in store and a schedule of shuttle boats. Continue toward the lake, stopping near Crater Lake Lodge for a view of that famous blue water, then pop in and check out the lodge itself, with its 1920s-era Great Hall. Then continue along West Rim Dr, stopping at Watchman Overlook for the first of many scenic views.

About halfway around the loop road is Cleetwood Cove Trail, which takes you to a boat landing at the shore of the lake (be warned: it's a steep and difficult hike). If time and energy levels allow, walk down to the boat shuttle and take a cruise around the lake – they range from an hour or two to a full day with a stop at Wizard Island. Here you can spend three hours hiking, fishing, or just wandering around.

Later, continue the drive along East Rim Dr, stopping at all the overlooks, until you're back at park headquarters.

02

A weekend

Same as day one, but instead of leaving the park at the end of the day, find a cozy campsite at Mazama Village Campground for the night. Stock up on cookout supplies (s'mores!) at the camping store in nearby Mazama Village, where you'll also want to top up the gas tank, fetch picnic supplies for the next day's lunch, and maybe pick up some souvenirs at the gift shop.

Next morning, after a hearty breakfast at the Crater Lake Lodge, head out for a hike up Garfield Peak. Make it a relaxing day of bird-watching and scenic photographs, with time for a picnic lunch and, of course, a few requisite selfies at the end of the hike. Afterward, hop onto a Crater Lake Trolley for a leisurely loop tour with a guide. Up for a longer trek? Aim instead for a spur trail heading southwest from Rim Village that connects to the Pacific Crest Trail (ask at the visitor center for maps), and wander as long as you please.

03

Three to four days

Extend your Pacific Crest Trail exploration into an overnight backpacking campout. The trail heading south leads you into Sky Lakes Wilderness – be sure to carry a detailed topographical map of this area, and take all the usual backpacking precautions. There are a number of intersecting trails that allow you to turn this into a nice loop hike of various distances. Ask at the visitor center for details about trail conditions, where you can camp, whether there are campfire restrictions and what the weather forecast looks like. The recommended routes are likely to vary considerably from one year to the next, depending on things like snowpack and damage from the wildfires that ravage the area, so be sure to stay flexible and heed the rangers' advice. After your hike, celebrate your accomplishment with a night in a comfy bed, a hot shower and substantial meal at the Crater Lake Lodge (book ahead).

15

OH

Cuyahoga Valley National Park

Amid the flowing curls of a crooked river, a verdant wonderland full of wildlife, waterfalls and historic trails transforms city folk into hiking, biking explorers.

Sandwiched between two cities and located in the middle of a tic-tac-toe grid of freeways, Cuyahoga Valley National Park is an unlikely outdoor utopia – yet it offers 125 miles (201km) of hiking and horseback-riding trails, myriad cycling, camping and canoeing opportunities and a wealth of winter adventures. Even more surprising are the additional activities that can be enjoyed here, including golf, live concerts and even hitching a lift on a locomotive: Cuyahoga Valley is a park less ordinary.

Ohio's only national park lies between the cities of Cleveland and Akron. Over 12,000 years of human drama have played out in this valley, formed by the Cuyahoga River (the name means 'crooked river' in the Mohawk language) as it wends towards Lake Erie. Early occupants, Native Americans known as the Whittlesey people, mysteriously vacated the valley in the early 1600s. Beaver trappers, mountain men and new tribes moved in, but the Native Americans' claims to the area were quashed with the 1795 Treaty of Greenville, after which Ohio saw an influx of settlers.

Over the next 150 years, cities germinated and swelled, a canal was dug, a railroad built and roads developed. Granted easy access to the valley, urbanites fell in love with their wild backyard. Land was donated by Cleveland businessman Hayward Kendall, and during the Great Depression the Civilian Conservation Corps built most of the park's infrastructure.

Development threatened, and a petition began to push for park status. In 1973, the director of the NPS stated that it would become a park 'over his dead body,' but in 1974 President Gerald Ford approved the Cuyahoga Valley National Recreation Area, which was rebranded a national park in 2000. Its railways and fairways now form part of the patchwork of this peculiar park.

Toolbox

When to go
The park is open year-round, but spring (when wildflowers erupt) and fall (as a colorful curtain draws across the forests) are the most stunning periods. Great hiking and biking can be enjoyed most of the year, but in winter swap trail shoes for skis, and bicycles for sleds.

Getting there
Interstates I-80 and I-271 run through the park, close to major attractions such as Brandywine Falls. Access is easy from Cleveland and Akron via the I-77 or Ohio State Route 8; visitor centers abound no matter which way you approach. Park entry is free.

Park in numbers

51.3
Area covered (sq miles)

125
Miles of hiking trails in the park

39
Mammal species active in the park

Stay here...

Camping
You're just a short drive from two major cities, but camping in the Cuyahoga Valley is an exercise in urban unwind that flushes out the fumes and rush-hour blues. Listen to raccoons, coyotes and owls at night and wake to a dawn chorus of warblers. From Memorial Day to the end of October, primitive camping is available to backcountry park users, close to the Towpath Trail by Stanford House.

Stanford House
Perfect for one-night park visitors, this restored 19th-century farmhouse offers accommodations in the heart of the park, right next to the Brandywine Falls trail, and close to the Boston Store Visitor Center and canal towpath. NPS-owned and -operated, it has a great atmosphere, with super-friendly staff and various communal areas, including a kitchen and a lounge with board games.

The Inn at Brandywine Falls
Those who prefer a bit of pampering will luxuriate in the ambience and service at the Inn at Brandywine Falls. Overlooking Brandywine Waterfall, this historic building dates to 1848. Its hospitality is legendary.

Do this!

Cycling
Do not forget your bike – cycling the Ohio and Erie Canal Towpath trail is virtually compulsory. There are various other bike-friendly paths to explore too, including the Bike & Hike Trail. Most tracks are sealed, but construction has recently begun on a new mountain-bike route, the East Rim Trail.

Skiing & sledding
Once snow starts to fall, Cuyahoga Valley transforms into a wonderland for cross-country skiers, snowshoe-sporting trekkers and sled heads. Skis and snowshoes can be hired, and all 125 miles (201km) of the park's trekking trails can be skied except for the Ledges and Brandywine Falls trail system.

Scenic touring
Trains have been huffing and puffing through Cuyahoga Valley since 1880 and taking a ride on the scenic service is a highlight experience – especially when combined with a ride along the Towpath Trail. From the platform, hail the train by waving your arms in the air.

◄ Blue Hen Creek Falls after heavy rainfall in Cuyahoga National Park.
► Enjoy summer's wildflowers.

Hike this...

01 Brandywine Gorge Trail
At the very minimum, hike the 1.5-mile (2.4km) track around Brandywine Creek and stroll the short path to the cascade itself.

02 Ohio & Erie Canal Towpath Trail
Around 20 miles (32.2km) of this historic route passes through the park, and hiking or cycling (or skating or skiing it) has become a must-do experience.

03 Buckeye Trail
This epic, 1444-mile (2324km) circular walk around Ohio passes through the park. Combine one section of the Buckeye with the Towpath Trail to make a 17-mile (27.4km) loop starting and finishing at Boston.

Alamy | Jason Langley; James Schwabel

What to spot...

The Appalachian Plateau and the Central Lowlands of America collide in the Cuyahoga Valley, creating a rich and healthy ecosystem. The skies above the park are busy with the activities of 194 species of birds, and in the forests and wetlands 900 plant species rustle as an eclectic collection of mammals, amphibians and reptiles go about their business. The river, too, is now in rude health, hosting 43 kinds of fish.

BALD EAGLE This iconic bird has returned to the park in numbers since the river's fish population rebounded. In November, watch them performing dramatic aerial courtship displays, diving and locking talons.

RACCOON Smart and crafty locals, raccoons can cope with the park's bitter winters, thanks to their dense underfur. Their distinctive face mask features in the mythology of several Native American tribes.

WANDERING GLIDER DRAGONFLY Ohio's wetlands are home to 157 species of dragonflies and damselflies, including the wandering glider (aka the globe skimmer), the planet's most common dragon.

Itineraries

Brandywine Falls beckons with its boardwalks of beaver spotting. Catch the Scenic Train or multitask on the Bike & Hike Trail.

◀ Covered bridges cross creeks in Cuyahoga Valley.
▶ The Peninsula Depot station on the Cuyahoga Valley Scenic Railroad.

01

A half-day

Free entry and easy access from surrounding cities make afternoon adventures entirely achievable in Cuyahoga Valley. Get a taste of the park's potential by wandering to one of the waterfalls, exploring a visitors center and spotting some wildlife.

The park's pin-up poster scene is Brandywine Falls, where the Brandywine Creek rushes off a 65ft-high (20m) drop in its haste to join the crooked river below. After an easy and short walk from the parking lot off Brandywine Road, you'll find boardwalks leading to observation platforms, where you can get up close and personal with the roaring cascade.

Grab lunch in the picnic area nearby and then head west to the Boston Store Visitor Center, housed in a building dating to 1836. This center tells the tale of the Ohio and Erie Canal that runs through the valley, connecting Lake Erie to the Ohio River.

Finally, go looking for beaver, otter, muskrat and waterfowl along the wetland boardwalk that runs around Beaver Marsh, a stroll of 1.5 miles (2.4km) from the Ira Trailhead.

02

A day

The classic day trip to Cuyahoga Valley involves one thing: an adventure along the Towpath Trail. Twenty miles (32.2km) of the historic Ohio and Erie Canal passes through the park – a bit much for a day walk, perhaps, but ideal for a bike ride, especially since you can pedal one way and catch the Scenic Train back.

Parking at the Boston Visitor Center, set off along the gloriously flat path. You could smash this in an hour or so, but with a packed lunch there's no point rushing – there are numerous picturesque picnic spots along the way.

Forests, fields, and wetlands line the trail as it flows through the Cuyahoga Valley. Occasionally the river itself makes an appearance, but the real highlight is spotting a couple of beavers in one of the wetlands.

Boarding the train at Rockside Station, grab a window seat and gaze out at the landscape you've just ridden through. It looks very different in winter, which might give you an idea – maybe come back in January to try skiing the Towpath…

03

Two or more days

To truly escape the city and explore this ancient valley, you need to spend at least a night here, preferably under canvas in the embrace of the wilderness – in blissful denial that the Ohio Turnpike is barely out of earshot.

Having spent the day in the saddle, cycling the towpath and circling back along a section of the Bike & Hike Trail (one of America's first 'rails to trails' conversions), you head to the Ledges in time for Cuyahoga's famous sunset. From the boulders on this clifftop vantage point you watch the day go down in a blaze of glory, setting the woodlands below aflame with autumnal colors.

After a night in the campsite near Stanford House, get a bigger taste of the backcountry with a footloose foray along the Buckeye Trail. Not long after leaving the trailhead you come across Blue Hen Falls – slightly smaller than Brandywine Falls, but every bit as impressive – and you have them to yourself.

This sets the tone for a full-day hike, finished off with a train ride back to the Boston Visitor Center.

Cuyahoga Valley

16

CA

Death Valley National Park

California's lowest, hottest and geologically oddest spot: Death Valley. It's surprisingly full of life, especially when spring wildflowers bloom.

The air shimmers with heat. Looking out the windshield, you glimpse sand dunes on the horizon, as if this were a Hollywood adventure flick set in North Africa. Salt flats, where the earth cracks jaggedly open, look as if they could swallow a city whole. Stones secretively slip across the playa, leaving behind tracks in the dust of an ancient lakebed. Inside twisting canyons, rocks carved by eons of wind reveal a desert rainbow of shades: rust red, ochre, mauve, acid green and electric blue. Swirling around everything is an ocean of sand.

Driving through Death Valley, you'll miss subtle signs of life if you never stop the car. Get out and step close to a prickly pear cactus (look, but don't touch!). Spy on a desert tortoise sleepily emerging from its burrow, or spot a desert bighorn sheep, its curved horns proudly curling up into the sky, picking its way along a rocky ridge. The valley's fragile web of life all depends on water, hidden in springs or seeps. After winter and spring rains soak the parched ground, a profusion of wildflowers burst skyward, including purple Mojave asters, desert gold and orange globemallow.

Death Valley's infamous name was bestowed by 19th-century emigrants in the gold rush, who became lost and almost died here. Later, prospectors moved in and dug mines for silver and other precious metals. The eerie relics of their endeavors stand along backroads through the desert, which preserves ghost towns as time capsules in its dry heat. Other unpaved roads lead to such spectacular vistas as Aguereberry Point, where you can see the 14,505ft-high (4421m) Mt Whitney, the USA's highest peak outside Alaska – then turn to look down over Badwater, North America's lowest point, plummeting to 282ft (86m) below sea level.

Toolbox

 When to go
Spring is the busy season, when wildflowers bloom; temperatures are balmy, though desert winds pick up. Autumn is another beautifully temperate time to visit. Winters remain mild at lower elevations, where summers are deadly hot.

 **Getting there**
The park is located in southern California, a two-hour drive from Las Vegas, Nevada, where you'll find the closest international airport. You'll need your own car to get to and around this enormous park.

Park in numbers

5270
Area covered (sq miles)

137°F
Highest temperature ever recorded (57°c)

282
Lowest elevation (ft below sea level)

Stay here...

Inn at Furnace Creek
At the park's historic, 1920s-era hotel, surrounded by palm-tree gardens, float in a hot springs–fed swimming pool or toast a special occasion with elegant cocktails on the patio. Minimalist rooms are serene, and some have inspiring mountain views and step-out terraces for catching the sunrise.

Ranch at Furnace Creek
In the middle of the park, this Old West–themed lodge emphasizes family fun. Duplex cabins can be a tight squeeze, yet still have plenty of Western charm, such as rocking chairs on the front porch. Amenities for active types, from golf to horseback rides, are a bonus.

Mesquite Spring Campground
Campers who have visited the park before often head to this uncrowded spot first. Almost 2000ft (610m) above the valley floor, temperatures are refreshingly cooler here. With just 30 campsites, you'll feel like a pioneer when you pitch your tent beneath sheltering hillsides. Warning: winds may whip through, especially overnight.

Do this!

Historic touring
Take a guided tour of Scotty's Castle, an eccentric mansion built by wealthy Chicagoans who befriended 'Death Valley' Scotty, a failed local prospector and raconteur. Ghost towns such as Skidoo and Rhyolite evoke the region's Wild West mining days, as do the strange, beehive-shaped charcoal kilns high in Wildrose Canyon.

4WD driving
To really get out and explore the wilderness, you'll need a high-clearance 4WD vehicle to tackle rough, rutted dirt roads, steep grades and sliding sands. The ultimate backcountry thrill is Titus Canyon, which slaloms downhill through the Grapevine Mountains, passing the ghost town of Leadfield and petroglyphs at Klare Spring. Rental 4WDs are available seasonally in Furnace Creek.

Stargazing
Death Valley is officially the USA's biggest 'dark sky' national park. Roll out your sleeping bag, grab a star chart and contemplate eternity as you stare into the depths of the Milky Way and watch shooting stars (meteors) blaze overhead.

◀ Rocks wander the dry lakebed of Racetrack playa, moved by strong winds and ice. Previous page: Zabriskie Point.

What to spot...

Adaptation to a harsh, arid landscape has produced a spectacular diversity of flora and fauna in Death Valley. Over a thousand species of plants thrive here, along with more than 400 animals, ranging from the endangered pupfish – which is actually smaller than your thumb – to braying wild burros that roam the range, the descendants of pack animals set loose by mining prospectors. Desert wildlife is most active in the cool early morning and just after sunset.

DESERT TORTOISE Inhabitants of the Mojave Desert for millions of years, these slow-moving reptiles are now threatened by habitat loss, predators and disease.

DESERT BIGHORN SHEEP These elusive, sure-footed mammals are hard to catch sight of, but look for them on mountain ridges and sheer cliff faces.

CALIFORNIA BARREL CACTUS These spiny, portly and ribbed succulents bloom with yellow flowers in spring – and occasionally grow taller than a human being.

Hike this...

01 Golden Canyon Trail
An easy, flat 2-mile (3.2km) walk into some of Death Valley's most colorful badlands, with views of the Red Cathedral's cliffs.

02 Mesquite Flat Sand Dunes
The lure of rolling, golden sand dunes is irresistible – take a 2-mile (3.2km) trek across them in dazzling sunshine, or at night under a full moon.

03 Wildrose Peak Trail
At cooler, higher elevations, a strenuous, 8.4-mile (13.5km) climb rewards hikers with awe-inspiring panoramas of the valley.

Itineraries

Explore ghost towns, the sunset palettes of Artists Drive or hike to Badwater, the continent's lowest point for the ultimate high.

← Sand dunes, Rhyolite Ghost Town, a coyote and Furnace Creek.
→ Motorbikers on Badwater Rd.

01
A day

Make the most of your short time in the park. After a quick peek at the ghost town of Rhyolite in the morning, drive over Daylight Pass into the park and descend over 4000ft (1219m) to the valley floor. Turn north and motor past rolling sand dunes, alluvial fan washes and wildflowers blanketing the hillsides in spring. Step back in time inside whimsical Scotty's Castle. Nearby, walk atop the impressive volcanic pit of Ubehebe Crater, which last exploded only a few centuries ago.

Get back on the road south to Furnace Creek, stopping for lunch and to take a cool dip in a springwater pool at the ranch. In the afternoon, detour down along Artists Drive, where a sunset palette of soft colors warms the eroded hillsides. Your finish line awaits at Badwater, the continent's lowest point – snap a photo by the sign to prove you finally made it here. Walk out over the crunchy salt flats at dusk when cool desert breezes blow, then wait for the night sky's star show to begin.

02
A weekend

Take your time on an overnight desert escape. Roll slowly into the park from the south, cresting Jubilee Pass. The long, winding road north to Badwater shows this valley's vastness. Pull over by the Badwater salt flats, which extend across the valley floor toward a phalanx of mountains. Continuing north, take a short hike through Golden Canyon, if it's not too hot. Pull into buzzing Furnace Creek and check into the ranch resort, the historic inn or a campsite. Around

sunset, head up to Zabriskie Point or Dante's View for panoramas of the badlands.

The next day, hop back in the car and head north for a spin through Mustard Canyon before turning west toward Stovepipe Wells. Next to the road, Mesquite Flat's sand dunes rise imperiously. You can walk across them, or continue west to scramble through cool, marbled Mosaic Canyon instead. After lunch, take a long, leisurely drive through the valley's most dramatic scenery en route to eccentric Scotty's Castle.

03
Five days

With a week to spare, you can poke into little-known corners of the park. Spend your first day in the south, hiking around the salt flats of Badwater, the badlands of Golden Canyon and underneath the Natural Bridge, then wind past viewpoints along Artists Drive. Make Furnace Creek your base camp, where you can spend the next day playing golf, taking a horseback ride, or renting a 4WD vehicle. Don't forget to head up to Zabriskie Point or Dante's View for sunset. On day three, check out

Scotty's Castle and volcanic Ubehebe Crater, then cross the Nevada state line to Rhyolite, a mining ghost town. Cool off at higher elevations on day four by following the Death Valley '49ers' tortured escape route up Emigrant Canyon, taking turn-offs to more ghost towns, breathtaking viewpoints and hardy hiking trails. On your last day, exit the park past Panamint Springs, pausing at impressive Father Crowley Vista Point and taking an easy ramble to hidden Darwin Falls.

Death Valley

17

AK

Denali National Park

Denali National Park encapsulates everything that is great about the Alaskan wilderness. Under the sheltering subarctic sky this majestic wild kingdom is vast, austere and exhilarating.

Here you'll discover nature in her most raw and at her most fierce. With over 6 million acres of intact wilderness, this massive park offers remarkable views and insights into the flora, fauna and active ecosystems of Alaska's immense interior.

Whether you take just a day to head up the Park Rd or plan a ten-day tromp across the virgin spaces of tundra, taiga forest, meadows, streams and hillsides that make this park so unique, a visit to Denali will not disappoint. With even the shortest of adventures, you are likely to see bear, moose and caribou. Stay a while longer and you very well could spot a wolf or a fox, plus any number of avian species.

Hovering above it all is the 20,237ft (6168m) Denali, known as Mt McKinley until a presidential decree restored its original Athabascan name – which means 'The Great One' – in 2015. This hulking peak is the highest in North America. Wait for a clear day to see the glacier-capped summit massif unfurl her loving arms across this mindblowing stretch of firmament, and the true power of nature manifests itself with an immediacy and an intimacy not easily found in the continental US. It's just bigger here. And going big is what an Alaskan adventure is about.

Denali is alpha and omega, the beginning and the end, and under her watchful eye, the remarkably orchestrated, dramatic plots of nature unfold each spring when the snows melt. The grizzly bears emerge from a long winter's nap; the caribou and moose shed winter coats as their fawn struggle to find balance on wobbly legs; wildflowers bloom; fox and wolf fatten themselves on small mammals; and visitors from across the globe move out through the wilderness,

astronauts in a foreign place, finding joy, balance and solitude in the whirl of life that spins around them.

⬆ A bull caribou in autumn.
➡ Taking the Talkeetna air taxi on Ruth Glacier.

Alamy | Design Pics Inc

Toolbox

When to go
Most people visit Denali from early June through late August for the best glimpses of wildlife, wildflowers and migratory birds. Come in winter or the shoulder seasons for solitude. The best wildlife viewing is in the early morning.

Getting there
Located along the road system in Alaska's Interior, the National Park entrance is easily accessed by car or train from Anchorage. From there, you hop on the shuttle for 92 miles (148km) of amazing wildlife viewing along the Park Rd.

Park in numbers

9492
Area covered (sq miles)

169
Species of birds

39
Species of mammals

Stay here...

Wonder Lake Campground
Deep inside the park, this tent-only campground offers the best views of Denali. The mountain is shy, and sometimes it takes a day or two for her to come out from the clouds that usually drape her summit, so book well ahead to reserve three days.

Camp Denali
Sitting on a 67-acre private reserve deep within the park, this backcountry lodge has rustic wood-hewn cabins that climb up a ridge from the original lodge, built by the founders in 1954. It's rustic, open and genuine. Highlights include naturalist-guided hikes that reveal fascinating details about this delicate ecosystem. Gorgeous views of the Alaska Range, well-planned meals and sustainable programs add to the mix.

Backcountry Camping
Solace and solitude are hallmarks of Denali's 87 backcountry units. Rather than hiking on specific trails to established backcountry camps, you can head out here across trail-less terrain and stay wherever you like within your designated unit. It's a choose-your-own-adventure with a wild twist.

Do this!

Backpacking
The park is roughly the size of Vermont, which means there's plenty of open space to go around. Planning the trip is an essential first step; rangers can take you through the ins-and-outs of trail-less hiking, wilderness survival, bear safety and more. Once you hit the backcountry, it's a singular experience that will push your limits, challenge your senses and foster a deep connection with this great land.

Cycling
You can bike the entirety of the 92-mile (148km) Park Rd, a remarkable ribbon that bisects the park. A ride along its expanse takes you through low tundra, open spruce woodlands and meadows, black spruce forest, and white spruce and paper birch forest.

Flightseeing
You think Denali looks big from your viewpoint at Wonder Lake? Take to the air for a change in perspective. From above, the immensity of this wilderness takes on new proportions that boggle the mind.

◀ Touring cyclists pedal up Grassy Pass. Opening spread: views of Denali and Wonder Lake.

What to spot...

The size and remoteness of Denali ensure a vibrant ecosystem that is intact and as untamed and real as it gets. You have a pretty good shot of seeing a handful of the park's most iconic megafauna with a simple tour along the Park Rd. Highlights include grizzly and black bear, wolf, caribou, moose and Dall Sheep. Migratory birds, and a startling diversity of plants, mosses, lichens and wildflowers add to the park's polychromatic eco-tapestry.

WOLF
This is one of the best spots in Alaska to sight these fabled apex predators. There are generally 60 to 100 wolves within the park, though numbers dropped alarmingly to just 48 in 2015.

MOOSE These awkward ungulates, the second-largest mammal in North America, are a mainstay within the park. Find them in forested areas by marshes and lakes.

GRIZZLY BEAR Mama bears often hang out by the Park Rd to protect their cubs, making this a great spot for grizzly viewing. Lacking a fish diet, they are smaller in size than their coastal cousins.

Hike this...

01 Triple Lakes Trail
This 9.5-mile (15.3km) trail takes you across creeks, lush forests and alpine passes, with awesome views of the Alaska Range to the gorgeous Triple Lakes.

02 Mt Healy Overlook Trail
Lucky hikers might just see Denali on a clear day from this short, steep 2.7-mile (4.3km) hike. The hike climbs 1700ft (518m), traveling from forested areas of spruce, alder and aspen into alpine country, where lichens, mosses and wildflowers rule.

03 Trail-less Hiking
Choose your own adventure across brooks, past lakes, through tundra, meadow and wood. Stick to ridgelines and avoid thick brush and terrain traps to make the journey easier.

Itineraries

Whether you're into glacier hiking, rafting down canyons or the more sedate (but equally scenic) sightseeing from the Denali Star Train, strap yourself in.

◀ Dall sheep in Denali National Park. A ranger hauls his gear up to Windy Corner on Denali.
➡ Fireweed lines the road at Sable Pass.

01

Two days

While you won't experience all that the park has to offer, you can easily see some amazing sights and a fair bit of wildlife in a day or two. The best start is aboard the Denali Star Train, a gorgeous sightseeing line that whisks you from Anchorage, past the Mantanuska Valley and the Susitna River to the park entrance. While you're there, don't miss a trip to the kennels to visit the sled dogs that rangers use in winter to patrol the park. Stop for the night in Canyon, McKinley Village,

Carlo Creek or Healy, waking up early to get the first shuttle bus along the Park Rd. The shuttle takes eight hours just to the Eielson Visitor Center, so expect a full day. Some of the best views are had between Savage River and Eielson, where you can spot Dall Sheep. At Sable Pass, marvel at the views from Polychrome Pass and head off for a short jaunt from the Visitor Center. You may choose to stop on the way back for an hour or two of trail-less hiking or outings on trails near Savage River.

02

A week

Denali National Park was created in 1917 with the express mission of protecting the park's remarkable flora and fauna. In 1980, the US Congress tripled its size. Despite its massive size, you can still see plenty of wildlands and wildlife in seven days. Plan well ahead to make backcountry and lodging reservations – getting a campsite at the famed Wonder Lake Campground is right up there with winning the lottery in terms of your odds – but well worth the risk.

Stay your first few days either at Wonder Lake, Camp Denali or one of the other remarkable lodges found at the end of the Park Rd in Kantishna. Spend a few days taking on shorter and longer day-hikes before heading back to park headquarters for your orientation and an extended three to seven days in the backcountry. Ideally, your trip will take you through a few unique ecosystems and backcountry units, before your final hitch out to civilization on the park shuttle.

03

Ten days

If adrenaline is your thing, there are some high-octane activities here to get your heart beating. Denali is about creating your own path, and there really is no limit to the number of off-the-wall adventures a serious outdoors person can have here. Start with some trail-less hiking for three or four days – the thrill of finding your own way in a roadless, trackless wilderness with map and compass is unlike any other.

If that's too tame for you, you can consider a flightseeing trip or some

guided glacier hiking. It's a three-week-long expedition-style ascent to get to the top of Denali. Over a thousand climbers attempt it every year, with fewer than half making it to the top. For river rats, there's some high-flying rafting on the nearby Nenana River, with Class III and IV water that features standing waves, bursting rapids and big holes down a sheer-cliffed canyon. Top off your trip with a few nights in nearby Talkeetna for bluegrass jams, killer fishing, zip-line tours and jet boats.

18

Dry Tortugas National Park

Splashed across a remote archipelago, Dry Tortugas features a titanic 19th-century fort balanced on a tropical reef, surrounded by shipwrecks and sensational sea life.

When Juan Ponce de León discovered Dry Tortugas in 1513, the Spaniard named the archipelago after the many *tortugas* (turtles) he encountered. (The word 'dry' was added to indicate the islands' lack of fresh water.) Nowadays, day-trippers come here to snorkel, dive and kayak around the reef and its seven atolls, spotting those languorous loggerhead turtles that are still numerous in these waters. But Dry Tortugas was originally scoped out for far less peaceful activities.

When the US acquired Florida from Spain in 1822, the strategic importance of Dry Tortugas was obvious. The keys' position at the mouth of the Bay of Mexico made them crucial for the defence of the young country's eastern flank. They were also considered for a base to combat the pirates of the Caribbean, though it wasn't until 1846 that construction finally began on the colossal coastal fortress.

During the Civil War, Fort Jefferson was used to hold Union deserters; it subsequently had a stint as a prison, famously hosting Dr Samuel Mudd after his conviction for involvement in Abraham Lincoln's assassination. Fortunately, though, since it never was properly finished, the only invasions the fort has witnessed have come in the form of flocks of birds that land here by the thousands while migrating.

The archipelago was made a national park in 1935, and these days the fort's sea wall and moat are popular with snorkelers.

A far-flung scattering of coral keys in the Gulf of Mexico isn't the first place you'd go looking for one of the largest brick buildings in the northern hemisphere. But here, 68 miles (109km) south of the famous Floridian outpost of Key West, is where you'll find Fort Jefferson – an epic, unfinished fortress that dominates Dry Tortugas, surely the most unusual of America's ever-surprising suite of national parks.

◄ Views of the hexagonal Fort Jefferson in Dry Tortugas National Park, built with more than 16 million bricks.

Toolbox

When to go
Visit in spring or fall to witness the twice-annual invasion of the islands by birds using Dry Tortugas as a stop-off on their migratory route between North and South America.

Getting there
Getting to Dry Tortugas is an adventure that involves either a boat ride or a flight in a floatplane; both can be arranged from Key West, Florida. Plane companies run half- and full-day experiences, while The *Yankee Freedom III*, a high-speed catamaran, offers day trips with 5 hours of island time (or you can camp overnight).

Park in numbers

101
Area covered (sq miles)

16
Bricks used to build Fort Jefferson in millions

100,000
Number of sooty terns that arrive from March to September

Stay here...

Camping
This is possibly the only place on the planet where you can get an entire national park almost completely to yourself for the night. Garden Key, close to Fort Jefferson, has eight primitive, first-come-first-served campsites. There's nothing here but a star-studded sky, so it's basic – but when the last boat leaves, campers are the kings and queens of the islands.

Do this!

Snorkeling & diving
Meet Ponce de León's turtles and a wealth of other marine life during a self-guided aquatic adventure around the park's pristine waters and colorful coral gardens – home to tropical fish, goliath groupers, lobsters, squid, octopi and reef sharks. While the sea is alive with incredible creatures, the park is a veritable ships' graveyard: divers can explore numerous wrecks, including the Windjammer.

Kayaking
Confident paddlers can island-hop across the translucent (but deep and sometimes challenging) water between the park's atolls, circumnavigating Bush and Long Key, or visiting the park's largest island, Loggerhead Key, which has stunning beaches.

Itineraries

Have catamaran, will travel – sail away to discover Fort Jefferson and its impressive moat then snorkel the coral paradise of this park's seven atolls.

01

A day

It's not a bad way to start the day: skimming across the Gulf of Mexico in a luxury catamaran, past the Marquesa Keys and Boca Grande, on your way to a septuplet of islands that form one of America's smallest national parks. An on-board naturalist educates you about what to expect, and just over two hours after leaving Key West you're in the protected waters of Dry Tortugas National Park, itching to slide into the gin-clear tropical water that surrounds these remote coral atolls. First, though, you explore Fort Jefferson, one of America's biggest and most impressive 19th-century constructions – complete with a moat! – which has an extraordinary tale to tell. The afternoon is a different story altogether, though, as you embark on an aquatic odyssey of discovery in the park's underwater world, where an astonishing universe exists among the corals. Boarding the afternoon boat back to the mainland, it's hard not to cast an envious eye at the campers who are staying on.

19

FL

Everglades National Park

Vast marshes of swaying sawgrass stretching as far as the eye can see have earned the Everglades its nickname: 'the River of Grass.'

Imagine strolling the Anhinga Trail, an elevated boardwalk over the sawgrass marsh of Taylor Slough, broad-leafed marsh plants rippling gently in the brown water. You notice a large log, and then – wait! – the log moves! It's a 7ft (2m) gator, raising its primeval head for a yellow-eyed perusal of its surroundings before settling back into the mud. A minute later, a green snake whips its way through the water and disappears in the grass. A bubblegum-pink roseate spoonbill sticks its long, goofy beak into the water and yanks out a wriggling fish. This profusion of nature, in all its swampy, sticky, scaly glory, is what the Everglades are all about.

This is the largest tropical wilderness in the US, 2410 sq miles (6242 sq km) of wet sawgrass prairie, sun-dappled mangrove swamps, dense hardwood hammocks, pine forest and estuaries teeming with sea life. It's the third-largest national park in the lower 48, covering the entire southwest tip of Florida.

Indigenous people have roamed these swamps and forests for more than 10,000 years, leaving behind evidence of their existence in the form of shell mounds, piled up over many years of habitation. Over the centuries, various Native American tribes and escaped slaves have used the Everglades as a hiding place, secreting themselves deep within the swamp. A little more than a century ago, water in Florida flowed freely down the peninsula in a shallow sheet. This 11,000-sq-mile (28,490-sq-km) wetland was an intricate network of marshes, ponds, creeks and forest. But early settlers attempted to drain the land to make it farmable, destroying much of the delicate ecosystem in the process. Everglades National Park was

established in 1947 to protect what was left of the unique biozone. Today, the area around the park maintains an 'only in Florida' hint of wildness, with kitschy roadside attractions, tumbledown crab shacks and the occasional biker bar.

 An airboat is the ideal way to get around the waterways of the Everglades. Previous page: a great egret stalks a meal.

Toolbox

When to go
The dry season runs from December through April, which is good for hiking and other land-based sightseeing, but bad for kayaking. Spring is better for watersports, but summer and fall bring heat, bugs and hurricanes.

Getting there
The park is less than an hour's drive from Miami. The two major access towns are Homestead/Florida City in the southeast, and Everglades City in the northwest. Both have accommodations and food. You'll need a car to get around here.

Park in numbers

2410
Area covered (sq miles)

15
Maximum adult size for an American alligator (ft)

60
Average yearly rainfall (in)

Stay here...

Everglades International Hostel
In a 1930s boarding house, this quirky Florida City hostel is big on atmosphere: mosaic floors, canopy beds, murals and book-filled dorms. But the real magic happens in the garden, a jungle Eden complete with a treehouse, waterfalls, a rock pool and a gazebo. Accommodations range from dorm beds to private rooms to family suites. If there's no space, you can camp in the garden!

Ivey House B&B
In Everglades City, this modern B&B is splashed with Florida touches, from tile floors to tropical prints. The 18 rooms are air-conditioned; cheaper digs are available in The Lodge down the walkway, which has a beach-house feel plus a courtyard with a swimming pool. The inn's nature tours and kayak trips earn high marks.

Long Pine Key Campground
Six miles from the Ernest Coe Visitor Center, this drive-in NPS campground has 108 sites, bathrooms and water (but no showers or electric hook-ups). What it lacks in amenities it makes up in cleanliness and proximity to nature. Wake in the morning to birdsong, the sun turning the water pink as it rises above the sawgrass. It's close to the Anhinga Trail – tops for gator-spotting – and other park sights. Bring bug spray!

Do this!

Kayaking
On Florida's southwest edge, the Ten Thousand Islands is an archipelago of tiny mangrove islands stretching some 60 miles (97km). Kayaking here will make you feel like Indiana Jones exploring a lost jungle. Paddle across stretches of pale jade water, alighting on an uninhabited white beach for a picnic lunch – before setting off beneath tunnels of mangroves.

Slogging
'What is slogging?' you ask, and why would you want to do it? Everglade-ese for 'walking through the mud,' slogging (or 'wet-walking') is a wonderfully messy way to get up close and personal with South Florida nature. Local companies offer guided slogs, where you'll be provided with special shoes for mucking through the wetlands, seeing swamp orchids, cypress trees, turtles and snakes.

Tram-touring
The Everglades' popular tram trip travels through the park's Shark Valley. Guides, all trained naturalists, point out wildlife – you're guaranteed to see gators here. In addition to gators, keep your eyes open for red-shouldered hawks, ibises and a plethora of snakes.

What to spot...

Famed for its alligators, the Everglades is home to so much more. The endless sawgrass prairie, tropical hardwood hammocks, mangrove swamps and swirling estuaries are home to a lush variety of birds, snakes (including more than 150,000 invasive Burmese pythons), turtles and more. If you're incredibly lucky you might see a manatee in the waters of Florida Bay; dolphins are much more common, though. Rare orchids grow deep in the wetlands, colorful quarry for intrepid flower-spotters.

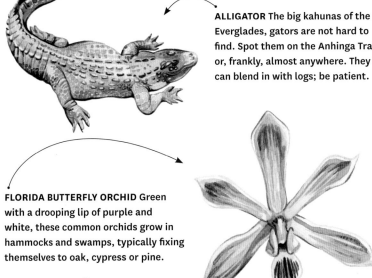

ALLIGATOR The big kahunas of the Everglades, gators are not hard to find. Spot them on the Anhinga Trail or, frankly, almost anywhere. They can blend in with logs; be patient.

FLORIDA BUTTERFLY ORCHID Green with a drooping lip of purple and white, these common orchids grow in hammocks and swamps, typically fixing themselves to oak, cypress or pine.

ROSEATE SPOONBILL Flamingo pink with a characteristic spoon-shaped bill, these large wading birds nest in mangrove trees and feed on crabs and small fish in shallow waters.

Hike this...

01 Anhinga Trail

You're guaranteed to see gators aplenty along this easy, 0.8-mile (1.3km) boardwalk trail; look for cormorants along the stone wall and nesting roseate spoonbills in the trees.

02 Bayshore Loop

Get an eyeful of mangrove islands as you skirt the edge of Florida Bay for 2 miles (3.2km), passing palm trees, blooming hibiscus and stands of buttonwood.

03 Snake Bight Trail

If the name doesn't scare you off, the mosquitos might. But stay and be rewarded with an adventurous 7.6-mile (12.2km) trek through hardwood hammock – keep your eyes open for flamingos.

Itineraries

It's gators guaranteed here, whether you bike through Shark Valley or cruise through mangroved Ten Thousand Islands in the US' largest tropical wilderness.

⬅ Baby alligators and an aerial view of Everglades' wetlands.
➡ The Mahogany Hammock Trail passes gumbo-limbo trees.

01

A day

Stick to one area if your time is limited; in this case we recommend Shark Valley. The two-hour Shark Valley tram tours will give you an entertaining introduction to the area and its wildlife, and you'll certainly get to check 'spotting an alligator' off your life's to-do list. Afterwards, rent a bike and cruise the 15-mile (24km) paved Shark Valley Trail, passing cypress and hardwood forests and crossing creeks – with barely any elevation gain. (But bring more water and sunscreen than you imagine you'll need. And food: there's nothing to eat in the park.) Picnic at the visitor center while looking for wood storks, Great White Herons and glossy ibises.

Afterwards, take the time to drive west to Big Cypress Gallery, where beloved Florida artist Clyde Butcher showcases his enormous B&W photographs of the swamps. Head back towards Miami with the sun sinking low behind you, turning the wetlands pink and gold. Finish up the day with a hearty plate of crackling roast pork with plantains at Exquisito Restaurant in Little Havana.

02

Two days

Base yourself in Everglades City, on the park's west side. Wake up early to kayak the Ten Thousand Islands, paddling through stands of gumbo-limbo trees and down mangrove-choked creeks, exploring ancient shell mounds and searching for ruins of Prohibition-era distilleries and trapper camps. Look for dolphins, otters, sharks and wading birds. Dine at Joanie's Blue Crab Café, a classic Florida seafood shack (try the Swamp Combo, a heaving platter of fried frog's legs, crab cakes and gator nuggets). The next day, head east along the Tamiami Trail, stopping for a giggle at the Skunk Ape Research Center in Ochopee, a cheesy 'zoo' and gift shop dedicated to South Florida's version of Bigfoot. Hit Shark Valley for a bike ride and a stroll through the hardwood hammock on the Bobcat Boardwalk. Exiting the park and heading south on Hwy 997, don't miss the Coral Castle, where an eccentric Latvian immigrant carved 1100 tons of coral rock into a strange fortress in the 1920s and '30s.

03

One week

On day one, hit the Ernest Coe Visitor Center and take an introductory walk around the raised platform trails through sawgrass prairie. Then move towards Royal Palm Visitor Center for a gators-guaranteed hike on the Anhinga Trail. Day two, ride bikes or take a tram tour around Shark Valley, keeping your eyes peeled for roseate spoonbills; anhingas (a water bird); rare, iridescent indigo snakes; gators and more. On day three, opt for a guided boat trip through the mangrove stands of the Ten Thousand Islands area, departing from the Gulf Coast Visitor Center. On day four, book a slog through the muddy waters of the cypress dome. Canoe the waters around Flamingo Point on day five, looking for wildlife. On day six, leave the Everglades for Biscayne National Park, which has the world's third-largest reef. Its crystalline waters, brimming with fish, make for world-class snorkeling. Spend day seven riding a glass-bottom boat around Biscayne and stare down at the jewel-colored reef, or dive one of the park's eerie shipwrecks.

20

Gates of the Arctic National Park & Preserve

Endless summer nights, a primordial ecosystem that is untainted by roads, and far-flung adventures on the edge of the planet.

You don't know nature. That is, modern humans don't know true nature. Wherever we go – be it on a backwoods day-hike or a longer trek through the wilds of the Rockies – our modern invasive human imprint is everywhere. You'll see it in passing planes, roads, telephone wires, litter and smog. But up above the Arctic Circle, where the winds howl wild and the caribou run free, true wilderness still exists – this is arguably the most primitive, most raw, most born-free stretch of wilderness in all of North America.

Interestingly enough, humankind has lived in harmony with this 8.4-million-acre swath of wilderness for over 13,000 years. And the 8.4-million-acre Gates of the Arctic has thousands of archeological sites that preserve the semi-nomadic traditions of the Inupiat and Athabascan peoples. To this day, the descendants of these original settlers – and a few non-native, modern-day back-to-the-Earthers – live, hunt and survive in this park. The days of nomadic hunting are over, but 11 small communities are still found within park boundaries.

Non-native explorers first came to the Central Brooks Range in the 1880s, looking for gold, military high ground and improved opportunities. But their footprints have long faded. What's left is an adventure-seeker's Valhalla, with uncharted wilderness stretching to that northern horizon and beyond.

As with any hard-to-penetrate wilderness, rivers are natural pathways for human travel. And the six rivers of Gates of the Arctic – the Alatna, John, Kobuk, Noatak, North Fork of the Koyukuk and Tinayguk Rivers – provide miles upon miles of unspoiled wilderness, big views of precipitous, glacier-carved valleys, and a unique connecting point between humankind and the river wild.

Getting to and through the Gates of the Arctic requires serious outdoors skills. Its sheer remoteness is the stuff of legends for serious boaters and hikers looking to go beyond the everyday.

Toolbox

☀ When to go
The summer is short here – luckily, having 24 hours of sunlight makes it easy to pack a lot of activity into a short period. Come June through August, unless you have a dogsled team or pair of skis.

🧭 Getting there
Planes can take you to the gateway villages of Bettles (where you'll find park headquarters) or Anaktuvuk Pass, where you can get floatplanes to drop you at the put-in for your river trip or backcountry hike. You can also simply walk out from these villages (or from the Dalton Hwy at Coldfoot) to enter this roadless national treasure.

Park in numbers

13,238
Area covered (sq miles)

16
Wild rivers

145
Species of birds

Stay here...

🏕 Camping
There are no designated campsites here, which means you can basically camp anywhere – on the edge of a lake, up in the roaring winds of a jagged ridgeline, down by the river on the edge of the great boreal forest.

🏠 Iniakuk Lake Wilderness Lodge
At the edge of the park, this fly-in luxury cabin offers all-inclusive stays in a 1974 log homestead. Trips include guided fishing, hiking, wildlife-watching and -viewing, but it's the intimacy and camaraderie that really make this place stand out. It also has 24-hour solar electricity, running water and a few remote cabins that will get you even further off the grid.

🏠 Peace of Selby Wilderness Lodge
Fly in to remote log cabins on the lakes and rivers of the southern Brooks Range, or spruce up your vacation with a few nights at the main waterfront lodge. The real winner here is the views.

Do this!

🛶 Paddling
Serious river rats can raft, canoe or kayak these undammed and uncontaminated waterways – much as Alaska Natives have been doing for time immemorial – on trips that last from a few days to a few weeks. The Noatak offers amazing paddling and wildlife watching for trips that usually stretch up to ten days. The Kobuk takes you through some solid Class III water. Continue on for a longer adventure all the way to the Chukchi Sea.

🎒 Backpacking
On land, there's no end to what you can see and do – your own ambitions and abilities are truly the only obstacles in your path.

Given that there are no trails, no roads and no cell-phone service, this challenging terrain is for expert outdoors enthusiasts only. Novices should hire a guide to lead them through this untamed wilderness.

〰 Pack-rafting
For a mix of hiking and paddling, some operators are offering pack-raft trips along the Alatna. It's hard work, but offers a high return.

◧ Dogsledding at the North Fork of the Koyukuk River, which flows through broad, glacial valleys.
➡ Watch out for wolf prints in the Brooks Range.

See this...

01 Flightseeing
You don't have to have MacGyver Swiss Army knife skills to enjoy the park. Hire a floatplane to take you across the park, spotting musk ox and caribou as you pass through the gates into the Brooks Range.

02 Archaeology
The human imprint goes back 13,000 years and you can still uncover archaeological finds such as abandoned camps and mining cabins throughout the park.

03 Birding
Stick near the waterways to spot osprey, eagles, yellow-rumped warblers, ptarmigan, snowy owl and any number of sparrows, longspurs, finch, growse, gull and tern.

What to spot...

It doesn't last long, but the arctic summer catches fire. Birds migrate here to feed on the billions of mosquitos; fish swim upstream; mammals fatten up for the long winter cold; caribou and moose take shelter in the boreal forest; and grizzlies eat until they're stuffed. While the migrating caribou, musk ox and big predators are highlights, it's the small rodents, birds and insect life that really bring this heavily sleeping wilderness to life.

CARIBOU The largest caribou herd in Alaska runs right through here. These stately animals weigh up to 500lb (227kg). Their hides and meat are a staple for Native Alaskans that still maintain a subsistence-hunting lifestyle.

MUSK OX
These ice-age bearded beasts roam across the wild like sage prophets from a time long since extinct. Look for them in open fields and tundra.

ARCTIC TERN The artic tern stop here – after the longest migration of any bird in the world – to fill up on insects before heading south to Antarctic waters.

Itineraries

Take a flightseeing tour over the Arctic Circle, raft the remote Noatak River and maybe spot a grizzly bear or two in this raw, rugged wilderness.

◧ Bushplanes are required for rafting trips.
⬆ Snowmachines are permitted in the park; morning light hits the Arrigetch peaks.

01

Five days

If you have limited outdoor experience or mobility (or just don't want to spend 10 days freezing in a tent by the river), this trip is for you. Begin with a day or two in Fairbanks, where you can take a flightseeing tour above the Arctic Circle, spend an afternoon at the excellent Museum of the North, or just bop around town, checking out the ruined dredges, riverboats and more. From there, hop an all-inclusive trip to Iniakuk Lake Wilderness Lodge. Fresh pastries will greet you every morning as

you plan short forays into the wilderness. From here, you can do canoe trips, head out in search of wildlife or just watch the water as it reflects the blue arctic sky. Set aside a day or two to stay off the grid in one of the lodge's remote cabins. The Arrigetch Peaks Wilderness Cabin is a rustic log masterpiece with a big porch and even bigger views. Each day, challenge your guide to take you to a new corner of the Brooks Range in search of wildlife, rare birds and views that stretch as far as your imagination.

02

Ten days

Your rafting trip starts in Fairbanks with an afternoon pub-paddle on the Chena River, rising early the next day for a flight into Bettles. Check in at the park HQ and arrange your gear, heading out into the wilds via floatplane to a drop along the Noatak River. As the floatplane buzzes into the distance, the reality that you are alone in a wilderness double the size of Switzerland sinks in.

Start your expedition right with a fresh-caught fish dinner and a night's

rest. A World Heritage site, the Noatak stretches for some 400 miles (644km) to the Chukchi Sea; you might paddle just 100 miles (160km), but it will feel like your adventure lasts a lifetime. Along the way, you'll see wolf, fox, moose, Dall sheep, spawning salmon and feeding grizzlies. After paddling 15 river miles (24km), you'll be exhausted; save some energy to pick blueberries and gaze at tundra wildflowers, such as Grass of Parnassus and Arctic poppies.

21

MT

Glacier National Park

Everything in Glacier is larger than life, from the ancient snowy mountains and the deep navy lakes to the fearless mountain goats.

Views of Glacier National Park. Previous page: fall kayaking on Bowman Lake

Driving along Glacier National Park's famed Going-to-the-Sun Rd feels rather ordinary at first. You drive through pine forest. You pass a lake. Then – whoa! – you turn a bend and you're 1000ft (305m) above the valley floor, surrounded prehistoric granite peaks straining towards the clouds. You turn your head to see a wall of waterfalls streaming down an ancient rock face. Turn again, and spot mountain goats leaping along flower-fringed crags so high they seem to touch the sun. This is Glacier National Park. Words like 'pretty' don't apply. Words like 'massive,' 'electrifying,' and 'fierce,' however, do.

Signed into existence by William Howard Taft in 1910, Glacier didn't become a major tourist destination until two years later, when the Great Northern Railway began building magnificent hotels and advertising the region as 'America's Switzerland.' WWII brought activity in the park to a screeching halt, and many of the chalets fell into disrepair. Today, nine of the original thirteen have been revived.

The 53-mile-long (85.3km) Going-to-the-Sun Rd was finished in 1932, ushering in the era of automobile travel. Traversing some of the park's most spectacular terrain via switchbacks and hairpin turns, it's considered by many to be one of the finest scenic drives in America. It's named for Going-to-the-Sun Mountain, which the local Blackfeet tribe considered a sacred spot. Today, it's closed for much of the year due to snow, sometimes not opening until as late as July.

In 1932, Glacier joined with Waterton Lakes National Park across the border in Alberta, Canada, to create the world's first International Peace Park, a symbol of the friendship between the US and Canada. Today visitors can hike or take a boat ride across the US–Canada border. In fact, this is the only place you can cross the border without clearing customs, but do bring your passport – hikers crossing the border by foot will get a unique mountain goat stamp.

Getty Images | Jordan Siemens; Noah Clayton

Toolbox

 When to go
As you might expect with a name like 'Glacier,' this park is freezing most of the year. Many facilities don't even open until July, and roads are often closed after the snows come in early fall. Hit the park in late August or early September for the best combination of warm weather and solitude.

Getting there
Glacier is in northern Montana, on the Canadian border. Glacier Park International Airport is in Kalispell, about 30 miles (48.3km) west. A public bus plies the park's main areas, but it's hard to get here without your own car.

Park in numbers

1583
Area covered (sq miles)

6646
Highest point on Going-to-the-Sun Rd: Logan's Pass (ft)

1500
Number of mountain goats in the park

Stay here...

🏠 Many Glacier Hotel
Everything about this rickety Swiss-style chalet charms, from the valets in lederhosen to the vintage tiled bathrooms and the library full of bird-watching books. Built in 1915, the lodge is far enough from Going-to-the-Sun Rd to be quiet even in mid-July. Rooms are basic but comfy. In the evening, pull on a sweater for drinks overlooking Swiftcurrent Lake.

⛺ Many Glacier Campground
First-come, first-served sites at Many Glacier Campground fill up fast, and no wonder – this is one of Glacier's loveliest campsites. Arrive early to snag a spot with good views.

Easy access to showers, laundry and a camp store means you won't be roughing it too much – and proximity to some of the park's finest hiking means you can roll right out of your sleeping bag and onto the trail.

🏠 Lake McDonald Lodge
Built in 1913, this pretty chalet is perched on the shore of Lake McDonald. The lobby is an example of early-20th-century 'parkitecture,' with half-timbered walls and a stone fireplace. Stay in the main lodge or a cabin, save money with a hostel-style dorm or splurge on a suite. Like all the park's lodgings, it books up early.

Do this!

🛞 Scenic driving
Bisecting the park diagonally from southwest to northeast, the engineering marvel that is Going-to-the-Sun Rd gives drivers dizzy views across the range and to the valley floor far below. Drive your own car, ride the park shuttle, or – our favorite – join a tour in one of Glacier's vintage red buses, complete with a guide.

🧲 Horseback riding
See Glacier from the back of a horse: Swan Mountain Outfitters has corrals throughout the park, where their cowboys and cowgirls will lead you on a half- or whole-day ride through the pine forests to mountain lakes and streams. You'll learn neat facts about the park's flora and fauna (sometimes because your horse is busy trying to eat a poisonous bush!).

🔭 Glacier-viewing
Glacier counts about 25 glaciers within its boundaries; back in 1850, there were 150. Many experts think the existing glaciers' days are numbered. So where's the best place to spot an endangered glacier? Some glaciers can be seen from Going-to-the-Sun Rd, including blue-gray Jackson Glacier. In the Many Glacier area, Grinnell Glacier is a bucket-list classic. Hike to the overlook to see it glimmering in the Montana sun.

What to spot...

Glacier teems with wildlife, especially when the summer thaws mean hibernating creatures come out to play. Chubby yellow-bellied marmots scurry across rocky pinnacles, majestic moose graze peacefully on the upper slopes of mountains, lumbering grizzlies forage for huckleberries in the lush meadows. The eastern side of the park is blown by dry chinook winds, making it drier and browner. The west side is wetter and more primeval, home to dark, dew-dripping cedar and hemlock forests.

MOUNTAIN GOATS
The park's official symbol, the fluffy, white mountain goat can be found scrambling up steep slopes – often they use the same hiking paths humans do.

GLACIER LILY In summer the avalanche slopes are carpeted in delicate yellow glacier lilies, which look like tiny six-pointed stars.

CANADIAN LYNX The silvery-brown lynx looks rather like a large housecat, but it takes work to spot them. Their numbers are threatened, and they are generally active at night.

Going-to-the-Sun Road is a popular alpine route for cyclists in Glacier National Park.

Hike this...

O1 The Highline
The park's most iconic hike cuts a narrow path along the famed Garden Wall (handholds included) before winding 7.5 miles (12km) into the mountains towards the rustic Granite Park Chalet.

O2 Avalanche Lake
Popular with families, this steady 4-mile (6.4km) round-trip traverses dense forest to the banks of a pretty blue alpine lake.

O3 Iceberg Lake
Hikers gasp when they hit the top of this 9-mile (14.5km) hike and the clear green water bobbing with small icebergs appears in front of them.

Itineraries

Ready for some life-changing hikes? Try Iceberg Lake or Logan Pass for glacial views, stunning vistas and bonus wolf sightings.

◀ Stand-up paddle-boarding on Hidden Lake.
▶ Backcountry cooking in Glacier National Park.

01

Two days

Wake early on your first day and inhale the piney air as you embark on the length of Going-to-the-Sun Rd. Heading southwest to northeast, stop first at Lake McDonald for a photo session and a peek at the timber lobby of iconic 1913 Lake McDonald Lodge. Ascend the hairpin turns of The Loop, where the road cuts across the continent-dividing Garden Wall. Keep your eyes open for the cascades at Bird Woman Falls and the Weeping Wall, then stop at Logan Pass Visitor Center to stretch your legs and gaze down across the valley from 6646ft (2026m). Descend to the viewpoint of Jackson Glacier Overlook, then stop for more pics by the navy waters of St Mary Lake. Finish up with a bison burger and a thick slice of huckleberry pie at the Park Cafe in St Mary. On day two, hit the Many Glaciers area for a plunge into the park's wilder side. Fortify yourself with lunch at the Ptarmigan Dining Room in Many Glacier Hotel before embarking on the 9-mile (14.5km) hike to impressive Iceberg Lake.

02

Four days

On day one, drive Going-to-the-Sun Rd as described in the two-day itinerary, but this time park at Logan Pass for the life-changing hike along the Highline Trail. You'll almost certainly spot a mountain goat or three along the trail; in spring and summer they sometimes have their fluffy white kids in tow. On day two finish Going-to-the-Sun Rd and stop at the mirror-smooth St Mary Lake for an afternoon of canoeing. On day three, head to Many Glacier and hike to either Iceberg Lake or Grinnell Glacier; both trails are stunners, full of sweeping vistas and primeval snowcaps. Dine at Two Sisters Cafe near Babb, beloved for their goofy-bumper-sticker–lined walls and their huckleberry milkshakes. On day four explore the more remote precincts of the park at Two Medicine Valley, where you're just as likely to see a wolf as another person. Upper Two Medicine Lake is a good day hike, passing through dense, ferny forest to reveal achingly beautiful mountain views.

03

One week

On day one get a feel for the park and its history with a day-long tour in one of the photogenic jammer buses; it'll give you the lay of the land for further adventures. One day two, hit the southwest portion of Going-to-the-Sun Rd, stopping for a warm-up hike at Avalanche Lake. Bring a picnic to eat on the sandy shores. On day three proceed to Logan Pass for the Highline Trail, again bringing lunch to eat at Granite Park Chalet while taking in the sweeping views of encircling mountains. On day four paddle St Mary Lake, watching for osprey, hawks and peregrine falcons. On day five head to the Swan Mountain corral at Many Glacier for a day-long trail ride through the dense forest to one of the area's milky-blue glacial lakes. Head to the wild Two Medicine Valley on day six for a scenic boat tour across the ice-cold, glassy lake. On day seven, pack your passport and cross the border for a day trip of hiking and boating in Waterton Lakes National Park in Canada.

22

AK

Glacier Bay National Park & Preserve

Quintessential Alaska, Glacier Bay is a forceful reminder of the strength, tenacity and power of Mother Nature.

Eleven tidewater glaciers cascade down from the mountains here and fill the sea with icebergs of all shapes and sizes imaginable. The park itself covers a wide variety of terrain over 3.3 million acres, from mountains and ice field to temperate rainforest and secluded fjords, but it's the glaciers, with their dramatic calving events, towering grandeur and visceral appeal, that are the star attraction.

The natural history of this bay is revealed in the deep fjord that was formed by rapidly retreating ice. When Captain George Vancouver sailed through here in 1794, Glacier Bay was little more than a mountain of ice. The next century, John Muir discovered that the ice had retreated within the bay by some 20 miles (32km) from the icy strait. Today, it goes back more than 60 miles (96.5km), revealing a hydrological history that is both fascinating and perhaps a little alarming.

You are unlikely to visit this rugged bay – marked by the thunderous roar of falling icebergs and the spirited vaults of migrating humpback whales – by land. In fact, no roads go here. Instead, you'll probably see it from the deck of a cruise ship – or, if you're lucky, from the water aboard a sea kayak. Two large cruise ships are permitted to enter the bay every day, and it's a highlight of many Southeast Alaska cruises. Independent adventurers can visit the park from Juneau, with stops in the remote offbeat village of Gustavus and park headquarters at Bartlett Cove. From aboard your vessel, you are likely to spot any number of remarkable sea mammals, such as whales and harbor seals; you might also spot a bear or moose paddling their way across a narrow section of bay. Part of the even larger 25-million-acre World Heritage site found here, this wilderness is rough and wild, untamed and unrelenting.

Toolbox

When to go

The park is open year-round, but the peak season is late May to early September. It rains up to 70in (178cm) a year here, so no matter what season you visit, expect it to be wet and cold.

Getting there

Most of the 300,000 yearly visitors get here on a cruise. If you're traveling independently, kick off your trip from Gustavus, an off-the-grid backwater so remote it didn't get electricity until the 1980s. From there, you can arrange a cruise or kayak from park headquarters at Bartlett Cove.

Park in numbers

5156
Area covered (sq miles)

11
Tidal glaciers

40
Weight of a humpback whale in tons

Stay here...

National Park Service Campground

Set in a ridiculously lush forest steps from the shoreline, this free campsite has a bear cache and little warming shelter. It's just 0.25 miles (0.4km) from Glacier Bay Lodge, where you can grab meals and warm up.

Glacier Bay Lodge

The only hotel and restaurant in Bartlett Cove, this granddaddy of a lodge has a warm, cozy air. The broad stone fireplace and restaurant are center-stage, where backpackers, just-back-from-the-wild kayakers, and well-heeled sightseers all gather. Nightly slideshows, guided day trips, ranger talks and the occasional movie upstairs add to the mix.

Blue Heron B&B

Located in Gustavus, the Blue Heron is a lilting little homestead, set in 10 acres, surrounded by fields of wildflowers and offering up killer views of the nearby Fairweather Mountains. The natural breakfasts are sumptuous and filling, and there's an overall feeling of close community. Ask the owner Deb for her help in customizing your trip, with kayaking, whale watching, biking or fishing.

Do this!

Kayaking

Take to the water, where the snap-crackle-and-pop of melting icebergs overpowers your senses. With a sea-taxi drop off you can explore a good bit in a day. Take a few more to further explore the Muir Inlet and West Arm, staying away from the open waters of the Bay. A fun overnight takes you to Beardslee Islands, where you can camp, spot birds and search for wildflowers.

Flightseeing

The majesty of the world of ice water and forest takes on new perspectives aboard a small airplane. You can head out from Haines to see the glaciers, bays and oceanfronts of the park. Numerous routes, running from 1 to 2½ hours, take you over the most dramatic scenery of the park.

Boat touring

Two-day tours to the park include an overnight at the Glacier Bay Lodge, and a long, eight-hour boat tour out to the glaciers. For something a little different, consider a whale-watching tour.

◄ Humpback whales visit Glacier Bay in summer to feed on small fish, consuming half a ton daily.

➡ A tufted puffin.

Hike this...

01 Nagoonberry Loop

For huge fields of wildflowers, spend a morning cruising this short, 2.2-mile trail. You'll pass from meadow to old-growth forest, giving great perspective on area flora.

02 Forest Trail

Hop on a ranger-led walk on this short nature trail that takes you past tiny ponds and stands of hemlock and spruce to the dock at Bartlett Cove.

03 Point Gustavus

You can walk along the beach from Bartlett Cove to Gustavus on this 12-mile trek, which usually takes two days. Look for pods of orca at Point Gustavus.

What to spot...

Most of your wildlife viewing will be from the sea, so expect plenty of maritime species and birds. There are Steller sea lion, harbor porpoise, harbor seal and mischievous sea otters. In the forested areas near the mouth of the Bay, you might sight brown or black bear; look to the cliffs for mountain goats. But the real stars are the whales that call this bay home, who are regularly spotted lobbing their tails on the water's surface.

HARBOR SEAL Thousands of seals breed and raise their pups on the floating icebergs found in the Johns Hopkins Inlet and near the Beardslee Islands.

HUMPBACK WHALE Anywhere from 40 to 200 humpback whales spend their summers bubble-net-feeding in these fruitful waters. You might also see Minke and killer whale, plus Dall's porpoise.

BROWN BEAR Bears live along the coast, where they eat barnacles, clams and other delicacies. You can also occasionally spot them swimming in the bay.

Itineraries

Spot puffins and Steller sea lions on a Glacier Bay boat tour or take it up a notch with a multiday paddle on the Alsek River.

◄ The skeleton of Snow, a humpback whale killed in Glacier Bay in 2001.

▲ A tree carving by indigenous Tlingit people. See the Beardsley Islands from a sea kayak.

01

Two days

If you aren't here on a cruise ship, you'll need to do a little pre-planning – and a lot of saving to get here. There are regular flights from Juneau, Alaska's capital, to Gustavus, or you can hop on a ferry aboard the Alaska Marine Highway, which offers beautiful sightseeing on its own. Stay at the Blue Heron B&B in Gustavus, sampling organic rolled oats with blueberries the next morning. Grab a picnic lunch at Sunnyside Market and hitch a ride over to Bartlett Cove. Stay the night in the campsite, with a little afternoon jaunt on the Forest Trail. The next day, get up early for a seven-hour boat tour of Glacier Bay. A park ranger provides commentary on the 130-mile (209km) circuit. At South Marble Island, expect to see tufted and horned puffins, along with Steller sea lions. You'll start seeing icebergs 20 miles (32km) out; after lunch is the pièce de résistance – close views of the tidewater glaciers that make this bay famous. If you're lucky, you might just see a chunk of ice the size of a building fall and crash into the water.

02

One week

With a heightened sense of adventure – and no aversion to risk, cold or wet – you can see and do remarkable things here. It all starts on the water. Begin from Gustavus and Bartlett Cove, where you can arrange sea taxis, guides and gear. The Glacier Bay Boat Tour will drop off independent parties, or a number of guided operations can take you for day-long or multiday paddles. All but the most experienced of paddlers should consider going with a guide (if for nothing else but the companionship).

You can do a short warm-up trip to Beardslee Islands to get your toes wet; another day trip takes you to Point Adolphus, a great spot for humpback sighting. Go bigger with a weeklong paddle up the East or West Arms. On your way home, continue north of the park to Glacier Bay National Preserve, a remote corner of wilderness best accessed from Yakutat, where you can raft the Alsek River, learn more about subsistence living, or find your own adventure in a wilderness without boundaries.

23

AZ

Grand Canyon National Park

To catch your first glimpse of this epic rent in the earth is to understand that some things are just as grand as they're billed.

The Grand Canyon, with its hypnotic folds of gold and red cliffs, its mesas rippling endlessly towards the horizon, is one of the most magnificent wonders of this planet. A mile (1.6km) deep, 18 miles (29km) wide and 277 miles (445.8km) long, its scope is truly hard to appreciate until you've seen it yourself. Come here to hike narrow trails down sandstone cliffs, to raft the roiling waters of the Colorado, to ride a mule through fragrant stands of piñon and sagebrush. Or just come to stand on the rim, camera in hand, marveling at the wonder of it all.

Some 90% of visitors come to the canyon's warmer South Rim, with its arid summers, silver falls, snowy fairyland winters and cool blue springs. The higher, colder North Rim is far more difficult to access, but is deeply rewarding for its crowd-free trails and silent nights powdered with stars. Further-flung areas are administered by Native American tribes – including the psychedelic blue falls of the Havasupai reservation and the vertiginous glass Skywalk of the Hualapai people.

The wild Colorado River has been sawing away at the Arizona landscape for some 6 million years. Along with wind, ice and continental drift, it has slowly cut through the earth, revealing a layer cake of Kaibab limestone, Coconino sandstone, Hermit shale and many other types of rock, creating the vast chasm we see today.

Home to various Native American groups for more than 10,000 years, the canyon's first European visitors were Spanish explorers in the 1540s. In the 1870s, geologist John Wesley Powell led expeditions through the canyon, drawing national attention to its beauty via a series of early photographs.

By the early 1900s, tourists were arriving in earnest via the Santa Fe Railroad. Today, some five million people from all over the globe come to be stunned by the canyon's epic size and beauty.

⬛ No cameras permitted, but that won't spoil the views from Grand Canyon West Skywalk. Previous page: Bright Angel Point on the North Rim.

Toolbox

When to go
The South Rim is open year-round, but summer crowds and winter cold make spring and fall the most pleasant times to visit. The North Rim has a more limited season of May to October.

Getting there
The entire canyon is within the state of Arizona. The South Rim is an hour north of Flagstaff, on I-40. Grand Canyon West, with the Skywalk, is a four-hour drive from South Rim. A major airport is four hours south in Phoenix. The North Rim entrance is 30 miles (48.2km) south of remote Jacob Lake.

Park in numbers

1902
Area covered (sq miles)

8800
Highest point: Pt Imperial (ft)

2
Age of oldest rocks in the Canyon (Vishnu Schist), in billion years

Stay here...

 El Tovar Hotel
Built in 1905 by celebrated architect Charles Whittlesey, this rim-side chalet has quite a history. Luminaries from Albert Einstein to Paul McCartney have slept in the limestone and Oregon pine lodge. Wake to jaw-dropping views with a pricey suite. For 30 years, El Tovar has been a National Historic Landmark.

Bright Angel Lodge
Pioneering female architect Mary Jane Colter created this and other landmark park buildings, inspired by the local landscape and native traditions. Made of stone with bright-painted trim, the 1935 lodge is the colors of a desert sunset. Its 'geologic' fireplace features all the rock layers of the canyon. Rooms range from doubles with shared bathrooms to log-lined suites.

Phantom Ranch
Overnighting at the Phantom Ranch is a true 'bucket list' experience. You can only get here by hiking, rafting or riding a mule, so forget about dodging tour bus crowds. Designed by Mary Jane Colter, these cozy stone cottages are tucked into the trees on the north side of the Colorado River. After a long day of tramping, there's nothing like sharing a beer with fellow travelers in the dining room.

Do this!

Sunset-watching
You won't be alone seeing the sun set over Lipan Point, but there's a reason for the crowds. Watching the light go red and violet over the Palisades of the Desert and the Echo and Vermilion Cliffs is a lifetime experience. You'll also have a terrific view of Unkar Rapid to the west. Arrive early and stay until the last drop of purple drains from the walls.

Climb the Desert View Watchtower
Designed by the southwestern architect Mary Jane Colter in 1932, this stone tower was inspired by ancestral Puebloan watchtowers. The top floor is at about 7522ft (2293m) above sea level, making it the highest spot on the South Rim, with views across the Painted Desert.

Rafting
Wannabe rafters often wait for a year or more to run the powerful Colorado, but the occasional lucky traveler gets a last-minute booking. However you get in, a rafting trip through the floor of the Grand Canyon is an experience you'll be telling your grandkids about. Trips range from about four to ten days, complete with riverside camping. Some sections are glass-smooth, while others will hurtle you over 30ft-plus (9m) rapids. Whee!

What to spot...

With an 8000ft (2438m) elevation gain from the Colorado River to the North Rim, the Grand Canyon hosts a startling variety of habitats. Gray foxes, mule deer and big horn sheep inhabit the piñon forests of the South Rim, while the cooler Ponderosa pine and blue spruce forests of the North Rim are home to mountain lions, bobcats and goshawks. The river itself is a habitat for endangered humpback chub and razorback suckers, while beavers, canyon tree frogs and coyotes can be found among the cottonwoods on its banks.

KAIBAB SQUIRREL The entire habitat of this tassel-eared squirrel is the Kaibab Plateau, along the Canyon's North Rim and just beyond.

CALIFORNIA CONDOR The largest land bird in America, this bald, black vulture became extinct in the wild in 1987. It was reintroduced to the Southwest, but there are still fewer than 500.

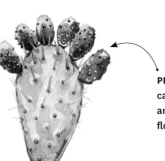

PRICKLY PEAR CACTUS These common cacti have wide, paddle-shaped pads and grow stunning pink, orange or yellow flowers and bulbous purple fruits.

Hike this...

01 Rim Trail
If you're not into altitude changes, this semi-paved, 12-mile (19.3km) trail covers the best viewpoints on the South Rim in one family-friendly walk.

02 Bright Angel Trail
See the canyon walls up close and personal on this popular stair trail, which descends 7.8 miles (12.5km) to the Colorado. There are several easy turning points for day-hikers.

03 Grandview Trail
One of the park's steepest trails, the 6-mile (9.7km) round-trip Grandview switchbacks down across rust-colored mesas, plunging 1600ft (488m) in less than a mile (1.6km).

Itineraries

Whichever itinerary you choose, don't miss a or sunset over the canyon. The hiking, mule trips and gorging on prickly pear are a bonus.

← Mule rides are available into the Grand Canyon; hiking Blacktail Canyon, a side-canyon.
→ Rafting the Colorado River.

01

A day

Arrive at the South Rim as dawn is breaking pink and lavender over the Painted Desert. Hit the best viewpoints in the most efficient way by walking the 12-mile (19.3km) Rim Trail. Stop first at the Pipe Creek Vista to gawk at the endless mesas' sea of red and purple waves. Then onward to the Yavapai Observation Station, where plate-glass windows offer panoramic views and topographic relief models explain the canyon's geology. Nearby Grandeur Point lets you look down at the hikers moving ant-like along the ribbon that is the Bright Angel Trail; stop here for a picnic lunch amid the pines. A bit further on, Mission-style Verkamp's Visitor Center is one of the park's oldest buildings, while the Mary Jane Colter–designed Hopi House was modeled after an old Hopi pueblo and built largely by Hopi tribespeople. Today it's a primo spot to pick up Native American jewelry and crafts. Several vistas later is Hopi Point – the place to see sunset drip its Crayola colors down the canyon walls (though nearby Mohave Point is a contender as well).

02

A weekend

Wake early amid the smell of piñon and juniper at one of the South Rim's campgrounds and fortify yourself with a hearty breakfast before hitting the Bright Angel Trail (with plenty of snacks and water). Wind your way down the canyon's rust-and-orange limestone and sandstone walls, passing mule trains as you go. Go as far as Indian Garden, an oasis of lush trees and waters 4.6 miles (7.4km) down. When you drag yourself, exhausted, back above the rim, have a shower and treat yourself to dinner in the dark-wood environs of the El Tovar Dining Room – duck with prickly pear glaze tastes that much better after so many miles of hiking. The next day, rest your aching calves by driving the 25-mile (40.2km) Desert View Dr. Start at Mather Point, where you can see the Bright Angel Trail winding into the rosy canyon. Don't miss the panoramic vistas of Lipan Point or the 70ft (21m) climb up the Watchtower. End the day watching the sun sink like a red penny behind the cliffs.

03

Five days

On day one, take in the multi-hued vistas along the 25-mile (40.2km) Desert View Dr. Finish by watching the sunset turn the cliffs a beautiful red from Lipan Point. On day two, plunge in with the steep 1.5-mile (2.4km) hike into the canyon's deep red folds on the Grandview Trail. Pack a picnic to eat when you've emerged back at the top, watching birds dip and dive along the rim.

On day three, pack your backpack and set out down the Bright Angel Trail, winding your way down the piñon-shaded trail, past the chartreuse oasis of Indian Garden and onto the canyon floor. With the rim a distant blur overhead, make your way to the rustic refuge of Phantom Ranch for a night of dreamless sleep.

On day four, do the same thing, but in reverse! Harder that way, isn't it? On day five, rest your legs with a half-day mule trip along the rim, riding through the pine and juniper forest to the Abyss overlook. Toast your trip with cocktails in the cozy wood lounge at El Tovar.

Mark Read

24

Grand Teton National Park

Yellowstone's lesser-known southern neighbor is a high-altitude stunner, with peaks, meadows and back roads that offer unbelievable views and blissful solitude.

G rand Teton isn't a 'drive-through' park, where you can see the best parts without straying more than a hundred paces from your car. Though it certainly does have some stunning scenic drives, this is a park for exploring. It's for hiking quad-burning trails up craggy peaks dotted with jade-green high-altitude lakes. It's for kayaking the choppy waters of Jackson Lake or rafting the undulating curves of the Snake River. It's for sitting silently in the tall grass watching pronghorns and bison graze in the wheat-colored afternoon sunlight. So if you're looking for an active, immersive park experience, the peaks and valleys of Grand Teton will make an unforgettable trip.

The sharp-spined Teton Range is the centerpiece of Grand Teton National Park. French fur trappers called its three main peaks *les trois tétons* – 'the three breasts.' (While we're not sure what Medusa-like creature has breasts as jagged as the Tetons, the name stuck.) In the early 1900s, the Jackson Hole area became crowded with tourist-centric development, from gas stations to dance halls to racetracks. Standard Oil heir John D Rockefeller Jr, concerned with the land's degradation, began secretly buying up property throughout the valley with the intent of giving it away as national park land. When the public found out, they revolted, angry about possible lost tax revenue. Though the park was established in 1929, it took more than 50 years and numerous acts of Congress to finalize its boundaries.

The terrain of Grand Teton varies vastly, its *Lord of the Rings*-like mountains erupting suddenly from the calm valley floor. Within the same day you can swim in a glacier-created mountain lake, hike through

dripping conifer forests, picnic beneath the cottonwoods of swift-flowing rivers and drive along the flat golden meadows of the valley. Watch the stars at night, or head to Jackson for a luxe bison-steak dinner.

⬆ Rangers assist with many activities in the park, mostly in the summer. Previous page: riding through the sage brush.
➡ John Moulton barn.

Toolbox

When to go
Grand Teton is open year-round but, like most high-altitude national parks, it is more popular – and crowded – in the summer, when wildflowers bloom and high temperatures are generally in the comfortable mid-70s F (low 20s C). Winter is gorgeous, though some roads may be closed due to snow.

Getting there
Grand Teton is just outside the town of Jackson, in Wyoming's northwest corner. The Jackson Hole Airport is actually inside Grand Teton, making it the only US airport within a national park. You'll need a car to see the park.

Park in numbers

485
Area covered (sq miles)

13,770
Highest point: Grand Teton (ft)

173
Average snowfall (in)

Snake River flows west through the park. Rafting is a popular way of exploring it (permits and fees apply).

Stay here...

Jenny Lake Campground

In summer, campers circle this lakeside haven as early as 6am, hoping to snag a coveted spot as the previous night's residents leave. We think it's worth the dawn wake-up to sleep under the evergreens at this central campground. With only 51 tent-only spots and no showers or dishwashing facilities, this is definitely not glamping – but that's the point.

Jenny Lake Lodge

The luxe log cabins go quickly at this upscale-rustic resort, which often fills up nearly a year in advance. Guests have been burrowing beneath Jenny Lake Lodge's handmade quilts since the 1920s. The high prices include breakfast, a five-course dinner as well as such activities as horseback riding and bike trips.

Jackson Lake Lodge

On a bluff overlooking Jackson Lake, this sprawling lodge is known more for its views than its accommodations. Rooms are standard (and somewhat dated), but the higher-priced ones have knee-weakening views over the Teton Range. Guests gather in the bar to watch the sun fall rosy over the mountains while sipping a lager. Kids adore the playground and heated swimming pool – a far sight warmer than icy Jackson Lake!

Do this!

Rafting

Raft down the Snake River as it wends its way through the valley, watching beavers and otters splash as eagles and osprey glide overhead. On the shore, you might spot pronghorn or elk grazing as you pass beneath green-gold willow trees. A number of outfitters offer this rafting trip, which lasts about 10 miles (16km). No white water here, just a peaceful meander, as guides point out animals.

Boat cruising

In summer, passenger boats shuttle between the Jenny Lake Visitor Center and the base of Mount Teewinot every 10 to 15 minutes. Alight on the west side of the lake for the short-but-stunning hike to Hidden Falls. Or opt for one of the thrice-daily scenic cruises, which ply the lake's glassy waters for an hour.

Cycling

A new, car-free multi-use path extends from Jackson to Jenny Lake, running parallel to major roads. Rent a bike at Moose, and cruise the valley with the Wyoming wind whipping your hair. Don't be surprised to spy a moose munching the grass as you fly by, especially early in the morning. In Jackson, fuel up on haute cowboy meals like bison burgers or elk steak before riding back.

What to spot...

Grand Teton has two major ecosystems: the mountains and the valley. The valley floor is blanketed in silvery sagebrush, a favorite snack of pronghorns and deer. On the riverbanks, cottonwood trees and willows give shade as otters frolic and elk stop for a drink. The lower slopes of the mountains are cool and green with conifers, the boughs of which are home to a plethora of songbirds. Further up, marmots and pikas scramble across rocky exposed peaks.

YELLOW-BELLIED MARMOTS Resembling beavers without the paddle-shaped tails, goofy-cute marmots are always a crowd-pleaser. They're easy to spot on the higher slopes of the Teton Range.

HUCKLEBERRY BUSHES In late summer, huckleberries begin to ripen on their spindly-branched bushes. Resembling darker, glossier blueberries, they're a favorite of humans and bears alike.

ELK In warm weather, elk graze in the park's valley. As the snow sets in, they make their way to the National Elk Refuge, just southeast of the park.

Hike this...

01 Surprise & Amphitheater Lakes

This lung-burning 9.6-mile (15.5km) round-trip hike follows switchbacks up the wildflower-spangled side of Disappointment Peak to these two chilly mountain oases.

02 Lake Solitude

Follow the swift-moving waters of Cascade Canyon through the conifer forest, up past fields of mountain bluebells to the deep green waters of Lake Solitude; it's 15 miles (24km) round-trip.

03 Hidden Falls

A popular family hike, this 1.5-mile (2.4km) meander begins at the western dock of the Jenny Lake shuttle and leads to this much-photographed 200ft (61m) waterfall.

Itineraries

Raft down Snake River, cruise tranquil Jenny Lake or hike alpine heights to Surprise and Amphitheater Lakes. Binoculars and a camera are a must for bird-watching.

◄ Hidden Falls and hikers in Grand Teton National Park.
➡ See the park from a bicycle saddle.

01

A day

Drive in from Jackson early in the morning to make the most of your day. Arrive in the valley as the sun is just beginning to kiss the valley floor with golden light, looking for grazing elk and moose. Take advantage of the good light to photograph the atmospherically decaying barns of Mormon Row in the park's southeast corner, home to a tiny community of Mormon homesteaders in the late 1800s. As the day begins to warm, make your way to Jenny Lake to ride the passenger boat across the mirror-smooth waters, snapping pictures of the jagged Teton Range as you near them. On the lake's western edge, take the 1.5-mile hike (2.4km) to the pounding waters of Hidden Falls. Spend the afternoon paddling along the shores of Jackson Lake. Don't forget your binoculars; this is a primo bird-watching spot. By now you've worked up an appetite for the chuckwagon dinner at Dornan's in Moose; enjoy plates of fire-cooked mashed potatoes, corn on the cob, BBQ beef, blackened fish and more at a picnic table under the starry sky.

02

Two days

Awaken in your tent (or in your lodge, if you've been lucky enough to snag a room) and take the first shuttle of the morning across Jenny Lake to the beat the crowds to the trailhead of Cascade Canyon. Spend the next six or seven hours traversing mossy forests, beach-like riverbanks and alpine meadows straight out of *Heidi* until you reach the icy waters of Lake Solitude. Then head back down in time for dinner with a view at the Mural Room in the Jackson Lake Lodge. The next morning, arrive at your pre-booked rafting trip down the Snake River, and spend the day drifting beneath the endless skies as birds sing in the background. Hit the chuckwagon dinner at Dornan's in Moose, or roast some wieners on an open fire. Set your alarm for a middle-of-the-night wake-up to marvel at the star-powdered sky. If you're ambitious, stay up for a dawn photo session of grazing mammals in the valley fields – early morning is the best time to catch them in action.

03

Four days

On day one, warm up with one of the park's most lung-blasting hikes, the 10-mile (16km) round-trip trek to Surprise and Amphitheater Lakes. Climb through mountain meadows to nearly 10,000ft (3048m), where year-round snow surrounds icy turquoise water, with marmots and pikas as your fuzzy companions. Dine on elk in huckleberry reduction at Jenny Lake Lodge before dropping into a dreamless sleep. On day two, canoe around Jenny Lake and enjoy a couple of easy hikes on the west side; the next day, cycle the dedicated trail all the way to Jackson, passing meadows of grazing cows, with purple mountains majestic in the background. Splurge on dinner at the Snake River Grill, where the likes of cornmeal-crusted Idaho trout and Korean-style venison are served in a snazzy, New West dining room. On the fourth day, saddle up with a trail ride from Colter Bay in the morning, then enjoy a little solitude and wildlife-watching in the Laurance S Rockefeller Preserve in the afternoon, once the Rockefeller family's getaway.

25

NV

Great Basin National Park

An imposing peak stabs into a star-splattered sky in central Nevada, surrounded by unbelievably ancient trees, incredible caves, an endangered glacier and awesome arches.

Less than 300 miles (483km) from the lairy neon glare of Las Vegas, Great Basin National Park is almost entirely free of light pollution, offering a spectacular window into the night sky – where five of our solar system's eight planets are often visible with the naked eye.

The White Pine county park sits almost a mile above sea level in Nevada, its elevation accentuating the clarity of the heavens above. The Snake Range climbs towards the stars here, reaching its zenith with Wheeler Peak, a high-flying horn sculpted by ice over many millennia, which shelters a tenacious glacier, laced with moonmilk and gypsum. This was the old hunting ground of the Fremont people and, later, Shoshone tribes. It lay on the route of the California Trail, which saw heavy wagon traffic when gold-rush fever began spreading like a contagion across America from the west coast in 1848.

The imposing Wheeler Peak overlooks an array of natural features that fall within the boundaries of an extraordinary park, named for the basins (valleys) that pockmark the region. Aboveground you'll find stone arches, thousand-year-old wall paintings, and trees that began growing from cones when Egypt's Great Pyramid was still being built.

But the discovery of the park's most famous feature is credited to Absalom Lehman, a wandering miner and sometime rancher who chanced across a great marble subterranean catacomb in the early 1880s. Lehman Caves, a chamber that burrows into the side of the Snake Range, is a treasure trove of stalactites, stalagmites and rare speleothems.

These caves brought the region its first layer of protection, with President Warren G Harding creating Lehman Caves National Monument in 1922. The surrounding area was made a national park in 1986.

Toolbox

When to go
Great Basin is open year-round. Lehman Caves stay a pretty constant 50°F (10°C) regardless of the season. Summer is best for hiking. Cross-country skiing is excellent in winter, but only one campground stays open all year.

Getting there
Located 290 miles (467km) north of Las Vegas and 250 miles (402km) south of Salt Lake City, Great Basin National Park is in Nevada, close to the Utah border. The visitor center is in the east of the park. It's easily accessed by car via the I-15 and US 50 highways. It's not possible to catch public transportation to the park.

Park in numbers

121
Area (sq miles)

13,065
Height of Wheeler Peak's summit (ft)

4900
Age of 'Prometheus,' a Great Basin bristlecone pine felled in 1964 (years)

Stay here...

Lower Lehman Creek
Fittingly, for a place with such a stellar reputation for its night sky, there's only one way to stay in Great Basin: you have to sleep out under the stars. Of the park's five developed campgrounds, only this one is open year-round. Facilities include vault toilets, picnic tables, tent pads, and campfire grills. The creek runs through the ground.

Wheeler Peak
At 9886ft (3013m), this is the highest of the park's campgrounds – temperatures can be cool. Open on a first-come-first-served basis between May and October (depending on conditions), it's great for tent campers, but large RVs will struggle. The views here are stunning, and trails leading to the park's top peak are close by.

Backcountry Camping
Shortly after the generators are switched off, a peaceful darkness descends on the primitive campgrounds along Snake Creek Rd, and the entire universe seems to rise above the brooding silhouette of Wheeler Peak. There are picnic tables and fire rings here, but little else – save for the million-dollar view.

Do this!

Stargazing
Cloudless nights in Great Basin offer an astonishing panoply of stars. Five planets can be seen with the naked eye, plus the Andromeda Galaxy, the Milky Way and meteor showers. Numerous nocturnal adventures can be enjoyed: take a tour through outer space with a laser-wielding ranger or, if there's a full moon, join a guided night hike.

Caving
Lehman Caves is a colossal marble cavern featuring a staggering collection of formations, including stalactites, stalagmites, helictites, flowstone, popcorn, and over 300 rare shields. There are two tour options: the 60-minute Lodge tour and the slightly more demanding 90-minute Grand Palace tour, which takes in the famous Parachute Shield.

Fishing & foraging
Brown, brook, rainbow and cutthroat trout are present in streams that run through the park, including Lehman and Baker creeks. In the fall, collect delicious pine nuts; these have formed part of the diet of Native Americans here for centuries (but if you're unsure about what you've collected, check with a ranger).

◄ A bristlecone pine tree in Wheeler Peak Grove, some of the world's oldest-living organisms.

➡ Aspens in Lehman Valley.

Hike this...

01 Sky Islands Forest Trail
A short, very accessible and informative 0.4-mile (0.6km) walk through high-alpine conifer forest, with interpretive signs explaining why this region is unique.

02 Bristlecone & Glacier Trail
With global temperatures rising, the park's glacier is expected to melt away within 20 years – see it while you can on this 4.6-mile (7.4km) trail. Nearby, bristlecone cone trees have been growing for millennia.

03 Wheeler Peak Summit Trail
Hike to the roof of the park and the summit of the Snake Range for stunning views. The 8.6-mile (13.8km) route follows the ridge from the Summit Trail parking area.

What to spot...

As a place where the desert meets the mountains in the midst of a great tract of largely untouched wilderness, the ecosystem here is vibrant. Great Basin is home to some of the world's most ancient lifeforms – bristlecone pine trees – plus another 800 species of plant and tree. Mammals here range from mountain lions to ground squirrels; snakes slither past prickly pear bushes; and birds such as Clark's nutcrackers flit around collecting pine nuts.

GREAT BASIN BRISTLECONE PINE
This species of tree can live for thousands of years. The oldest non-clonal organism ever found was a Great Basin bristlecone pine tree, felled near Wheeler Peak and dated at 4900 years old.

THE MILKY WAY
Our galactic neighborhood burns brightly above Great Basin at night, with 100 to 400 billion stars creating a great white smudge across the sky.

PYGMY RABBIT
The world's smallest rabbit is a resident of Great Basin; it's one of only two American species of rabbit to dig its own burrow.

RING-TAILED CAT A relative of the raccoon (and not actually a cat at all), ring-tails are shy, nocturnal creatures who live very solitary lives, meeting only to mate.

138

Itineraries

Take a guided tour of Lehman Caves, trek the mighty Wheeler Peak or tackle the backcountry along the Baker Lake Loop Trail.

 12 miles (19km) of beauty on Wheeler Peak Scenic Drive.
➡ Lehman Cave features hundreds of rock formations.

01

A half-day

You're driving I-15 between Salt Lake and Vegas and want to break the journey with a night in a motel and an afternoon of activities. A quick exploration of Great Basin is the perfect antidote to freeway fatigue.

After having a good look around the visitor center, join a park ranger for a 90-minute guided tour of Lehman Caves, marveling at the natural grandeur of the Grand Palace and spotting century-old signatures on the walls of the Inscription Room.

Back out in the open air, get behind the wheel of your car and take a spin along the 12-mile (19.3km) Wheeler Peak Scenic Dr, drinking in inspiring views of the mountain and panoramic vistas of the valleys all around.

At the end of the road, pull up in the Bristlecone Parking Area and stretch your legs by strolling the 0.25-mile (0.4km) Sky Island Forest Trail through high-alpine conifer forest. Then continue, refreshed by the blast of natural beauty.

02

Overnight

Just after daybreak, drive into the Summit Trail parking lot and begin the 8.6-mile (13.8km) trek to the top of Wheeler Peak. Get started early to minimize the risk of getting caught out in the open during one of the storms that sometimes blast this park. The trail traces the ridgeline, and by the time you reach the summit you feel as though you've truly earned the vista that sprawls before you.

Invigorated by the views, set off to explore further around the Bristlecone Pine Trail, which leads to the oldest lifeforms on the planet – some of them thousands of years old. It would be a shame to be so close and not see Nevada's only glacier – especially since it could be gone within a couple of decades – so carry on beyond the pines to seek out the park's most endangered feature.

After heading back to the base of the mountain and touring the famous cave, it's time to set up camp. The sun is setting in a cloudless sky, and you don't want to miss the guided ranger tour through space.

03

Three or more days

From your base camp in the heart of the park, there are multiple adventures to look forward to. The first day you'll spend getting a feel for the place, doing the self-guided Mountain View Nature Trail, inhaling the aroma of the piñon-juniper forest, and checking out the visitor center.

A hike to the top of Wheeler Peak, a stroll to see the bristlecone pines and the glacier, and an underground exploration of the Lehman Caves are all on the list, of course, but you're also looking forward to venturing a bit further. Investigate the excavated Fremont Indian Village at Baker Archaeological Site; search for ancient rock art at Pictograph Cave; and hike to Lexington Arch in the far south of the park.

The biggest adventure, though, promises to be the backcountry escapade along the Baker Lake/Johnson Lake Loop Trail. Come armed with a lightweight tent, and break the 13-mile (21km) hike with some primitive camping. Just you and the stars – a heavenly experience indeed.

26

CO

Great Sand Dunes National Park

This sea of sand banked up against snow-dusted peaks is no optical illusion. It's nature at its most whimsical and surreal.

Getty Images | Whit Richardson

After a long approach through the flats of the San Luis Valley, this shimmering Saharan landscape seems like a mirage. The dunes stretch for 30 sq miles (78 sq km), flanked by the steep Sangre de Christo range on one side and glassy wetlands on the other.

It's a place of stirring optical illusions. The ceaseless wind works like a disconsolate sculptor, constantly creating or erasing elegant ripples underfoot. One can lose all perspective in the shadow of the dunes – the largest of which rises over 700ft (213m). In this monochromatic landscape, the only reference to judge distance is the sight of other hikers, like ants on the faraway dunes.

The Great Sand Dunes are a playground for both grown-ups and children alike, who can glide down dunes in saucers and on snowboards, build castles, bury limbs and rejoice in the joys of this unusual gift. Hold a grain under a magnifying glass to see the spectrum of its shapes and colors: 29 different rock and mineral types – from obsidian and sulfur to amethyst and turquoise – are represented in the sand's makeup.

Where did all this sand come from, and why does it stay here? The answer lies in the unique geography and weather patterns of the San Luis Valley. For millions of years, streams, snowmelt and flash floods have been carrying eroded sand and silt out of the San Juan Mountains, about 60 miles (96.5km) west, to the valley floor. From there, prevailing southwest winds gradually blow the sand into the natural hollow at the southern end of the Sangre de Cristo range. At the same time, streams and stronger prevailing winds from the eastern mountains reciprocate, causing the sand to pile up into what have become the highest dunes in North America.

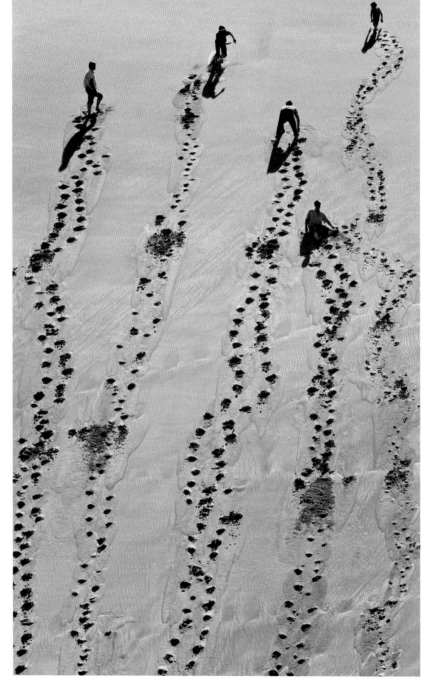

Toolbox

⚙️ **When to go**
The moderate temperatures of late spring and early fall are best for visitation. (In summer, the sand can reach 140°F/60°C during the heat of the day.) It's also exquisite during a full moon. The campground is open May through mid-November.

🧭 **Getting there**
Colorado's Great Sand Dunes National Park is 33 miles (53km) northeast of Alamosa and 240 miles (386km) from state capital Denver, which has an international airport. There's no public transportation, so a car is necessary.

Park in numbers

132
Area covered (sq miles)

150-20
High and low dune temperature (°F)

750
Tallest dune (ft)

Stay here...

Pinyon Flats Campground
The park's official campground boasts a great location not far from the dune field. Pitch your tent, gather around the campfire and take advantage of the star-riddled sky of the valley for amazing nighttime views.

Zapata Ranch
Ideal for horseback-riding enthusiasts, this exclusive preserve is a working cattle and bison ranch set amid groves of cottonwood trees. Owned and operated by the Nature Conservancy, the main inn is a refurbished 19th-century log structure, with distant views of the sand dunes.

Orient Mine & Valley View Hot Springs
Offering campsites and affordable cabins, this off-the-grid, little-known hot springs resort is a magical place snuggled into the foothills of the Sangre de Christo mountains. Geothermal waters flow downhill through a series of natural ponds in one of Colorado's most beautiful hot springs. It's also clothing optional. The location is 66 miles (106km) from the Sand Dunes.

Do this!

Sledding
The heavy wooden sled may seem like a bad idea when you're trudging out to the dunes, but the gleeful rush down the slopes is worth every footstep. Conditions are best after a recent precipitation. Boards can be rented at the edge of the park.

Tubing
The snowmelt stream of Medano Creek flows down from the Sangre de Cristo Mountains. At times, you can even float down the creek on an inner tube, right besides the dunes. Peak flow is usually in late May or early June. Water rippling over the sand creates a temporary beach popular with families.

Wildlife viewing
Alamosa National Wildlife Refuge hosts bald eagles, elk and coyotes. In the spring and fall look for migrating sandhill cranes. Visit at dawn or dusk, when wildlife is the most active – and when you'll hear the amazing auditory soundscape of bird calls and whistles. It's 3 miles (5km) from Alamosa.

◀ What goes up must come down; climbing dunes at Great Sand Dunes National Park. Previous page: dunes and the Sangre de Cristo mountains.

What to spot...

The sand dunes are a strange centerpiece in a diverse landscape of grasslands, wetlands, conifer and aspen forests, alpine lakes, and tundra. The unique high-altitude desert environment is a place of extremes, with big fluctuations in temperature. Constant moisture from precipitation allows some species, including kangaroo rat, blowgrass and various beetles, to survive on the actual dunes. Scientists estimate that the dunes are about a half-million years old.

RIO GRANDE CUTTHROAT TROUT
With a flaming belly stripe, this lovely native trout survives well in Medano Creek because exotic fish cannot invade the closed drainage system.

PEREGRINE FALCON This monitored and once-endangered falcon is the fastest bird in the world. It nests in cliffs and swoops down on these grasslands in search of prey.

ROCKY MOUNTAIN BEE PLANT During wet summers, pink patches of this wildflower attract diverse pollinators to damp grasslands and woodlands. Locals call it 'skunkweed' for its signature stink.

Hike this...

01 Great Sand Dunes

There are no trails through these expansive dunes, but it's still the star attraction. It's hard – trudging hills of sand, you'll feel like an ant in a sugar bowl. Try for High Dune, a 2.5-mile (4km) round-trip with panoramas.

02 Mosca Pass Trail

A moderate, 7-mile (11km) round-trip hike up into the Sangre de Cristo Wilderness through meadows and aspen stands along Mosca Creek.

03 Zapata Falls

This short, 0.5-mile (800m) family hike scrambles through ankle-deep, ice-cold water and over slippery rocks to the end of a slot canyon.

← Mule deer and summer sunflowers in the park.
→ Bring a sandboard for sliding down the dunes.

Itineraries

Hike the dunes, sled down them or take on daunting Blanca Peak. Cool down your adrenalin in Mosca Creek or get steamy in Valley View Hot Springs.

01
A day

Arm yourself with good sunblock, a hat and plenty of water. If it's summer, an early start on the dunes will help you avoid both heat and afternoon thunderstorms. Although sandals might seem ideal, closed-toe shoes provide better protection against the heat and a firmer grip.

Hike the dunes in any direction. There are no trails or obstructions – this is free hiking at its best. Keeping track of landmarks, such as distant peaks, will help with orientation. Bring a sled and you have entertainment for as long as your calves can drag it uphill. If you can't resist goal-setting, head for High Dune and Star Dune – at 750ft (229m) it's the tallest dune in the park.

At lunchtime, take a break at the picnic area and cool your heels in Mosca Creek. In early summer, the flow is usually high enough to float in inner tubes. Spend your afternoon exploring the other facets of the park. That's right – the dunes make up less than half of it. Head south 10 miles (16km) for a short, scrambling hike at Zapata Falls.

02
A weekend

Spend your first day on the dunes. Sleeping over at the Pinyon Flats Campground earns you the privilege of photographing the dunes in the moonlight. Keep an eye out for nocturnal wanderers: kangaroo rats, toads, coyotes, bobcats and owls.

On day two, head further afield. The Zapata Falls hike can be extended to reach the alpine South Zapata Lake (8 miles/13km round-trip). Look for chirping marmots and pikas on the slopes.

And then there's the obvious staring you down. Blanca Peak (14,344ft/4372m) is the tall, diamond-shaped summit that's the backdrop to the sand dunes. While for most it will just be a photo op across the valley, experienced hikers will want to take it on. From the Lake Como trailhead it's a full-day odyssey with an early start. The 11-mile (17.7km) round-trip has 3900ft (1189m) of elevation gain. Access requires a 4WD vehicle.

Cap your weekend off with a soak in the nearby Valley View Hot Springs. Hike into these natural rock ponds to soothe your muscle aches.

Great Sand Dunes

27

NC / TN

Great Smoky Mountains National Park

The Rockies may be dramatic, but the mist- and moss-shrouded peaks of the ancient Appalachians have mystery.

Getty Images | Sean Pavone

Imagine watching the sky go from ink-black to periwinkle-blue as pink dawn clouds ripple across the endless, wrinkled chain of peaks stretching towards the horizon. It's like nowhere else on earth. From the fog-choked summit of Clingman's Dome to the photogenic ghost town of Cades Cove to the tinkling music of a dozen silvery waterfalls, there's something deeply magical about these mountains. Experience it by hiking the park's trails, sleeping in its many remote campgrounds, splashing in its icy swimming holes and driving its craggy back roads.

The Cherokee people who called this land home for thousands of years were forcibly removed by President Andrew Jackson's decree in the 1830s, marching to Oklahoma along what's now known as the Trail of Tears. But some decided to stay behind, hiding in the mountains in what is now the national park; some of the ancestors of these rebels still live outside the park, in the Qualla Boundary area.

White settlers had arrived in the early 1800s, homesteading, building railroads, and cutting timber from the deep primeval forests. Worried the logging would spoil the landscape, private citizens, the US government and Standard Oil heir John D Rockefeller Jr banded together to buy up land and evict those living in the park in the 1920s.

Unlike most national parks, Great Smoky Mountains charges no admission to visitors, thanks to a proviso in the park's original charter as part of a grant from the Rockefeller family. Its lack of entry fee and its convenient location to many Eastern cities make Great Smoky Mountains America's most visited national park, with more than 10 million travelers a year. But

most visitors don't stray far from their cars, which is their loss – once you get a few hundred steps away from the road you're in your own personal fairyland.

 The watermill at Roaring Fork.
 Hiking in the park. Previous page: sunset at Newfound Gap.

Toolbox

When to go
The park is open year-round, but is definitely most crowded in summer. Fall is especially stunning, though chilly. In winter, certain roads and facilities may be closed.

Getting there
The park straddles eastern Tennessee and western North Carolina. In Tennessee the major access town is Gatlinburg, a kitschy holiday resort of minigolf courses and pancake houses. In North Carolina it's the town of Cherokee; the city of Asheville is about two hours' drive away and has an airport.

Park in numbers

816
Area covered (sq miles)

907
New plant and animal species discovered here

78
Preserved historic buildings

Stay here...

🏠 LeConte Lodge

LeConte is no ordinary hotel. Perched on the summit of Mt LeConte, this electricity-free lodge is reached on foot. Supplies are packed in on llamas (see them hoofing it up Trillium Gap Trail on Monday, Wednesday and Friday mornings). Hikers dine by the light of kerosene lamps before retiring to bunks to doze through the silent Appalachian night.

🏕 Cades Cove Campground

Cades Cove has a social vibe, with summer ranger programs, bike rentals and a camp store. The 160 campsites are shaded by forest, with flush toilets nearby. The trailhead to Abram Falls is outside your tent flap, as is a stable offering trail and carriage rides through the valley. Cades Cove is heavenly during fall.

⛺ Balsam Mountain Campground

In a forest 'island' of red spruce and balsam fir, this small campground is off the beaten path – watch bunnies hop past your tent. The overlook offers one of the most stunning sunsets in the Smokies. Lack of RV hookups keep Balsam Mountain peaceful, and the high elevation keeps things cool – bring a sweater!

Do this!

🚲 Cycling

Cades Cove, a mountain valley ('cove' in Appalachian-speak), was settled by gritty English, Welsh and Scots-Irish pioneers in the 1800s. Today, the area is a photogenic ghost town of mills and homesteads. An 11-mile (17.7km) loop road gets slammed with traffic in the high season; rent a bike and ride on a Wednesday or Saturday morning, when it's car-free.

📷 Vista-viewing

At 6643ft (2025m), foggy Clingman's Dome is the Smokies' highest peak. A drive and a 0.5-mile (0.8km) hike lead to an observation tower that looks rather like a flying saucer. On a clear day, you can see 100 miles (161km) and seven states from its panoramic windows. It's also a primo sunset-viewing spot, with wispy clouds turning the sky into a pink-and-purple watercolor painting. In fall, views over the gold and red mountains are absolutely luscious.

〰 Waterfall-hopping

More than 85in (216cm) of rain fall every year in the high country, ideal conditions for lots of waterfalls. Near Cades Cove, Abrams Falls plunges down 20ft (6m) of rocks, sending mist high into the air. You can walk behind bridal-veil-like Grotto Falls, deep within the old-growth hemlock forest. At Mingo Falls, silvery water streams down for 120ft (36.6m).

What to spot...

The Smokies are home to such an astounding richness of plant and animal life they've been declared an International Biosphere Reserve. Mountain meadows light up with trillium, columbine, violets and fire pinks in spring. In summer, mountain laurels, rhododendrons and azaleas bloom wildly on heath balds. Deep spruce, pine and hemlock forests shelter a profusion of mosses and ferns, some yet unnamed by science. Throughout the territory, black bears, owls, brook trout, salamanders and hundreds of other animals make their homes.

BLEEDING HEART
Just as their name suggests, these pink wildflowers are shaped like valentine hearts with a drop emerging at the bottom. Look for them on slopes in April and May.

LUNGLESS SALAMANDER The park is home to 24 varieties of skin-breathing salamanders, which can be spotted in streams and under damp logs and leaf litter.

YELLOW BIRCH These common trees can be identified by their bronze bark, which smells faintly of wintergreen. In fall their leaves turn a stunning gold.

A bull elk bugling during the rutting season in the park.

Hike this...

01 Laurel Falls

This classic, 2.6-mile (4.2km) round-trip hike climbs gently through oak and mountain laurel to an 80ft (24.4m) cascade with two wading-friendly pools.

02 Chimney Tops

This 4-mile (6.4km) quad burner ascends steeply through rhododendron thicket and across several streams, finishing at two knobs of metamorphic rock known as 'the chimneys.'

03 Alum Cave Bluffs

Old-growth forests, the craggy portal of Arch Rock and a heath bald carpeted with blueberry bushes are highlights of this 4.5-mile (7.2km) climb up Mt LeConte.

Itineraries

Waterfall fans are spoiled for choice: look for black bears near Laurel Falls, hike Abrams Falls or hit Townsend Wye to jump off rocks into Little River.

 Purple phacelia flowers. The Little River Trail follows on a railroad bed.
▶ Llamas at Grotto Falls on the Trillium Gap Trail.

01

A day

Concentrate on the park's main artery, 30-mile (48.3km) Newfound Gap Rd, which winds through forest so deep it feels like a tunnel on the way from Cherokee, North Carolina, to Gatlinburg, Tennessee. Starting from the North Carolina side, you'll hit Mingus Mill, a restored 1886 gristmill, and Mountain Farm, a collection of 19th-century buildings giving visitors a peek into the life of Appalachian homesteaders. Gawk at the patchwork quilt of the Oconaluftee River Valley from the overlook, then take the turnoff for Clingman's Dome for 100-mile (161km) views across the mid-South. At Newfound Gap you'll cross from North Carolina into Tennessee; a few miles later you'll hit the trailhead for Alum Cave Bluffs – take it if you fancy a hike through misty alpine forest. Do the loop-de-loop at The Loop, a section of road that goes through a tunnel and crosses over itself. Near the Tennessee-side exit you'll have opportunities to snap the iconic stone peaks of Chimney Tops. Top the day off with pancakes in delightfully cheesy Gatlinburg.

02

Two days

Drive Newfound Gap Rd as in the first itinerary, but when you get near the Tennessee border, hang a left onto Little River Rd to find the trailhead for Laurel Falls, one of the park's most popular waterfall overlooks. It's not uncommon to see a black bear snuffling in the bushes beyond this 80ft (24.4m) torrent. Splash around in the chilly base pool here, or head a little further to the beloved Townsend Wye swimming hole, where families jump from rocks into Little River. Camp amid the fragrant pines at Cades Cove Campground.

In the morning, wake early to drive (or cycle!) the Cades Cove loop, poking into old log cabins, watching a grist mill in action and climbing the hill to the old graveyard to get a feel for life in this mountain valley in the 1800s. Later, take the 5-mile (8km) hike to Abrams Falls, a short but wild waterfall deep in the cool forest. Finish the evening hanging out outside the camp store with fellow travelers, swapping tales of trails hiked and bears seen.

03

Five days

Start off on day one in the park access town of Cherokee, where you can ignore the fast food and cheesy gift shops in favor of the top-notch Museum of the Cherokee Indian. To truly appreciate these mountains you must learn about the people who named the region Shaconage ('land of the blue smoke'). On day two, hit Newfound Gap Rd, gawping at the overlooks and stopping to explore caves and falls alone the way. On day three, hit the Trillium Gap Trail up to Mt LeConte (why yes, you've reserved this wildly popular lodge a year in advance – good planning!), passing through virgin hemlock forest and stands of prehistoric-looking ferns. Bunk down in your electricity-free dorm, awaking in the silent dark on day four to see the sun rise over the smoky blue mountains. Head back down the mountain and continue on to the kitsch-ville of Gatlinburg, where you can spend day five visiting a moonshine distillery, playing hillbilly-themed minigolf or simply gobbling down a stack of pancakes the height of a small child.

28

Guadalupe Mountains National Park

Soaring high above the desert floor, the untrammeled wilderness of the Guadalupe Mountains is one of the best-kept secrets in Texas.

Mountain, forest and desert intersect in this rugged landscape wilderness, which attracts only a handful of visitors each year, despite its diversity. Gazing out across the shimmering Chihuahuan Desert from the tallest peak in Texas, it's hard to believe that this national park remains so little known. On even a one-day hike, you can get a taste of Guadalupe's unusual features, traversing arid, cactus-lined open country, then dipping into woodland-lined canyons and crossing trout-filled streams before beginning a steep ascent past windswept grasslands to craggy ridges with the scent of pine all around you.

Hidden in a small pocket of the southwest, you could almost miss this place if it weren't for the sheer, 8085ft-high (2464m) rockface of El Capitan, one of the park's most dramatic features. But in fact there's more to this region than meets the eye. The mountains here comprise one of the finest remnants of an ancient fossil reef. Around 250 million years ago, when the world was dominated by a single supercontinent called Pangaea, a vast tropical sea covered this area. This reef might have remained forever entombed were it not for uplift, with powerful geological forces creating sheer canyons and jagged mountains – as well as exposing huge sections of the reef and its age-old fossils, which today draw scientists from across the globe.

Fast-forward to 10,000 BC, when the Guadalupe Mountains played a crucial role to early indigenous populations, who hunted mammoth and other animals in the waning days of the Ice Age. They also gathered edible vegetation and lived in caves in the range, where they left behind pottery, baskets and rock art. Later on the scene were Apaches and gold-seeking Spaniards, followed by pioneers in the 19th-century. The mountains were also the unlikely setting for a station on the Butterfield Overland Mail Route, a 2800-mile (4502km) run that connected St Louis with San Francisco.

⬆ Reaching the summit of Guadalupe Peak, looking over the Chihuahuan desert.
➡ Pratt Cabin, McKittrick Canyon.

Toolbox

When to go
A spectacular time to visit the park is in late October and early November, when you can see a blaze of colorful fall foliage. Spring (March to May) is also a nice time to visit, with cooler temperatures for long hikes.

Getting there
Guadalupe Mountains National Park is in Texas' northwest corner. Dog Canyon is accessed via NM137 in New Mexico, while McKittrick Canyon and Pine Springs lie along US62 in Texas. There are no roads inside the park, making for a 120-mile (193km) drive between north and south entrances. The closest airport is in El Paso, 100 miles (161km) west.

Park in numbers

135
Area covered (sq miles)

8751
Highest point, Guadalupe Peak (ft)

1000
Number of plant species

Stay here...

Dog Canyon Campground
Located in tree-covered canyon on the north side of the park, this is the more appealing of Guadalupe's two established campgrounds. Sites are in a scenic, well-protected location beneath steep cliff walls. The 6280ft-high (1914m) elevation can make nights cool here, so plan accordingly.

Rodeway Inn
If you're not camping in the park, this simple chain motel is your closest lodging option. It's located in White's City, about 36 miles (58km) north of the McKittrick Canyon entrance – also handy for visiting nearby Carlsbad Caverns. There's a pool, which is most welcome after a day of hiking in the hot sun.

Hotel El Capitan
Named after the dramatic rockface in the Guadalupe Mountains, El Capitan is a historic Mission-revival style hotel built in the 1930s. The best rooms are spacious, with French doors opening onto private balconies overlooking a courtyard. The restaurant serves up some of the best cooking in a hundred-mile radius. It's located 65 miles (105km) south of the park in Van Horn.

Do this!

Bat-watching
The unique ecosystems of the Guadalupe Mountains make it attractive for a wide range of birds migrating through the Chihuahuan Desert. You can spy such desert dwellers as canyon towhees and roadrunners, with golden eagles soaring overhead. Early evening in riparian areas yield other rewards: violet-green swallows flitting over springs, broad-tailed hummingbirds feeding on nectar, and black phoebes hunting insects over the water.

Backpacking
The Guadalupe Mountains is an ideal destination for a multiday trek. You'll find 10 backcountry campgrounds spread along some 80 miles (129km) of trails. The variety of terrain means that you can get a taste of the low-desert country, riparian woodlands and pine-covered mountains all in one trip.

Wildlife-watching
No matter what time of year you visit, the park offers some fine opportunities to view wildlife. The few permanent water sources in the park (McKittrick Canyon, Smith Springs and Manzanita Spring) are the best places to look for creatures – as well as signs of animal life (tracks, scat, burrows and dens).

Hike this...

01 Guadalupe Peak
This challenging, 8.4-mile (13.5km) out-and-back hike takes you up the highest peak in Texas – 8751ft (2667m) – and includes a 3000ft (915m) elevation gain.

02 McKittrick Canyon Trail
One of the most popular trails in the park is a 7-mile (11.3km) round-trip hike that leads though scenic canyon woodlands to a historic cabin and out to the Grotto, set beside a gurgling stream.

03 Smith Spring Trail
Walk this pleasant, 2.3-mile (3.7km) trail in search of wildlife. You can sometimes spy mule deer and elk, along with abundant bird life near the lush Smith Spring.

What to spot...

Rising up out of the desert landscape, the Guadalupe Mountains encompasses several varied ecosystems. Its rocky canyons, lush wooded streams and forest-fringed mountaintops provide habitats for 60 mammal species, 55 reptile species and some 300 bird species. There are also nocturnal desert creatures, such as coyotes, badgers and 16 bat species. Many of Guadalupe's reptiles can be spotted in the daytime (such as the crevice spiny lizard).

TRILOBITE FOSSIL BATS
Trilobites were an arthropod group that flourished some 400 million years ago before dying out in the mass extinction that happened at the end of the Permian era (250 million years ago). More than 400,000 of these insectivores roost in the caves.

JACKRABBBIT A commonly spotted inhabitant in the Guadalupe Mountains, the jackrabbit uses its large ears to shed excess heat and stay cool in the desert heat.

BROAD-TAILED HUMMINGBIRD
This jewel-like bird, with an iridescent-green back and crown and a white breast, is able to survive cold mountain nights by dropping its heart rate, lowering its temperature and entering torpor.

156

Itineraries

Hike the highest point in Texas, admire the cactus and agave on the iconic Canyon Trail, or picnic by a grotto.

◀ Sunrise at Guadalupe Peak, with yuccas.
▲ A spotted owl and a hunters' cabin in McKittrick Canyon.

01

A day

Start the day at opening time (8am) at the McKittrick Canyon entrance. The crisp, early morning air is a fine time to spy wildlife so head off on the iconic Canyon Trail without delay. The route leads across a scrubby desert landscape sprinkled with cactus and agave to reach a stream where the woodlands begin; after the open desert, walking in the shade of oak and maple (beneath a canopy of fiery colors in fall) is bliss. A few miles further on, arrive at the Pratt Cabin, the old family dwelling of Wallace Pratt, a petroleum geologist and conservationist who fell in love with the area and built this home in the 1930s (later donating it to the national park). Although you can stop here for lunch, it's worth pressing on to the Grotto for a scenic picnic beside a stream; it's a lush setting, and you can even spy rainbow trout in the water. After the return hike, drive down to the Pine Springs Visitor Center, to peruse exhibits on the park's natural history and fauna and watch a short film on the Guadalupe Mountains.

02

A weekend

A two-day backpacking trip is ideal to catch magical sunset views: a good overnight destination is Pine Top. Or, spend day one hiking in McKittrick Canyon and the second day tackling the challenging ascent up Guadalupe Peak. Set off early in the morning from Pine Springs Campground; the hardest part is at the start, when you'll climb a series of steep switchbacks over the first 1.5 miles (2.4km). The views, which only get better with each rise, will impel you onward. The next part of the hike has a gentler ascent and takes you through a cool forest of pine and Douglas fir, which flourish on the north slopes. After another 3 miles (4.8km), you'll reach a false summit – but don't despair, it's just 1 mile (1.6km) further to the end. Pass a backcountry campsite, then cross a wooden bridge, then it's just a few more uphill switchbacks and you're at the summit. This is the highest point in Texas, and the panorama over the desert below is sublime. Allow six to eight hours for the hike.

29

· HI ·

Haleakalā National Park

Step inside what Native Hawaiians named 'The House of the Sun,' an ancient volcano spreading from sky to sea.

Standing on the edge of Haleakalā's summit crater, you'll shiver in the pre-dawn cold as you peer down into what looks like an ancient battlefield of cinder cones and lava rocks. But you won't give the chilly temperature another thought once the sun finally blazes over the eroded edge of this ancient volcano, its rays slanting across a colorful cinder desert and lighting up an ocean of clouds floating as far as you can see. It's a spiritual experience in a spot that is sacred to Native Hawaiians, who tell a story about how the demigod Maui lassoed the sun from this peak, giving light and life to his people.

Soaring over 10,000ft (3048m) high, Haleakalā Volcano is the park's resplendent centerpiece. Its summit is a winding 37-mile (59.5km) drive uphill from Maui's paradisiacal beaches, making a higher ascent in a shorter distance than on any other road on earth. Hiking trails dive into the volcanic crater's wilderness, where rare, endangered wildlife such as the Haleakalā silversword plant and the nēnē (Hawaiian goose) thrive. Wild summit weather can change in a heartbeat, from blisteringly sunny to icy cold, windy and rainy – yet the volcanic landscape remains an alien beauty. For an unforgettable night, camp out or sleep in a primitive cabin on the crater floor as the Milky Way glows overhead.

Though the volcanic summit is Haleakalā's most famous attraction, there's another side to this park. Follow the jungle road beyond Hana to coastal Kipahulu, an ancient Hawaiian village site on the volcano's lower slopes. There, in 'Ohe'o Gulch, stream-fed pools tumble downhill into the Pacific Ocean; on calm days, you can even take a dip. Afterward, trek uphill through a forest of green bamboo, which rustles musically in the wind, to lacy Waimoku Falls.

Getty Images | John Elk

Toolbox

When to go
Visit at any time of year. Winters are cooler and wetter in Hawaii, though, and rainstorms can close the park's summit and coastal areas. The weather atop the summit is fickle, so check the forecast before driving up.

Getting there
To the summit, it's a 1½-hour drive from Kahului, Maui's main airport, where domestic US and inter-island flights land, and rental cars are available. To Kipahulu, it's a 60-mile (96.5km) drive via the slow road to Hana; allow 2½ hours.

Park in numbers

52
Area covered (sq miles)

10,023
Highest elevation (ft)

19
Size of summit crater (sq miles)

Stay here...

Holua Cabin & Wilderness Campground

From the park's summit road, Holua is less than a 4-mile (6.4km) hike into the volcanic crater via the switchbacking Halemau'u Trail. Book ahead to stay in a rustic cabin built by the Civilian Conservation Corps (CCC) or pack your own tent and gear for a wilderness campsite (permit required).

Kapalaoa Cabin

If you're lucky enough to score a reservation for this basic, bunk-bedded wilderness cabin, you'll sleep inside the belly of the beast: the crater's cinder desert. Stargazing and sunrises are unbelievably awesome here. It's a 5.5-mile (8.9km) hike downhill via the Keonehe'ehe'e Trail from the summit road.

Kipahulu Campground

Of the park's two drive-up campgrounds, one is near the summit and one is by the coast – and Kipahulu wins for its ocean panoramas and open, grassy camping area. Bonus: it's free. Just bring your own water.

Do this!

Bird-watching

Traipse along the 0.5-mile (0.8km) Hosmer Grove Loop Trail through a forest high on the volcano's slopes and spy myriad birds. Make reservations in advance to join a longer, naturalist-guided trek through the magical cloud forest of the Waikamoi Preserve, normally off-limits to the public.

Stargazing

The skies are so clear over the summit of Haleakalā that solar observatories have been built there. Skywatching after dark is equally good. Bring your own binoculars, which can be rented from island dive shops. Rangers often lead stargazing programs at Hosmer Grove Campground in summer.

Swimming

As long as rain isn't in the forecast, you can realize your tropical fantasy of swimming in jungle pools along Pipiwai Stream, which falls in cascades as it makes its way downhill into the ocean. To swim in the sea, head to idyllic Hamoa Beach – less than 10 miles (16km) away from the park's Kipahulu district.

◄ There are more than 30 miles (48km) of hiking trails in the summit area of Haleakalā National Park. Stick to the trail. Previous page: the volcanic caldera.

What to spot...

As elsewhere in the Hawaiian Islands, Maui's endemic flora and fauna have evolved into an astonishing array of species, many found nowhere else on the planet. Along with Hawai'i Volcanoes National Park, its sister park on the Big Island, Haleakalā has been designated a Unesco International Biosphere Reserve for its diverse ecosystems and rare wildlife – which is under threat from habitat loss, global climate change and invasive species brought by the first Europeans and Americans who landed on Hawaiian shores.

NĒNĒ (HAWAIIAN GOOSE) This endangered bird nests in the volcano's summit crater, where it evolved webbed feet for walking on lava.

HALEAKALĀ SILVERSWORD A rare plant that belongs in the daisy family, silverswords bloom spectacularly only once in their lifetime, which can last up to 90 years.

'UA'U (HAWAIIAN PETREL) Also endangered, these seabirds nest at high elevations on the volcano's slopes, then fly down to the distant sea to hunt squid.

Hike this...

O1 Halemauʻu Trail
Starting from cloud level, descend 1000ft-high (305m) cliffs into the volcano's crater. Don't miss the fascinating Silversword Loop detour. The trail ranges from 2.2 to 9.2 miles (3.5 to 14.8km).

O2 Keoneheʻeheʻe Trail
Nicknamed 'Sliding Sands,' this thrilling trail wraps around cinder cones as it switchbacks from the summit to the crater floor. The trail ranges from 0.5 to 11.2 miles (0.8 to 18km)

O3 Pipiwai Trail
In the coastal Kipahulu district, this family-friendly 4-mile (6.4km) hike climbs through lush bamboo forest to stop beneath 400ft-tall (122m) Waimoku Falls.

Itineraries

Hike the grand loop of the volcanic crater, swim in the pools of 'Ohe'o Gulch or in a jungle waterfall. Colorful cinder sunsets come for free.

← A silversword plant. Makahiku Falls can be viewed from Pipiwai Trail.
→ An 'I'iwi bird, a variety of honeycreeper, in Haleakalā National Park.

01
A day

Set your alarm for very early – and don't you dare hit 'snooze.' Depending on where on the island you're staying, it'll take two hours or more to drive to the volcano's summit. You'll want to be standing on the crater rim well before dawn breaks, when the sun performs its light show among the clouds and cinder cones. Evade the crowds huddled at the summit overlook by climbing a short way up Pa Ka'oao (White Hill) for a better perch. After sunrise, hike down the Keonehe'ehe'e (Sliding Sands) Trail into the utterly wild cinder desert, then head out across the crater floor, bordered by cliffs, to wilderness Kapalaoa Cabin. Eat your lunch at the picnic table outside the cabin (but please don't feed or give any water to the nēnē, no matter how sweetly they beg!). If you've got energy to spare, detour north toward the most striking cones in the crater area, nicknamed Pele's Paint Pot after the Hawaiian goddess of fire and volcanoes. End your hike where it began, back uphill at the summit.

02
Two days

Spend your first day at the park's volcanic summit, catching sunrise from the crater rim and then looping around Hosmer Grove to spot forest birds. Mid-morning, start hiking down into the crater on the Halemau'u Trail, where you can eat lunch at the rustic picnic table outside Holua wilderness cabin. After lunch, detour to the Silversword Loop, a de-facto botanical garden growing on the crater floor, before hiking out of the crater and driving downhill to the ocean.

On day two, hit the road early again. Drive the serpentine highway, which passes over 54 one-lane bridges, to sleepy Hana town. Take a break and swim in a jungle waterfall or have lunch at a roadside, island-style BBQ shack. Keep going to the park's coastal Kipahulu district to see the pools of 'Ohe'o Gulch – you can even go for a dip if rain isn't imminent. The family-friendly 4-mile (6.4km) Pipiwai Trail, heads uphill through a tunnel of bamboo trees to a waterfall deep in the forest.

03
Four days

For hikers and backpackers, the ultimate park experience is making a grand loop on foot around the volcanic crater. Organize wilderness cabin bookings well in advance, or bring all the gear you'll need for camping at high elevations in highly variable weather. On day one, after watching sunrise at the summit, drop into the crater on the Keonehe'ehe'e (Sliding Sands) Trail and head to Kapalaoa Cabin (no camping). Take time to explore the colorful cinder desert just north of the cabin before sunset. The next day, strap on your pack for the hike over to the wet, windy side of the volcano, where you can camp outside or sleep inside Paliku Cabin. On day three, trek back across the crater floor, winding through the cinder desert to reach the campsite and cabin at Holua, which boasts the crater's best sunrise views. On your last day, hike up the switchbacks of the Halemau'u Trail back to the crater rim, reluctantly leaving the volcanic wilderness behind.

Haleakalā

30

HI

Hawai'i Volcanoes National Park

Newly born earth churns and fiery lava glows in the chaotic realm of Pele, the Hawaiian goddess of volcanoes.

For over 70 million years, volcanoes in the deep have been giving birth to the Hawaiian Islands. After emerging as bare rocks from under the sea, the islands later become oases for unique plant and animal life, then eventually tumble down into flat coral atolls flung over thousands of miles of open ocean. Today Hawai'i, also known as the Big Island, sits directly atop a 'hot spot' deep beneath the Earth's crust, making it the only Hawaiian island that's still volcanically active. Don't be alarmed, though: Hawaiian volcanoes rarely explode – instead, they usually just ooze streams of molten lava. And when that red-hot lava hits the ocean, you'll witness apocalyptic plumes of steam billowing upward.

Life and the landscape here are never static. Kīlauea Volcano has been erupting continuously since 1983, when lava fountains dramatically spewed into the sky. In 2008 Halema'uma'u Crater, home of the hot-tempered Hawaiian trickster god Pele, was transformed into a lava lake, just as it was when famous 19th-century travelers Isabella Bird and Mark Twain ventured here on horseback. Today, atop Kīlauea's jet-black lava flows, vibrant green ferns, lichens, moss, 'ohelo plants with bright-red berries and 'ohi'a lehua trees (blossoming with pom-pom flowers) colonize the new terrain. In lush *kipuka* (oases) spared by earlier lava flows, lucky forest birds sing.

Whether you come for a startling geology lesson or to get in touch with living Hawaiian traditions, this park doesn't disappoint. Native Hawaiians first walked this land, etching petroglyphs and burying the *piko* (umbilical cord) of newborns in lava rocks. They left behind footprints fossilized in the volcanic ash and performed sacred

hula dances on the crater rim. They also summited Mauna Loa, at 13,680ft (4170m) the world's most massive shield volcano – which is higher than Mt Everest when measured from the ocean floor.

⬆ Molten lava on Kīlauea volcano, the most active on the island (and previous page).
➡ Lava hardens when it reaches the Pacific ocean.

Getty Images | Greg Vaughn

Toolbox

When to go
Open year-round, the park experiences wetter, cooler winters. Before visiting, check for eruption updates, which can close some viewpoints, roads and trails.

Getting there
On the east side of Hawai'i's Big Island, the park is an hour's drive south of Hilo airport, or 2½ hours from busier Kailua-Kona airport on the west coast. Interisland flights from Hawai'i's major international airport in its capital Honolulu are fast and frequent. To reach the park, rent a car in Hilo or Kona.

Park in numbers

505.4
Area covered (sq miles)

33
Years that Kilauea Volcano has been erupting

500
Acres of new land created since eruption began

Stay here...

Volcano House
Being the only hotel in the national park (and, being founded in 1846, actually predating the park) means that nowhere else can you wake up to views of the Kilauea Caldera and a rainforest through your window. Even if you don't stay overnight at this historic (and recently renovated) venue, stop for an epicurean meal at the hotel's Rim Restaurant or for a drink in Uncle George's Lounge, where Hawaiian musicians play.

Namakanipaio Cabins & Campground
Nestled within a peaceful grove of eucalyptus trees, this park campground will let you pitch a tent – if you rent one from them, they'll even set it up for you – or bunk down in a rustic cabin with a barbecue grill and fire pit outside your door.

Chalet Kilauea
There's something for everyone – hikers, families, even honeymooners – at this rambling lodge located in the sleepy town of Volcano, just outside the park. For privacy and a two-person hot tub, cozy up inside the Hapu'u Forest Bungalow, secreted down a short trail bordered by green ferns.

Do this!

Lava viewing
Kīlauea's lava flow is unpredictable. Ask at the visitor center if it's currently possible to see the flow inside the park. Recently, the only accessible viewpoint was at the Jaggar Museum on Crater Rim Dr, which affords distant views of the lava lake roiling inside Halemau'uma'u Crater. There may be better viewing areas outside the park in the Puna district, requiring either a long hike or a boat ride.

Caving
When molten lava erupts, it leaves behind lava tubes. Some are even big enough to drive a school bus through! You can walk right into Nahuku (Thurston Lava Tube), which is hidden in a fern forest just off Crater Rim Dr.

Learning about Hawaiian arts & culture
Traditional *hula halau* (schools) dance and Hawaiian artisans demonstrate their crafts at the Volcano Art Center Gallery, next door to the park's visitor center. Sign up in advance for art classes and workshops.

◄ The island forests are exceptionally fertile, with lots of unique indigenous species.

What to spot...

Both a Unesco World Heritage site and an International Biosphere Reserve, the park protects unexpectedly diverse habitats: lava deserts, rain forest, coastal beaches, and even an alpine mountain summit. More than 50 threatened or endangered species find refuge here. Birds are especially abundant, from petite, rainbow-colored Hawaiian honeycreepers that flutter through rain forest oases to the solitary royal Hawaiian hawk (i'o) swooping overhead as its hunts for prey.

'OHI'A LEHUA Growing as a plant, a shrub or a tree, 'ohi'a is easily recognized by its twisting stems, and branches with flowers that vary in color from cream to red.

'APAPANE This Hawaiian honeycreeper sports crimson feathers and a curved black beak for drinking flower nectar.

HONU'EA (HAWAIIAN HAWKSBILL TURTLE) This endangered amphibian hauls out on remote beaches to lay eggs. Hatchlings dig themselves out of the sandy nests, emerging only at night and heading straight back into the sea.

Hike this...

O1 Kilauea Iki Trail Trek 4 miles (6.4km) from the crater's rain forest down across a lava moonscape on this loop trail through a recent volcanic eruption.

O2 Pu'u Loa Petroglyphs Off Chain of Craters Rd, a short, 1.4-mile (2.3km) hike leads to an archaeological field of ancient Hawaiian rock art.

O3 Napau Trail Experienced backcountry hikers who come fully prepared can venture to the edge of the active volcanic zone, where the Pu'u O'o vent looms. The trail is 14 miles (22.5km).

Itineraries

Take a night walk through spooky Thurston Lava Tube, hike Devastation Trail or opt for sheer wilderness and native birds on the Kahuku Unit.

◀ A hapu'u fern. Traditional dress at the investiture of the Big Island's Royal Court.
▶ Steam rises from volcanic vents.

01

A day

Don't fret if rain clouds and vog (volcanic smog) greet your early-morning arrival at the park – the mercurial weather at the volcanic summit could just as easily bring sunshine later in the day. Stop by the park visitor center and get oriented inside its educational museum. Cruising west along Crater Rim Dr, stop at the Jaggar Museum to peruse its geology displays inside, and, out back, to view plumes of smoke rising out of Halema'uma'u Crater. Backtrack to the Sulphur Banks, where volcanic gases have left colorful mineral deposits, before having lunch at the historic Volcano House. In the afternoon, you'll feel like an astronaut exploring another planet on the Kilauea Iki Loop Trail, which dips from the rainforest into a volcanic crater. After sunset, take a spooky walk (bring flashlights!) through Thurston Lava Tube, just across the road. Then hop back in your car and return to the Jaggar Museum to glimpse Halema'uma'u's lava lake smoking like a hellish inferno in the dark.

02

Two days

Start with the day one itinerary then get a leisurely start after breakfast in Volcano town. Drive back into the park and wind downhill toward the ocean on Chain of Craters Rd, passing evidence of violent past eruptions – craters, cinder cones, and lava shields. Take some short nature hikes, including the Devastation Trail and the walk out to the Pu'u Loa petroglyph field, one of many archaeological sites protected by the park. Of all the viewpoints overlooking the park's lava flows, don't skip Kealakomo Overlook, where a picnic table makes the perfect lunch spot. Near the bottom of Chain of Craters Rd, which ends where lava flows once buried it, look offshore for the landmark Holei Sea Arch.

Drive back uphill to the park entrance, then head west to little-traveled Mauna Loa Rd. It begins as a one-lane paved road near Kipukapuaulu (Bird Park), where birders hike along a forested loop trail, then climbs partway up Mauna Loa volcano to a mesmerizing lookout.

03

Three days

Proceed as per days one and two. On your third day in the park, take some time to get off the beaten path and explore the Kahuku Unit, the newest addition to this already massive park. To get there, follow the island's belt road south through the Ka'u district, known for its small coffee farms and the sea turtles that haul out on the beach at Punalu'u. You'll drive past the turnoff to Ka Lae, the southernmost point in the US, and Green Sands Beach, located beyond the wind farms on the coast; both are worth a detour.

Back on the belt road, keep driving toward Ocean View. The turnoff to the Kahuku Unit will be on your right, and the gates are usually open daily (though for limited hours).

On the grounds of an historic ranch, this pocket of wilderness is a place of peaceful pastures, lava flows and dense forest. On any of several short hiking trails, you may be the only person crunching over these ancient lava flows and listening for the songs of the islands's unique native birds.

31

Hot Springs National Park

A small park surrounding a natural wonder – people have been soaking in the curious, curative waters of this steamy sanctuary for centuries.

T he smallest (and arguably the oldest) of America's national parks, Hot Springs revolves around 47 boiling brooks of geothermally warmed water that once enveloped this corner of Arkansas in an ethereal cloak of steam – and are invested, many people insist, with healing powers.

The water is regurgitated rainfall, deep-heated during a dramatic 4000-year journey from mountaintop into the bowels of the earth and back again. Hot Springs doesn't suffer from the sulfur stink that most spa towns have to endure, and the colorless water is pumped to 'jug fountains,' where you can taste the famous magic mountain juice with rumored restorative qualities.

Font of youth or simply nature's gift, the spring has been phenomenally popular for centuries, and the area has attracted human activity for millennia. Native American tribes – including the Caddo, Choctaw and Cherokee – were drawn to the 'Valley of the Vapours' long before Europeans arrived. Spanish Conquistador Hernando de Soto stopped for a soak in 1541, beginning a long-standing tourist tradition, and Dunbar and Hunter visited during their mission of discovery after the US acquired the region in the 1803 Louisiana Purchase. The first American settlers arrived by 1807.

But it's also caused some hot debates, not least about its place in the history of the country's parks. Yellowstone is commonly considered the world's first national park, but the Hot Springs Reservation, predecessor of Hot Springs National Park, was signed into being by President Andrew Jackson in 1832 – four decades before Yellowstone received protection. Numerous generations of buildings have housed hot tubs here over the years, until the current Bathhouse Row was built between 1912 and 1922 – by which time Hot Springs was officially a national park.

The confusion is understandable. This isn't what most people picture when they imagine a national park – no grizzly bears, but instead bare bodies in the Buckstaff Bath House – but there are indeed outdoor adventures to be enjoyed in this historical setting.

← Steaming hot springs at Arlington Lawn, at the north end of historic Bathhouse Row.

Getty Images | Richard Rasmussen;

Toolbox

When to go

The park is open all year, but it can get very busy in the summer months, especially during July. Winters are mild and wildflowers begin bursting into bloom on the mountainsides from February.

Getting there

The National Park is found downtown in the Arkansas city of Hot Springs – 300 miles (483km) east of Dallas, Texas, and 200 miles (322km) west of Memphis, Tennessee. Bathhouse Row is flanked by the mountains that catch the rain and send it on its long journey into the earth.

Park in numbers

8.6
Area covered (sq miles)

143
Average temperature of the hot springs' water (°F)

700,000
Gallons of hot water collected each day in the reservoir

Stay here...

Gulpha Gorge

Hot Springs offers various accommodations, but the only place to stay in the park itself is this campground, beautifully positioned on a creek (complete with crawfish) and directly connected to the trail network that leads to Hot Creek Mountain. There are no showers – but you're located next to the most famous bathhouse in America.

Do this!

Bathing

You've come here to get into hot water and this, the park's last surviving operational bathhouse, is where to take the plunge; there are separate men's and women's baths. People have been washing their worries away here since 1912. The full traditional treatment takes approximately 1½ hours.

Hiking

The park has 26 miles (41.8km) of trails, mostly short, steep and sweet options. For a bigger challenge, hike the 10-mile (16km) Sunset Trail, which traverses West Mountain, threads the hardwood forest of Sugarloaf Mountain and crosses Fordyce Mountain to end in Gulpha Gorge campground.

What to spot...

Hot Springs has a mild climate and the park features forests populated by pine, oak and hickory. Bird species include ruby-throated hummingbirds and golden eagles.

RED RIVER WATERDOG
This local mudpuppy uses feathery gills to breathe underwater. Like other salamanders, they retain the freaky – but useful – larval ability to regenerate lost limbs and even repair parts of their brains.

Itineraries

For geothermal good times, hike Hot Springs Mountain before succumbing to a traditional spa treatment.

01

A day

Wake to a dawn chorus of bird chatter in Gulpha Gorge Campground. This might be America's smallest national park, but there's still plenty to fit into a day.

A perfect start is to hike Hot Springs Mountain. From outside your tent a choice of paths all lead to Mountain Tower, where, before heading down via Dead Chief Trail, you see the city flicker into life.

Wander past century-old spa buildings on Bathhouse Row to imagine the scene that would have greeted Dunbar and Hunter when they arrived in 1804. Back then the 47 steaming springs would have been open to the elements; now the only 'Open Spring' can be seen behind Maurice Bathhouse.

Stop by the visitor center in the old Fordyce Bathhouse to see how the place looked in 1915 before braving the Buckstaff to experience what a traditional spa treatment feels like. You had intended to hike the Sunset Trail later, but such energetic plans get entangled with the hot-water vapors and begin evaporating – maybe stay another night...

32

MI

Isle Royale National Park

A wild kingdom of moose and wolves in the middle of Lake Superior, Isle Royale is the least-visited national park in the Lower 48.

Everything about Isle Royale is intriguing. The 893-sq-mile (2313 sq km) island – surrounded by 400 smaller satellite islands – is thick with spruce and birch and sits in the middle of the largest and coldest of the Great Lakes. It may look like pristine wilderness, but Isle Royale's abundant natural resources have been mined for centuries. Native Americans were hammering chunks of copper out of bedrock using smooth stones found along the shoreline 4500 years ago. After the US took possession of the island from the French in 1783, commercial fishermen used gillnets to catch whitefish, lake trout, and siskiwit off the shore. In the mid-1800s, workers set fire to satellite islands to prospect for copper and logged off the massive white pines on the mainland to make way for human development. In the early 1900s, Isle Royale was such a popular summer haven for wealthy families from St Louis and Chicago that Belle Isle, off the northeast shoreline, had a nine-hole golf course.

Today, the trees have grown back and 99% of the island is designated as wilderness. In that wilderness, zigzagged by hiking trails and dotted with campsites, lives a constantly fluctuating number of wolves and moose. It's not likely a visitor will see one of the three elusive wolves remaining on the island, but it is relatively common to see a massive bull moose, its antler rack spanning 6ft (1.8m), crashing through the lowland swamps and diving the inland lakes to eat the roots of water lilies.

For the last 50 years scientists here have been conducting the longest-running study of a predator-prey system in the world. The wolf population is at an all-time low – partially because of a five-decade decline in the frequency of an ice bridge forming from mainland Canada and Minnesota – but the park recently created a new management plan to address the diminishing wolf numbers.

Toolbox

When to go
The park is open from mid-April until mid-October, but even in summer, fog or rough water can delay flights or ferries, the only public mode of transport to the island. The park is most crowded in August. For a quiet trip, go in May. For the most reliable weather, visit in July or August.

Getting there
Isle Royale belongs to Michigan and is 55 miles (88.5km) northwest of its Keeweenaw Peninsula, but the island is only 22 miles (35.4km) east of Minnesota and even closer to Canada. Four ferries and one seaplane provide service from Houghton or Copper Harbor, Michigan, or Grand Portage, Minnesota.

Park in numbers

893
Area covered (sq miles)

3
Number of wolves (2015)

1250
Estimated number of moose (2015)

Stay here...

Rock Harbor Lodge Housekeeping Cottages
Tucked in the woods behind the main lodge, the cottages have sleeping space for four, a fully equipped kitchenette, a bathroom, and a wall of picture windows that overlook placid Tobin Harbor. The quality of the serenity in these cabins is priceless.

Three Mile Campground
Three miles (5km) east of the main park entrance of Rock Harbor, this campground sees a lot of hiker traffic. But it also sits on a gorgeous southern shoreline of pebbly beaches and granite rocks that slope straight into Lake Superior. There are at least two screened-in camping shelters right on the shoreline and an overnight dock for campers arriving by private boat.

Feldtmann Lake Campground
Six miles (10km) southwest of Windigo, the eastern park entry, this campground sits on a sizable inland lake, but is also a short 10-minute hike to Rainbow Cove, a pebbly crescent-moon red beach on the island's southwest shore. Many moose have been sighted in both locations.

Do this!

Sea kayaking
Rent a sea kayak from the dockmaster at Rock Harbor and spend at least a half-day exploring the archipelago, where hundred-year-old cabins sit on granite sloping down to the lakeshore. Beware: the weather here is very changeable and currents around Blake Point, the easternmost tip of the island, can be tricky.

Deep-sea fishing
It's more like 'deep-lake fishing' but sign on for a fishing charter in Rock Harbor to catch Lake Superior trout or salmon. A Michigan fishing license, which can be bought at Rock Harbor, is required. Fishing for trout or northern pike on the island's inland lakes is within National Park boundaries and doesn't require a Michigan License.

Scuba diving
The waters off Isle Royale are riddled with ten major wrecks, all relatively easy to see in Lake Superior's clear water. But divers beware: surface water temperatures rarely rise above 55°F (13°C) and deeper water rarely surpasses 35°F (2°C) degrees. A dry suit is mandatory.

← Isle Royale lighthouse on Menagerie Island.

➡ Spot squirrels here.

Hike this...

01 Minong Ridge Trail
Often described as the toughest hike in Michigan, this rocky, hard-to-navigate trail starts at Windigo Harbor and ends 31.6 miles (50.9km) later at McCargoe Cove, an inlet on the island's north shore.

02 Greenstone Ridge Trail
The main 40-mile-long (64.4km) island thruway barrels through the backbone of Isle Royale and tops out at 1300ft (396m), with glorious views to Lake Superior. Plan three to five days to do the whole thing.

03 Scoville Point Loop
It may be short, but this 4-mile (6.4km) loop trail starting in Rock Harbor offers some of the most gorgeous scenery on the entire island. Time the hike for sunrise to spot moose, or sundown over Tobin Harbor.

What to spot...

A classic, second-growth northern boreal forest, Isle Royale is thick with spruce, pine and birch, and riddled with freshwater inland lakes lined by water lilies and the occasional purple orchid. Moose, wolves, and fox thrive here, but the island has no bears or raccoons, making it unnecessary to hang food at night in the backcountry.

MOOSE Because the wolf population has diminished so greatly in recent years, the moose population is soaring, which makes these majestic beasts easy to spot. If you to see a sow with a calf or a bull in rutting season (mid-September to late October) steer clear.

PILEATED WOODPECKER These yellow-eyed, black-bodied, scarlet-headed woodpeckers are a delight to spot as they dart from tree to tree, pecking away at dead trees for carpenter ants. Their signature calling card: a rectangular hole.

WOLF The odds of spotting one of the three remaining and very elusive Isle Royale wolves are not great – but one can always hope. Interestingly, the three were most recently often spotted on the east end of the island, close to the most populated part of the park in the summer.

Itineraries

Sail the thrice-weekly ferry for a classic overview of the island, kayak or canoe Rock or Tobin Harbor, or the truly adventurous can hike the whole island.

← Isle Royale from the air, largest of the national park's islands.
→ Check the weather forecast before exploring Isle Royale's inlets.

01
Two days

For a grand overview of the entire island, buy a ticket on the *Voyageur II*, a comfortable and sturdy 65ft (20m) aluminum ferry that leaves three times a week from Grand Portage, Minnesota. By 7:30am the boat is well underway to Windigo, the first stop on Isle Royale. Traveling clockwise around the densely wooded shore, the next stop is McCargoe Cove, where the boat picks up hard-core hikers who have toughed the Minong Ridge Trail. After rounding Blake Point, the boat turns southwest toward Rock Harbor. Check into a lakeside room at Rock Harbor Lodge, take a quick 4-mile (6.4km) round-trip hike to Scoville Point, and then dine on fresh lake trout at rustic Lighthouse Restaurant. The next morning, catch the sunrise from your northeast-facing room before boarding the ferry to see south-shore highlights, such as an old commercial fisherman's cabin and a classic lighthouse. If the weather cooperates, the boat will have fully circumnavigated the island and get back at Grand Portage by 3pm.

02
Three days

If island time is of the essence, opt for the rock-star entrance: a round-trip floatplane flight from Houghton, Michigan. It's more expensive than a ferry, but the takeoff-to-touchdown time is just 35 minutes and the flight lands right at Rock Harbor. Book a stay in a housekeeping cottage, buy a map of the park at the park service office, then set off on foot for Mt Franklin, an island high point that rises more than 1000ft (305m) and has glorious views of the north shore and Lake Superior beyond.

On day two, if the weather is right, rent a kayak, canoe, or 15-horsepower outboard and troll Rock or Tobin Harbor for lake trout, brook trout, or whitefish. On the last day, hike the southern shoreline toward Three Mile campground, where there are plenty of granite slabs – perfect spots to launch into the cool water before drying off in the sun. Or else book a full-day of trout or salmon fishing from Rock Harbor.

03
Six days

The rite of passage on Isle Royale is to hike the length of the island. Five nights is ample time to complete the 42.5-mile (68.4km) hike along the Greenstone Ridge Trail. Take the *Voyageur II* from Grand Portage, start in Windigo on the west side of the island and hike 6 miles (9.6km) to Island Mine or 12 miles (19.3km) to South Lake Desor. The campgrounds, which are nicely spaced out at 6- to 10-mile (9.6 to 16km) interims, are first-come, first-serve. On the fourth night, hang a right at Mt Franklin and hike the 2 miles (3.2km) to Three Mile Campground, hopefully getting there in time to secure a lakeside campsite, which includes a screened-in shelter.

The last day will be an easy lakeside stroll into Rock Harbor, where a hot shower and a cold draft beer will be waiting. Just remember: this may be the flat Midwest, but there are eight points along the trail that rise above 1300ft (396m). (Be prepared for sore feet and legs!) On the morning of day six, hop on the ferry at Rock Harbor.

33

CA

Joshua Tree National Park

Twisted trees pointing skyward, epic playgrounds of rocks and rare palm oases beckon you to this Southern California desert crossroads.

Joshua Tree

Feel an irresistible urge to go wild in this untamed park. Go find where giant boulders look as if they were rolled across the desert floor, ending up jumbled together in oddly shaped heaps, with evocative names like 'Skull Rock.' The park's bizarrely bent namesake trees stand out starkly against the sere landscape, especially under the bewitching light of a full moon. Climbing over a parched, rocky hill, you may stumble upon the biggest surprise of all: a cool spring shaded by Californian fan palms, towering trees that can live for almost a century.

Joshua Tree is uniquely placed, with one foot in the higher, cooler Mojave Desert and the other foot in the lower, hotter Colorado Desert. The latter is part of the much larger Sonora Desert that stretches into Mexico – you can sometimes see that far from the park's Keys View on a clear day. On the road down to Cottonwood Springs, watch through your car's windshield as the deserts slowly transition while you wind through Pinto Basin, which has been inhabited for over 8000 years. Native Americans, including the Serrano, Chemehuevi and Cahuilla tribes, still call this desert home, traditionally gathering its plants for food, medicine and for weaving baskets with bold patterns.

Along dirt trails and roads, you'll find that historical artifacts abound in Joshua Tree. Gun-slinging, horseback-riding American miners arrived in the 19th century seeking silver and gold, though most never found it. Homesteaders also tried to make a go of it here, but left when the rains disappeared. Today, rock climbers come to test world-class routes up granite monoliths and towering slabs – the most eye-catching results of ancient volcanism and plate tectonic action. The terrain is crisscrossed by dozens of earthquake faults, including California's famously shaky San Andreas, which create the very springs and oases that make life possible here.

Toolbox

When to go
The biggest crowds arrive in spring, when wildflowers are in bloom. Temperatures are pleasantly mild in both spring and autumn, which are ideal seasons for most outdoor activities. Winter can be cold, but with clear, starry skies.

Getting there
The park is in Southern California, just over an hour's drive northeast of the resort town of Palm Springs. It's at least two hours by car east of Los Angeles, where busy LAX international airport is located.

Park in numbers

1235.4
Area covered (sq miles)

8000
Rock-climbing routes

5
Desert fan-palm oases

Stay here...

Black Rock Campground Just a 15-minute drive from the town of Joshua Tree, this family-friendly spot is the place to pitch a tent without feeling too far from civilization. Campsites are reservable up to six months in advance, which is handy for planning spring trips.

Jumbo Rocks Campground Are you dreaming of sleeping under the stars next to the park's iconic rock formations? This first-come, first-served campground is smack dab in the middle of all that gorgeous scenery. Show up early to get a site, especially on weekends. Don't forget to bring your own water.

Harmony Motel A simple roadside motel has one big claim to fame: the rock band U2 stayed here while working on their groundbreaking album *The Joshua Tree*. Unwind in the outdoor hot tub or cool swimming pool after a satisfyingly long day of hiking and climbing. Book the Jack Kerouac Cabin for a more private getaway.

Do this!

Rock climbing Monzogranite boulders, slabs and sheer faces issue a siren's call for you to climb, whether you're an enthusiastic novice or an expert. Outdoor outfitters in the town of Joshua Tree rent and sell climbing gear and teach hands-on lessons. Before you head out on your own, though, join the park's climbing ranger for morning coffee during the climbing season (roughly October to April).

Backcountry driving Some of the most fun you can have in a desert park is bumping down dirt roads into the wilderness in a car or on a mountain bike. Follow the 18-mile (29km) Geology Tour Rd for a sped-up version of 100 million years of natural history, or explore Covington Flats, where the park's biggest Joshua trees grow.

Guided touring Buy tickets for a tour of fascinating Keys Ranch, where homesteaders staked a claim, or take a full moon hike guided by a ranger naturalist (free!).

Joshua Tree National Park attracts rock climbers of all ages. Previous page: the parks eroded rocks provide plenty of handholds.

What to spot...

Uniquely positioned at the boundary of two deserts, this park offers visitors an astounding collection of plants and animals to look for. To the south, the Colorado Desert is earmarked by ocotillo plants, with their spiky red blooms, and cholla cactus, whose spines seem to 'jump out' at passersby (watch out!). Farther north, the milder Mojave Desert provides habitat for rare Joshua trees, as well as desert tortoises and migratory birds stopping over along the Pacific Flyway.

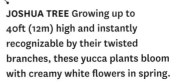

JOSHUA TREE Growing up to 40ft (12m) high and instantly recognizable by their twisted branches, these yucca plants bloom with creamy white flowers in spring.

GREATER ROADRUNNER One of the park's few resident avian species, these tan cuckoos can run over 25mph (40kph) and are fast enough to kill attacking rattlesnakes.

MOJAVE COLLARED LIZARD Look for the distinctive black-and-white rings around the neck of this reptilian predator found in rocky areas of the park.

Hike this...

01 Hidden Valley
Children will enjoy this short, 1-mile (1.6km) nature trail, an all-in-one introduction to the park's geology, flora and fauna.

02 Lost Horse Mine
Walk 4 miles (6.4km) through a desert wash to the remains of a 19th-century gold mine. If you follow the full loop, plan on hiking just over 6 miles (9.7km).

03 Lost Palms Oasis
Become an explorer of a lost world on this remote, 7.2-mile (11.6km) hike to a California fan-palm oasis.

Itineraries

Visit the ruins of Lost Horse Mine, hike Hidden Valley and Barker Dam, and don't miss the Keys View sunsets over the iconic Joshua trees.

◄ A coyote. Park up to admire the Milky Way; there's an annual Night Sky festival in the park.
► The joshua tree is a variety of yucca.

01

A day

It may leave you wanting more, but one day is still enough to hit the highlights of this desert park. Driving in from Palm Springs through the Yucca Valley, the tiny town of Joshua Tree is your last chance for food, water and gas – there are no tourist services inside the park. Driving down Park Blvd, you'll spot those iconic Joshua trees even before you reach the park's entrance station. Inside the park, hop out of the car at Hidden Valley for a brief nature walk and a picnic lunch. Nearby, a short trail rounds the cool reservoir at Barker Dam and passes Native American petroglyphs. Head up to Keys View for panoramic photos, then drive east through the 'Wonderland of Rocks' wilderness, where granite boulders are heaped up in every conceivable shape – kids especially love Skull Rock. Peruse educational exhibits inside the visitor center by the Oasis of Mara, then take a late afternoon hike over a hill to Fortynine Palms Oasis, where California fan palms shade a clear pool of water that attracts wildlife.

02

Two days

If you've got two days to spend, make more time for the heart of the park. Tour historic Keys Ranch with a ranger as your guide, or hike out into a desert wash to visit the ruins of Lost Horse Mine. Bump down Geology Tour Rd, passing rock climbers clinging to rock slabs that jut up from the sand. Snag a prime campsite at Jumbo Rocks before sunset and later watch the stars twinkle high above your sleeping bag.

The next day, drive lazily south through Pinto Basin, stopping to walk around the cactus garden of weird-looking succulents, including crooked ocotillo plants and fuzzy-looking 'teddy bear' cholla cactus (which are, in fact, painfully barbed). Dropping into the Colorado Desert, the road finally reaches Cottonwood Spring, which has a small visitor center and campground. Gear up and bring plenty of water for the meditative hike to Lost Palms Oasis, a native fan-palm grove standing in a lonely canyon, where desert bighorn sheep might be your only companions.

03

Three days

Three days gives you plenty of time to get to know this park inside out. Spend an entire day around Hidden Valley and Barker Dam, hiking, picnicking, and taking a rock-climbing lesson from a local guide. There's no better sunset perch than Keys View, although the top of Ryan Mountain offers equally magnificent vistas with more solitude, if you're up for a hardy ascent. Pitch your tent at Hidden Valley for the first night. The next day, tour Keys Ranch and bring mountain bikes to pedal around Queen Valley, where you can inspect the remains of an enormous mine. Before sunset, head to Black Rock Campground and drive the dirt roads around Covington Flat to see gigantic Joshua trees. On day three, drive down to Cottonwood Springs, where you can hike to fantastic Lost Palms Oasis before leaving the park. Or drive north instead to the small roadside Oasis of Mara, then hike to Fortynine Palms Oasis, just off the highway heading back to the town of Joshua Tree.

34

A K

Katmai
National
Park &
Preserve

*Some of the best brown
bear–watching in the world
can be found at this remote
park on the hazy-bayed
Alaskan Peninsula.*

NATIONAL PARKS *of* AMERICA

Getty Images | Paul Souders

Remember watching wildlife shows as a kid and seeing a 1000-pound (453.6kg) brown bear scooping salmon from a waterfall? That was shot – almost without a doubt – in Katmai National Park's Brooks Camp. If you have the money to get here, you can see this postcard-perfect scene from wild America play out in real life and in living color.

Head a little further afield in the 6400-sq-mile (16,576 sq km) park – that's about the size of Wales – to explore lost lakes, revel in Alaska Native cultural traditions that go back thousands of years, enjoy some excellent fishing and visit the enchanting and evocatively named Valley of Ten Thousand Smokes.

Formed as a national monument in 1918, Katmai was recognized as a national park in 1980. Its original purpose was to study the active volcanism of the Valley of Ten Thousand Smokes and the extensive coastal habitats that make this area ecosystem so rich. The Valley of Ten Thousand Smokes is a 40-sq-mile (103.6 sq km) ashflow that resulted from the eruption of Novarupta in 1912. For years the entire valley was filled with smoking fumeroles; today, only a few remain on the nearby hillsides. What's left behind is a naked moonscape that's powerful, bleak and just a little surreal.

The real reason you go here is to see bears – big ones. Fattened up from massive salmon runs, the brown bears of Katmai are immense, powerful and awe-inspiring. While most people head to Brooks Falls to sight these ursine masterpieces, you can spot bears throughout the park. You'll also find excellent canoeing and kayaking on the hundreds of miles of river, lake and stream that crisscross this coastal environment.

Backcountry explorers can easily extend their trip into the wilderness that marks this untrammeled corner of the earth. There are only 5 miles (8km) of trail in the park, but where your adventurous spirit and compass take you is up to your abilities and wanderlust.

Getty Images | Paul Whitfield

Toolbox

 When to go
July and September are the best months for bear viewing at Brooks Camp; come in July to see the salmon still alive and fighting their way upstream. Park services run from June to mid-September.

 **Getting there**
Located on the Alaska Peninsula, it's not easy to get here. You first fly in to King Salmon, then get on a floatplane to Brooks Camp. With a bit of planning, and an adventurous spirit, there's unlimited backcountry hikes and paddles to be had.

Park in numbers

6400
Area covered (sq miles)

2200
Number of brown bears in the park

9000
Years of human habitation

Stay here...

Hallo Bay Bear Camp
Specializing in bear-watching, this tour operator has a safari camp on the coastal edge of the park. You'll sleep in tents and get plenty of proximity with guided nature tours. The groups are small, making for intimate encounters with the big bears that roam the park.

Brooks Lodge
Just a short walk from Brooks Falls, this lodge offers easy access to fishing and bear-viewing, plus awesome views of Naknek Lake. It's a rustic yet expensive treat. Expect to stay on bunk beds in back-to-basics rooms – and stay up late swapping tales with fellow travelers.

Fure Cabin
On Naknek Lake's Bay of Islands, this public-use cabin was the home of famed trapper Roy Fure, who built the cabin in 1926 from hand-hewn spruce logs. It's a welcome, simple stopover for kayakers and canoers adventuring into the further reaches of the park; reserve it through the park service.

Do this!

Canoeing & kayaking
Hop in a kayak or canoe to paddle this spectacularly scenic route through the Katmai Backcountry. It's 86 miles (138.4km) long, and takes anywhere from five to 10 days, making this a trip fit only for experienced paddlers.

Fishing
For thousands of years, fishing has been a central part of the culture and commerce of the region. Within the park, you can fish for rainbow trout, arctic char, Dolly Varden trout, arctic grayling, char, and of course the five species of Pacific salmon that run through here.

Bear-watching
This is the reason around 50,000 people make it here every year. The best viewing is of course at Brooks Falls, where in high season you can see around 10 bears gathered by the falls, where salmon make dramatic leaps and the bears happily claw them out of the air and into their bellies. Go further afield for smaller crowds, and always – always – practice good bear safety.

Camping beside Naknek Lake; Brooks Falls, where bears catch salmon, is nearby. Previous page: a coastal brown bear.

What to spot...

Alongside the hallmark brown bears, 42 species of mammal inhabit the park. Brown bears and moose are found in the coastal and lake regions. You can also spot caribou, red fox, wolf, lynx, wolverine, river otter, mink, marten, weasel, porcupine, snowshoe hare, red squirrel and busy little beavers. Along the coast, red salmon are a lifeblood, but you can also spot barking sea lions, sea otters and the occasional whale or porpoise along the Shelikof Strait, just beyond the park borders.

BROWN BEAR
Weighing in at over 1000lbs (453.6kg) at the end of the summer – when they can down up to 30 salmon in a day – brown bears are one of the world's most iconic apex predators.

BEAVER The lakes, ponds and marshes of this coastal area attract an amazing variety of animal life. Watching beavers build their lodges and ponds is a wonderful afternoon activity.

SEA LION
Head to the coast to spot seals and sea lions, and the ever-endearing (and sadly endangered) sea otters. The large sea lion colonies are a sight (and sound) to behold.

Hike this...

01 Brooks Falls
It's just a 0.5-mile (0.8km) hike from the drop-off to Brooks Falls. Along the way are three viewing platforms and the final deck, where camera-toting tourists battle for the best shot.

02 Dumpling Mountain
The only developed trail, this half-day trek takes you to the top of 2520ft (768m) Dumpling Mountain, where you catch superlative views of the surrounding lake country.

03 Three Forks Overlook
There aren't many trails in the park, but you can ask to be dropped off at this overlook, where you can trek into the rugged backcountry.

Getty Images | Patrick Endres; Barcroft Media

Itineraries

Bear-watching around Brooks Camp, roadtripping to Three Forks Overlook, kayaking the Savonski Loop – this park has it all, and Ten Thousand Smokes views.

◀ The annual feeding frenzy at Brooks Falls sees brown bears fatten up for winter.
▶ A floatplane on Naknek Lake; a red fox in Katmai National Park.

01

Three days

It's expensive staying at Brooks Camp, so you may wish to limit your time and focus on just the essentials. Fly into Brooks Camp on floatplane from the gateway village of King Salmon. On a budget, you can either set up shop in King Salmon, with day trips to the park, or enter the lottery to stay at the Brooks Camp Campground (which is, understandably, surrounded by an electric fence). If you've got money to spare, splurge and stay at the rustic Brooks Lodge or Hallo Bay Bear

Camp. Your first day should definitely be spent watching bears on the platforms around Brooks Camp – you'll probably want to dedicate at least a few hours every day for this.

On day two, hop on the 23-mile (38km) road (the only one in the park) to the Three Forks Overlook, for arching views of the Valley of Ten Thousand Smokes. You can head off here for some killer trail-less hiking. On your third day, consider a short kayak or spring for a flightseeing tour.

02

Ten days

If time, budget, outdoor experience and ambition are no object, you can do some only-dreamers-and-daredevils-need-apply activities. Start with a day of bear viewing at Brooks Camp, where you can gather information and solidify plans for a backcountry expedition. From there, paddlers should hop in a kayak or canoe for either a five- to 10-day circuit on the Savonski Loop. You could also do a shorter 30-mile (48.3km) paddle to the Bay Islands with a floatplane pickup or a quick, 10-mile

(16km) out-and-back to Margot Creek. Expect high winds and rough waters on big lakes. If you aren't wiped out already, venture from the Valley of Ten Thousand Smokes for unlimited backcountry hiking, using riverbeds and ridgelines to traverse this trackless terrain. A few operators offer all-inclusive trips that include hiking, paddling and bear-watching. For an added kick, end your trip with a journey to Lake Clark National Park & Preserve, a seldom-explored park of hills, glaciers and more.

35

Kenai Fjords National Park

With cascading glaciers, sky-high fjords teaming with bird and sea life, and easy access, this maritime park is an enchanting mix of sea, ice and mountainside.

The nearly 40 glaciers that carve their way through stone and rock down to the rugged fjords are the crowning jewels of this popular national park.

Alas, due to global warming, these glaciers are in retreat. But they are still massive, incredible, awe-inspiring and remarkably forceful. Atop it all is the Harding Ice Field. This majestic glimmering block of ice, created more than 23,000 years ago, covers 700 sq miles (1813 sq km) of Alaska's Kenai Mountains. From it, glaciers flowed to the sea, carving the deep fjords you see today in such legendary waters as Resurrection and Aialik Bays.

The *de rigeur* trip here is a boat tour from the lyrical fishing village of Seward. Along the way, you will see fjords, glaciers and a remarkable tapestry of maritime wildlife that includes sea otters, Dall's porpoise, harbor porpoise, Steller sea lion, harbor seal and orca. Whalewatching is also spectacular, with opportunities to sight fin, gray, humpack, minke and sei whale.

For another perspective on this waterworld, get closer to nature on a kayak tour – paddling between icebergs and listening to the crackle of melting ice is magical. You can head out for a day amid the bergs or scale-up your adventure with multiday paddles.

The Exit Glacier is the most often-visited land area in the park. You can hike here easily in a day, even extending your trip to make it to the top of the world on the Harding Ice Field. From here you can also access a trail that traverses the entire Kenai Peninsula. This broad spit of land on the southern coast of Alaska is home to black and brown bear, mountain goat and moose. You might even sight a marmot or northern bog lemming if you look close enough.

Toolbox

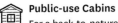

When to go
In these northern latitudes, the best time to visit is during the summer months of June to August. On the shoulder season, you might catch some good weather, but the visitor centers aren't open.

Getting there
From Anchorage, hop on the Alaska Railroad to get down to the gateway city of Seward and its cute shops. Boat and kayak trips into the park depart from here, or you can head inland for a hike to the Exit Glacier.

Park in numbers

917

Area covered (sq miles)

191

Species of bird

545

Miles of coastline

Stay here...

Public-use Cabins
For a back-to-nature treat, book one of the three public-use cabins located along the fjords for a long weekend. The Aialik Cabin sits on a beach, offering great whale-watching. From the Holgate Arm Cabin, you can wonder at the nearby glacier, while the North Arm Cabin is far from everything – requiring some serious paddling to get here.

Kenai Fjords Glacier Lodge
The only wilderness lodge within the park, this all-inclusive lodge on a glorious lagoon has 16 rustic cabins that exude just the right balance between modern comfort and Alaska-backwoods atavism. A series of boardwalks connect your cabins, and everything is included – guided boat trips, kayaks, gourmet meals and transport from Seward.

Alaska Paddle Inn
These custom-built rooms tower over a private beach on Resurrection Bay, outside Seward. The arcaded ceilings, cozy appointments and gas fireplaces add to the considerable charms that make it feel like home. Explore the beach, hop out for an afternoon kayak or simply sit by the waterfront and watch the horizon.

Do this!

Sea kayaking
While you can go on a short day paddle, multiday blue-water excursions here are where it's at. From Seward, you can hire a boat to take you out to Aialik Bay, spending three or four days paddling south past Pedersen Glacier and into the Holgate Arm. Aboard a kayak, with the wind in your hair and the water lapping at your side, you'll feel an intimate connection with the water and nature that makes this place special.

Boat touring
From a boat, you'll see plenty of birds and coastal wildlife, also taking in the dramatic sights, waterfalls and calving glaciers of Resurrection Bay, Holgate Arm and the Northwestern Lagoon. This experience takes you close to the wild, steep fjords of the park. Trained naturalists offer running commentary and, when it's cold, hot chocolate.

Glacier touring
Strap on some crampons, ready your ice ax and tie-in for adventure with an ice-climbing excursion onto the Harding Ice Field. Guided trips take you past crevasses and ice caves, where remarkable blues shine in the bright Alaskan sun.

← Spire Cove in Kenai Fjords is a geology lesson.
→ Orca pods cruise nearby.

Hike this...

01 Exit Glacier
From the Exit Glacier nature center, head out for a ranger-guided trek to a viewing point above this glacier (one of the few spots accessible by land in the park). The hike takes just an hour or two round-trip.

02 Harding Ice Field Trail
It's only 4 miles (6.4km) to the top, but because of the steepness, it can take you up to eight hours' round-trip to make it to the Harding Ice Field.

03 Resurrection River Trail
Outside the park, this trail is a spectacular backwoods romp. Strap on a backpack for a multi-day hike from Seward to the village of Hope on the northern coast of the Kenai Peninsula.

What to spot...

If you love sea life, then Kenai Fjords is the place for you. Top on nearly everybody's list is sighting marine mammals such as various whales or porpoise – in fact the park's mission includes protecting these sea animals and maintaining their breeding areas. You'll want your binoculars and mega-zoom lens to spot some of the signature bird species, including tufted and horned puffins, bald eagles and oystercatchers.

ORCA There are approximately 250 orca in 15 pods roaming the waters of Prince William Sound. In May and early June, you might just spot them cruising at 35mph (56km/h) past your bow.

PUFFIN These fanciful birds with their colorful beaks nest here starting in mid-May. They are incredible swimmers and, like penguins, they mate for life.

SEA OTTER Playful, hilarious to watch and curious as anything, these water weasels are seen throughout Alaska's southern coasts. You will most certainly see a handful on your trip.

Itineraries

Take a boat tour of the fjords, a guided ascent of the Harding Ice Field or meet the challenge of Mt Marathon before dining on the world's freshest halibut.

◄ A stand-up paddle board lets you get close to an iceberg canyon on Bear Lake in Kenai Fjords.
➔ Snack time at Bear Lake.

01

Three days

Head down to Seward from Anchorage on the Coastal Classic Train, stopping to view beluga whale running up the Turnagain Arm. Once you get here, take a stroll through town, enjoying the wonderful murals that add color to every corner. Have dinner dockside at Chinooks, and hire your boat tour for the following day. Two major operators run the boat tours. You won't see much on the three-hour tour, so splurge instead on the full eight-hour deal to see more of the fjords. A naturalist will provide running commentary. Keep your eyes on the horizon for whale, orca and other sea mammals. Party that night Alaskan-style at the rough-and-tumble Thorn's Showcase Lounge, which happens to serve some of the best halibut around. The next day, get up early for the guided ascent of the Harding Ice Field, stopping on the way home at the Exit Glacier Salmon Bake. On day three, you may wish to consider taking a guided sea-kayak trip, or else head out for a long day-hike in the wild countryside that surrounds the village of Seward.

02

Five days

The best way to explore this water-bound national park is aboard a sea kayak. With no rumble of motors, you'll get closer than you ever imagined to the sights, sounds and energy of this marvelous corner of our earth. It requires some planning, as only expert paddlers should challenge the waters outside of Resurrection Bay. For the rest of us, you'll need to hire a sea-taxi to drop you in the relatively calm waters of Aialik Bay. Expect to be cold and wet the entire time. Afterwards, stay in a public-use cabin in Aialik or one of dozens of remote campsites. There's nothing better than sitting by a fire after a long day in the rain and warming up over a few beers. Over the next four days, you can slowly make your way past Pedersen Glacier and into Holgate Arm, where another public-use cabin awaits. A sea-taxi can pick you up after day five, or else you can continue on, exploring the seldom-viewed corners of this remote park. Finish your trip with refreshing beers and a very fancy dinner at Ray's Waterfront.

03

Seven days

Start with the essentials, then move out into new ground with a little improvisation. After you've exhausted the tours and kayaks of the park, there's still plenty to do in and around Seward. The Lost Lake Trail goes up 7 miles (11.3km) and offers some of the most spectacular views of Resurrection Bay you will ever see.

If that's not enough, really challenge yourself with an ascent of nearby Mt Marathon, where loco locals run a killer footrace every July 4th. The following day, rent a fat-tire mountain bike to ride along the Iditarod National Historic Trail.

In the afternoon, you can spend three hours whisking amid the Sitka spruce at Stoney Creek Canopy Adventures. Dog sledding isn't for everybody, but if you must, you should consider going with Godwin Glacier Dog Sled Tours, where you fly up to a glacier to spend an afternoon skating across the ice. Top off everything with some deep-sea fishing for halibut and salmon.

36

Kings Canyon National Park

Giant sequoia trees, sheer granite cliffs and a dizzyingly deep river canyon all combine in this hidden Sierra Nevada beauty.

Getty Images | Jens Karlsson

The poet and conservationist John Muir once called Kings Canyon 'a rival to the Yosemite.' You'll understand why as you drive down the serpentine Kings Canyon Scenic Byway, cut narrowly into the edges of canyon walls carved by glaciers and polished by rushing water and creeping time. At roadside vista points like Junction View, steel your nerves and peer over the precipice toward the roaring white-water river far below. Arriving at the end of the road in Cedar Grove, get out and ramble beside the powerful Kings River, where Muir himself gave impromptu lectures while standing atop an enormous rock.

Only a fraction of the crowds that swarm Yosemite National Park, found farther north in the Sierra Nevada, make their way to Kings Canyon. As you hike deep into the peaceful forest to a tumbling waterfall, the only sounds along the trail may be birdsong, canyon breezes, and your own footsteps. Down by the Kings River, you can go for a dip in summertime swimming holes, or show up in spring to spy black bears grazing in wildflower meadows. In winter, strap on snowshoes and tramp among some of the world's largest trees, including the towering General Grant Tree, the official Christmas tree of the US.

Backpackers revel in the wilderness of the High Sierra, so readily accessible from Cedar Grove. One classic route is the Rae Lakes Loop, which follows the famous John Muir Trail and Pacific Crest Trail over mountain passes and past alpine lakes that will leave you awestruck by nature's majesty. Expert rock climbers find epic challenges – without the crowds of Yosemite's El Capitán – in the park's backcountry, too. For kids, camping next to trees that measure over 20 stories tall is a thrill not soon forgotten.

Toolbox

When to go
Summer is the most crowded time to visit. Waterfalls peak in late spring, while early fall is still warm enough for camping. In winter, the Kings Canyon Scenic Byway closes.

Getting there
The park is a four-hour drive east of San Francisco via Fresno, a city in California's Central Valley. In summer, buses to Grant Grove stop at Fresno's airport and train and bus stations. You'll need a car to drive the Kings Canyon Scenic Byway.

Park in numbers

721.7
Area covered (sq miles)

8200
Maximum depth of Kings Canyon (ft)

268.1
Height of General Grant, tallest tree (ft)

Getty Images | Larry Gerbrandt

Stay here...

John Muir Lodge
In Grant Grove Village, secluded down a side road away from the crowds of campers, this woodsy inn is the best place to bed down in the park. Relax in a rocking chair on the front porch in summer, or cozy up by the fireplace in winter.

Sheep Creek Campground
At the bottom of Kings Canyon, this riverside campground lets you pitch a tent without being squeezed against your neighbors. It's a quick walk to the outdoor amphitheater, where campfire ranger programs happen in summer, or to the Cedar Grove Village market and grill for a meal.

Azalea Campground
Within walking distance of the General Grant Grove, this forested, family-friendly campground allows you to camp quite close to giant sequoias. It's a quick shuttle ride to the Grant Grove Village market, which sells all the supplies you'll need to make s'mores in the crackling fire pit at your campsite.

Do this!

Swimming
When the Kings River water levels drop in mid-summer, swimming holes appear. Look for them near Roads End in Cedar Grove, especially around the beach by Muir Rock and underneath the Red Bridge. (Check with park rangers before taking a dip, just to be sure current conditions are safe enough.)

Horseback riding
Saddle up for a short trail ride among giant sequoia trees at Grant Grove. Drive all the way down into the canyon to the rustic Cedar Grove Pack Station for trots beside the Kings River and multi-day wilderness trips to High Sierra lakes and meadows.

Skiing & snowshoeing
When the Kings Canyon Scenic Byway is closed in winter, you can still rent snowshoes in Grant Grove Village and trek among the giant sequoias. In the nearby Sequoia National Forest, family-friendly Montecito Sequoia Lodge rents snowshoes and cross-country skis and has miles of groomed ski trails.

← Grant Grove, home to some of the world's largest trees, the giant sequoia. Previous page: The Lakes Trail to Pear Lake is a highlight of Kings Canyon National Park.

What to spot...

Kings Canyon has all the diversity of more famous Sierra Nevada national parks, and then some. Black bears, mule deer and yellow-bellied marmots inhabit mixed conifer forests, high mountain meadows, granite peaks and the canyon's slopes. So do 150 rare and unusual species, such as the endangered mountain yellow-legged frog, which survives only by alpine lakes in the High Sierra. The park is also a paradise for birders, with more than 200 varied species thriving here.

BLACK BEAR
Urus americanus is the king of the forests. Don't let the name fool you, though: their fur can be black, brown, golden or even cinnamon-colored.

GIANT SEQUOIA These venerable trees grow in abundance in Grant Grove and in historically misnamed Redwood Canyon, where few people now go.

CALIFORNIA SPOTTED OWL
Count yourself lucky if you see this nocturnal hunter with inky dark eyes – Kings Canyon is one of its few protected strongholds.

Hike this...

O1 General Grant Tree Trail

Amble past giant sequoias and peek inside the Fallen Monarch, a tree so big it once served as horse stables. The trail is 0.4 miles (0.6km).

O2 Zumwalt Meadow Loop

Tramp 1.5 miles (2.4km) along the boardwalk through a grassy meadow, where wildflowers bloom next to the Kings River.

O3 Mist Falls

From the end of the scenic byway, climb up the canyon's granite walls through shady forest to a rocky waterfall that thunders in spring. The trail is 9 miles (14.5km).

Itineraries

Hike Redwood Canyon for a serene sequoia experience, see the world's second largest tree at General Grant Grove or tour the marble magic of Boyden Cavern.

← Zumwalt Meadow. The mountain yellow-legged frog is a lakeside resident.
→ Horses and mules haul gear in the High Sierra.

01

A day

From the park's Big Stump entrance station, it's just a few more miles to the park's visitor hub, Grant Grove Village. Step inside the Kings Canyon Visitor Center for natural history displays and to pick up hiking maps and information; there's even an educational play room at the back for kids. Drive or ride the free seasonal shuttle bus to General Grant Grove, where an easy nature walk loops past fine specimens of giant sequoias, including the world's second-largest living tree and the hollowed-out Fallen Monarch. After a

pleasant picnic lunch in the sun-dappled forest, head over to Grant Grove Stables for a short horseback or mule ride. If you crave more solitude while hiking among the giant sequoias, drive south to Redwood Canyon for its interlocking network of trails.

Before sunset, return to Grant Grove Village and follow Panoramic Point Rd as it winds narrowly upward; on foot, hike up a short hill for sweeping views of Kings Canyon – at its best when the fading sunlight paints the rocks in serene pastels.

02

Two days

Wake up to the smell of pine trees at your forest campsite in Grant Grove. After breakfast, start driving down the Kings Canyon Scenic Byway, which drops deep into the canyon for 35 miles (56.3km), passing through the Giant Sequoia National Monument on its way down to Cedar Grove. Stop at Junction View for unbelievable vistas of one of North America's deepest canyons and to take a tour of Boyden Cavern, a marble cave set in the canyon's walls. Pulling into Cedar Grove Village,

grab some cold drinks and ice cream at the market or lunch at the grill, then kick back on the riverside deck. Afterward, drive another 6 miles (9.6km) down the road, passing Roaring River Falls and pretty Zumwalt Meadow, a favorite haunt of black bears.

From aptly named Roads End, hiking trails lead to waterfalls and lakes, or else you can just laze by the small beach at Muir Rock. Pitch your tent next to the Kings River at Sheep Creek Campground, west of Cedar Grove Village.

03

Three days

Pack up your tent and drive back up out of the canyon. Detour to forested Hume Lake, where you can swim in the cool waters or rent a canoe or kayak for a placid morning paddle. Driving deeper into the Sequoia National Forest, follow bumpy dirt roads to historic Buck Rock Lookout. Climb 172 steps up to a restored, still functional fire lookout for bird's-eye views of the Great Western Divide. (The lookout is open to the public in summer, except during lightning storms and fire emergencies). Make your

way west to the Generals Hwy, then take another short detour down a side road to Redwood Canyon. The name is a misnomer, because it's giant sequoias that grow here – large groves of them, in fact. Hiking trails loop through the canyon, affording you a rare chance to commune with the enormous trees in meditative peace. With a wilderness permit, you can camp overnight in the canyon, or keep driving south toward Sequoia National Park for more campgrounds and lodging.

37

AK

Kobuk Valley National Park & Preserve

Discover sand dunes, massive herds of migrating caribou and mile upon glorious mile of remote solitude in this Great Land park.

Above the arctic circle, the wilds of Alaska get just a little wilder. And the remote Kobuk Valley National Park and Preserve – with its patches of oddly placed sand dunes, the rambling Kobuk River, bookended mountain ranges, and lasting Alaska Native cultural imprint – is as wild as it gets.

The Baird and Waring Mountain Ranges encircle this park, protecting unique geological features, such as the 25-sq-mile (64.8 sq km) Great Kobuk Sand Dunes, which formed over millennia as particles of fine sand produced by the grinding action of nearby glaciers were blown into the valley. Along the 61-mile (98km) stretch of the Kobuk River, you'll find 150ft-high (46m) river bluffs marked by the ages with permafrost ice and fossils dating back to the ice age. The Little Kobuk and Hunt River Dunes add to this Technicolor mix.

Twice a year hundreds of thousands of caribou migrate through the park: north in the spring and south in the fall. You'll find their tracks along the lofty sand dunes and in the surrounding wetlands wilderness. Witnessing this great migration is a spectacle on par with the great movements of the Serengeti – except, of course, it's a lot colder.

At Onion Portage, Alaska Natives have gathered for 9000 years to harvest these migrating herds as they ford the stream. To this day, subsistence hunters remain active in the park, harvesting caribou to feed their families over the long Alaskan winter.

Kobuk is hard to get to and frightfully cold, presenting an excellent challenge for experienced backpackers, boaters and wildlife watchers. You'll be rewarded with supreme solitude, vistas that stretch on to infinity and 24 hours of sunlight. More than anything, a visit here to the top of the world is about reconnecting to the earth as it was – before human progress affected the courses of our waterways, the shapes of our mountains and grandeur of our valleys.

Toolbox

When to go
Flightseers and wildlife enthusiasts time trips around the great caribou migrations in spring and fall (though changing temperatures may be affecting migration patterns). For boating and backpacking come in the summer.

Getting there
There are no roads into the park, and getting here will require some planning and patience. From Anchorage, you fly to Kotzebue, then take a puddle-jumper to the Native villages near the park or get dropped off on a chartered floatplane to see the Kobuk River and sand dunes.

Park in numbers

2656
Area covered (sq miles)

400
Plant species

119
Unique bird species

Stay here...

Bettles Lodge
This vintage 1952 lodge is a National Historic site. The six rooms are back-to-basics, but you get a spirited dining room and bar with the requisite moose-antler decorations. They also offer tours and operate a number of remote summer cabins, including the Aurora Viewing Cabin, 3 miles (4.8km) from the lodge.

Camping
Camping in the Great Kobuk Sand Dunes – just a 2-mile (3.2km) hike up from your floatplane drop-off on the river – is an otherworldly experience that will last a lifetime. Find a corner of sand to pitch your tent and set off for miles of exploration in this out-of-place sandscape on the edges of the arctic.

Kobuk River Lodge
After floating the Kobuk River for several days, nothing feels better than a hot shower. Overlooking the confluence of the Kobuk and Ambler Rivers, this homegrown lodge has simple rooms, plenty of taxidermy (including a big-tusked walrus) and enough hot water to warm away the day's shivers. It offers guided day hikes to Onion Portage and the Great Kobuk Sand Dunes.

← A caribou herd crosses Kobuk River in fall.
→ An aerial view of the Great Kobuk Sand Dunes.

Do this!

Kayaking
From Walter Lake in the Gates of the Arctic National Preserve, you can travel some 115 river miles (185km) down to your take-out in Kobuk village; the trip takes anywhere from five to eight days. You'll start with some Class IV water in Gates of the Arctic, moving into floatable Class I. Entering the park, you'll encounter fishing camps and hunting parties, along with a rich variety of wildlife. It's a gorgeous adventure.

Flightseeing
Book a half-day flightseeing tour from Kotzebue or Bettles to see the park from the air, a good way to spot migrating caribou and other wildlife. Or hire a floatplane to drop you off for backcountry hiking (along the ridgelines in the Baird Mountains).

Itineraries

Go flightseeing for migrating caribou or day trip to Great Kobuk Sand Dunes.

01

Five days

This is one of the least-visited national parks. There are no roads, no established trails, no official campsites – so whether you come here on a one-day flightseeing tour or spend eight days on the river, you'll need to plan ahead. Start with a flight from Anchorage to Kotzebue, where you can stay at the Nullaġvik Hotel and check out the Northwest Arctic Heritage Center, which also serves as park headquarters. From there, take a flightseeing tour of the park, hoping for views of migrating caribou. The next day, transfer to Kobuk. From here, take day tours to Onion Portage and the Great Kobuk Sand Dunes, where you can spot caribou, climb through the dunes and search out wildlife. Spend your final day angling for Dolly Varden trout, sheefish, salmon, grayling and pike near Kobuk.

38

AK

Lake Clark National Park

This under-the-radar, four-million-acre park is the epitome of Alaska, with coastal bays, glaciers, volcanoes, tundra, deep freshwater lakes, wildlife, and centuries of Native American history.

The abundance in Lake Clark National Park is over the top, even for Alaska. Two major mountain ranges, the Neacola and the Chigmit, merge here; Lake Clark Pass, which separates them, was once surrounded by 24 glaciers. While most have since receded, left in their wake are glacial lakes and streams swimming with such a bounty of salmon that the park has one of the highest concentrations of brown bears in the world.

Descendants of the Dena'ina Athabascan Indians have been fishing Lake Clark, a 128-sq-mile (332 sq km) haven for salmon and trout, for 12,000 years. The lake's native name, Qizhjeh Vena, means 'a place where people gathered.' In the early 20th century the Dena'ina abandoned their village of Kijik, which they had occupied for almost a thousand years; today the ghost town is the largest Athabascan archaeological site in the state of Alaska. The surviving Dena'ina descendants still live in Nondalton, a village of 164 residents on the southwestern shoreline of Sixmile Lake at the southern tip of Lake Clark.

Accessible only via floatplane (or a beach-landing bush plane), the park may seem out of reach for short hops, but it's only 100 miles (161km) southwest across the Cook Inlet from Anchorage, and many exciting regions are accessible via a 70-minute flight. The park's marquee attraction is its 130-mile-long (209km) coastline along the Cook Inlet, where mother bears and their cubs migrate every June in search of sedge, razor clams, and fish.

Humans can migrate to the park to fish for salmon, too – in the summer of 2014, more than 730,000 red salmon returned to Lake Clark alone. Beyond fishing, visitors can hike high-alpine tundra of the western slope, kayak-camp in Lake Clark, or take a day trip to view bears along the coastline.

Toolbox

When to go

There is no official park entry, but its visitor center in Port Alsworth, on the shore of Lake Clark, is open from late May to mid-September. Camping is good within that window, but plan what you want to do: June for bear-viewing along the Cook Inlet coast, or July or August for salmon-fishing.

Getting there

Unconnected to the Alaskan road system, the park is 100 miles (161km) southwest of Anchorage and is accessible via floatplane from Homer, Kenai and Anchorage. Weather and tides permitting, the east side of the park along Cook Inlet is accessible via boat.

Park in numbers

6297

Area covered (sq miles)

0

Number of roads in the park

147,000

The number of red salmon that annually migrate into Lake Clark

Stay here...

Redoubt Mountain Lodge

This six-cabin lodge spread over five acres and surrounded by an electric fence to keep out the brown bears, is the only property on Crescent Lake, a glacial-fed lake in the shadow of 10,197ft (3108m) Redoubt Volcano. It's a boat ride away from some of the best sockeye, coho, chinook, and king-salmon fishing in the world.

Backcountry camping

A trail-free wilderness, Lake Clark has an infinite number of superb places to pitch a tent. One of the most highly coveted, which requires a 40-minute flight from Port Alsworth, is the spit of land that juts out of Turquoise Lake – tucked between 8000ft (2438m) towering peaks to the east and high-alpine tundra to the west.

Silver Salmon Creek Lodge

Set between volcanic peaks and tidal marshes beside Cook Inlet, the cozy lodge with a communal lounging area and bedrooms with sleigh beds is a wilderness oasis. The lodge's tented camp, ten miles (16km) to the south, operates from July to September to coincide with the salmon run.

Do this!

Fishing

Fishing here is a full sensory experience. As if fly-casting in the shadow of 10,000-foot peaks isn't enough, there's also the very real possibility that a brown bear is lurking on the shoreline, waiting for you to reel in your catch. Luckily, the salmon are so abundant here, that there's plenty for everyone.

Bear-viewing

It would be nearly impossible to visit Lake Clark in June and not see a brown bear (the same as a grizzly except that it lives along the coastline instead of in the interior). It's an easy hop from Anchorage, Kenai or Homer to the Cook Inlet shoreline to watch the largest land-based predator on earth forage, fight, and play.

Kayaking

This 42-mile (67.6km) lake lined by the Chigmit Mountains is an ideal place to experience backcountry Alaska on a budget. With advance planning, campers can fly into Port Alsworth and rent a kayak, then hop a water taxi to take them to a campsite furnished with a tent, firewood and a pit toilet – and a killer view. Choose a meeting spot and spend a night or a week exploring the massive lake.

← Glacier Creek cascades towards Upper Twin Lake.
▶ Snack on alpine blueberries.

Hike this...

01 Tanalian Mountain: It may be only 4.1 miles (6.6km) to the top, but the trail climbs 3600ft (1097m) from Port Alsworth to the top of 3900-ft (1189m) Tanalian Mountain, where you'll find exhilarating views of Lake Clark.

02 Turquoise to Twin Lake This 25-mile (40km) point-to-point hike loops through high-alpine tundra. There's 8000 feet (2438m) of climbing, but the payoff is possible sightings of bear, sheep, caribou, eagle, or moose.

03 Silver Salmon Creek Beach to Chinitna Bay This 25-mile (40km) coastal hike is a straightforward amble along the beach with a few exceptions: brown bears and river crossings, some of which aren't passable at high tide.

What to spot...

BROWN BEAR Black and brown bears wander throughout the entire park, but the most impressive numbers can be found along the park's coastline in June. Watch The Wild Kingdom unfold before your eyes, with mamas teaching cubs how to dig for razor clams and males catching up to 30 fish per day.

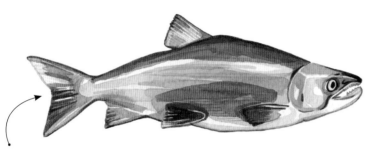

SOCKEYE SALMON This brilliant red fish is what has kept brown bears, sea mammals, and humans alive in this harsh region for centuries; one of the main reasons for the park's existence is to protect the fish's spawning grounds. The sheer numbers of sockeye that enter the park's watershed through the Newhalen River each year are staggering – from 1.5 to 6 million.

ALDER Better known as 'tanglefoot,' the densest clusters of this silvery-green shrub are so thick that it's almost impossible to hike through them. If hiking is your objective, stick to the park's western slope, where the alder is less intrusive.

Itineraries

This is all about the bears, not to mention glaciers and snow-capped volcanoes. Hiking is tough but mix it up with whitewater rafting and easy fishing.

← Horned puffins live in Lake Clark National Park.
→ A coastal brown bear ignores a pair of planes on Chinitna Bay.

01

A day

With its trifecta of nutritional sources – razor clams, sedge and salmon – Chinitna Bay, a coastal salt-marsh habitat, is a magnet for brown bears, who congregate en masse along the beach. There are two vantage points from which guests can photograph them digging for clams, catching salmon or chasing each other down the beach. The thought of getting close enough to take a decent photograph of the world's largest land-based predator is a little intimidating at first, but the bears are so busy foraging for food that unless you disturb them, they won't disturb you. Bear Viewing in Alaska is the only operator in the national park allowed to access Chinitna Bay via boat, which means that guests also get a bonus 40-mile (64km), 1½-hour crossing of Cook Inlet from Homer, offering a panoramic view of glaciers ending abruptly in the sea, snowcapped volcanoes, sea birds and other marine life. The 10-hour tour includes five to eight hours with the bears, plus an additional option of halibut fishing or clam digging.

02

Five days

When the red Cessna from Anchorage-based Rust's Flying Service touches down on Crescent Lake, the scenery seems almost too impossibly Technicolor to be true. On the northwest end of the turquoise glacial lake is snowcapped Redoubt Volcano; to the southeast is the 2-mile-long (3.2km) Lake Fork of the Crescent River, a world-class sockeye and silver salmon fishery. In between are precipitous, mountain-fringed shorelines where brown bears troll for easy prey. Photograph them fishing from the distant comfort of a flat-bottomed boat, or drop a line in to catch lake trout. Hiking here can be a little tough as the alder along the shoreline is dense and catchy, but there are at least seven treks that spur off of the lake, one of which ends at a 60ft (18m) waterfall. Every night guests gather at the rustic Redoubt Mountain Lodge, where the chef serves up a fresh catch of the day, followed by a fireside nightcap and an early bedtime in one of six cozy log cabins with tin roofs – an ideal place to bunk down in a rainstorm.

03

Ten days

Considering that the park is four million acres and you can camp just about anywhere in it, there's a lot of backcountry to explore – but if you don't have extensive Alaskan wilderness skills, it's best to travel with a guide who does. Dan Oberlatz, the owner of Alaska Alpine Adventures, has been exploring the park since 1992. One of his most interesting offerings in the park is a ten-day hiking-and-river trip that starts with a drop-off on Lower Twin Lake and eventually winds down the Wild and Scenic Chilikadrotna River via inflatable canoe. From start to finish you'll spend three days on foot, hiking 25-plus miles (40km) on high-alpine tundra in view of snowcapped peaks, followed by 80 river miles (129km) of Class II and III whitewater and a mellow float on the Mulchatna River, where the easy pace allows for spincasting for rainbow trout and arctic char. It's not uncommon to see wolves, bears, and caribou en route. The last night includes a hot shower and a cozy bed at a lodge on Lake Clark.

39

CA

Lassen Volcanic National Park

Where the Sierra Nevada mountains, Cascade volcanoes and the Great Basin Desert collide, this geologically active spot is exhilarating to explore.

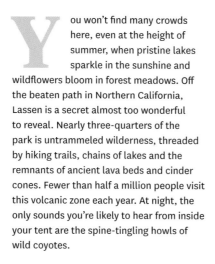

You won't find many crowds here, even at the height of summer, when pristine lakes sparkle in the sunshine and wildflowers bloom in forest meadows. Off the beaten path in Northern California, Lassen is a secret almost too wonderful to reveal. Nearly three-quarters of the park is untrammeled wilderness, threaded by hiking trails, chains of lakes and the remnants of ancient lava beds and cinder cones. Fewer than half a million people visit this volcanic zone each year. At night, the only sounds you're likely to hear from inside your tent are the spine-tingling howls of wild coyotes.

At the northern edge of the Sierra Nevada range, Lassen Peak is the southernmost active volcano in the Cascade Range, which extends throughout the Pacific Northwest. Astoundingly, all of the world's different volcano types – shield, plug dome, cinder cone and composite – are found here, along with boiling mud pots, steaming vents and sulfurous hot springs. Geologically speaking, the hubbub began 825,000 years ago – and it's still going on. Lassen Peak last erupted in 1915, just one year before it became a national park. Witness the chaos of a morphing landscape in the park's unique hydrothermal areas, which still hiss and bubble dramatically today.

At the boundary of three distinct ecological regions, Lassen has long been a meeting point for Native American tribes. The Maidu, Yahi, Yana and Atsugewi peoples traditionally came here during the summer to hunt and to gather plants for food, medicine and weaving coiled baskets with geometric patterns. During the 19th century, wagon-train emigrants to California passed through; later still, fortune-hunting miners, loggers and ranchers all made their way here. You can learn more about the park's cultural history inside the Loomis Museum and at Kohm Yah-mah-nee Visitor Center; its name means 'Snow Mountain' in honor of Lassen Peak.

Toolbox

When to go
Most visitor facilities are open during summer only. The main road through the park typically closes after the first major snowfall in October and doesn't reopen until the snow melts the following year – usually sometime in June.

Getting there
Located off the I-5 Fwy in Northern California's mountains, the park is less than a four-hour drive from San Francisco, which has a major international airport. You'll need a car to get here and around.

Park in numbers

166.3
Area covered (sq miles)

10,463
Lassen Peak, the tallest mountain (ft)

1915
Last volcanic eruption (May 22)

Stay here...

Manzanita Lake Campground
Sprawling at almost 6000ft (1829m) in elevation, this family-friendly campground near the park's northern entrance stays open from early summer until the first snow falls. Book ahead for a lake-view campsite, or a cozy, modern log cabin that can sleep a family of up to six people.

Drakesbad Guest Ranch
Hidden in the pastoral Warner Valley, this old-fashioned mountain resort dates from the late 19th century. It rents rustic cabins and lodge rooms and serves three square meals a day. You can keep kids busy here with swimming, horseback rides, campfire sing-alongs and stargazing through telescopes.

Summit Lake Campgrounds
In the middle of the park, these woodsy campgrounds are great for families. They're ideally positioned for day hikes, lake swimming and peak climbing, too. Rangers give campfire talks in the outdoor amphitheater nearby. It's smart to reserve a site in advance at this always-popular campground, which is open only during summer.

Do this!

Swimming & boating
In summer, the park's higher-elevation lakes call to swimmers, especially those who are willing to hike out to more secluded spots off the park's main road. Paddlers can rent kayaks, canoes, 'catarafts' and stand-up paddle boarding (SUP) sets from the camper store at Manzanita Lake.

Stargazing
One of California's best dark-sky parks, the heavens above Lassen are undimmed by artificial light pollution, thanks to the park's distance from major urban areas. Rangers give free astronomy programs in summer. Show up during the annual Perseid meteor shower in early August for Lassen's cool Dark Sky Festival.

Cross-country skiing & snowshoeing
When the main park road is closed in winter, you can still go snowshoeing or cross-country skiing if you bring your own equipment. Ungroomed trails start from both the south and north park entrances, leading to frozen lakes and up mountain peaks – the latter for experienced backcountry enthusiasts only.

← Bumpass Hell is the largest hydrothermal area in the park with some of world's hottest fumaroles.

Hike this...

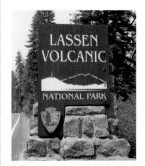

01 Bumpass Hell
Follow the 3-mile (4.8km) boardwalk around a netherworld of wildly colored, steaming pools and mud pots, with inspiring views of Brokeoff Mountain.

02 Lassen Peak
Rise more than 2000ft (610m) as you climb on a recently rebuilt, 5-mile (8km) trail to the summit of the park's highest, most active volcano.

03 Echo Lake
Starting from Summit Lake Campground, it's a refreshing 4.4-mile (7km) hike through the forest to find this blue-green gem, where folks picnic and swim.

 Lassen Volcanic National Park's Painted Dunes are visible from the challenging Cinder Cone trail.

What to spot...

The contrast of cool forests and hot cinder deserts, along a mix of craggy volcanic and mountainous terrain, result in an unusual variety of resident wildlife. More than 200 species of birds have been spotted, including those that stop over during annual spring and fall migrations, as well as more rarely seen birds, such as bald eagles, peregrine falcons and California spotted owls. The mixed conifer forests and alpine peaks here provide habitat for a rainbow of wildflowers too.

SIERRA NEVADA RED FOX Lassen is one of only three places in California where you may spot this small mammal, one of the state's most endangered species.

RED FIR These mighty trees can live for a few hundred years; they grow over 175ft (53m) tall in Lassen's dense forests.

WHITEBARK PINE These stunted, twisted conifers growing at the edge of the tree line are easily recognized, but they're threatened by climate change.

Itineraries

Kayak Manzanita Lake, hike the volcanic summit of Lassen Peak or get some 4WD action out to the turquoise Juniper Lake for stunning views from Mt Harkness.

◄ Pilot Pinnacle, a volcanic remnant.
► Lake Helen, at 8200ft (2500m), is named after Helen Tanner Brodt, the first woman to summit Lassen Peak.

01

A day

Entering the park on winding Hwy 89, the Kohm Yah-mah-nee Visitor Center should be your first stop. Peruse the natural and cultural history exhibits, catch a free nature film in the auditorium and look out over the landscape from inside a LEED platinum-certified green building. Keep driving uphill on the main park road to the Sulphur Works, where stinky vents hiss steam into the air. Pull over at Bumpass Hell to traipse along a wooden boardwalk into the heart of the park's biggest hydrothermal area – its eerie landscape is unforgettable. Picnic on the shores of nearby Lake Helen, above which rises the painterly dome of Lassen Peak. The road continues toward the park's northern entrance, passing through the scars of the volcano's 1915 eruption, where a trail leads around the Devastated Area, and the Chaos Crags and Jumbles, created by dramatic rockslides. Spend the rest of your afternoon by Manzanita Lake, taking a dip or paddling a canoe or kayak in the placid waters. Bed down in a camping cabin or pitch a tent in the lakeshore campground.

02

Two days

Follow the itinerary for day one then on the morning of day two, get up early and backtrack south along the main park road to the trailhead for Lassen Peak. Starting out from a breathtaking elevation of 8500ft (2591m), this adventurous trail tops out on the volcanic summit at 10,457ft (3187m), where you can peer down over the evidence of 300,000 years of eruptions that have shaped this park. Back at the trailhead, hop in your car and drive north to Summit Lake for a picnic lunch and maybe a quick sunlight snooze by the shore. If you're up for it, take a gentle hike out to tranquil Echo Lake, which is less than 2 miles (3.2km) away. You could spend the whole day hiking this chain of lakes, including jaunts to larger Upper and Lower Twin Lakes (if you didn't already while away the morning on Lassen Peak). Before sunset arrives, set up camp at Summit Lake, then join a ranger-led campfire program after dark.

03

Three days

For three days in the park, continue the two-day itinerary then pack up camp at Summit Lake and get back on the main park road heading south. Exit the park and loop (via Hwys 89 and 36) over to the park's remote Warner Valley; it's at least a 90-minute drive from Kohm Yah-mah-nee Visitor Center. In a grassy valley fed by Hot Springs Creek, you'll find the historic Drakesbad Guest Ranch, along with easy trails to pretty lakes that are more serene and less often visited than those along the main park road. Call ahead for reservations to treat yourself to a hearty buffet lunch at the ranch. In the late afternoon, backtrack out of the valley, then take the potholed side road (a 4WD may be required) out to turquoise Juniper Lake, with its beautiful shoreline campground. It's less than a 4-mile (6.4km) round-trip hike from the lake up to the fire lookout on Mt Harkness, affording spectacular views over the countryside.

40

KY

Mammoth Cave National Park

With stalagmites as tall as trees, cathedral-sized chambers and subterranean rivers full of strange, blind cave creatures, visiting Mammoth is like being on another planet.

Descend into an eerie underground world, walking down a damp pathway into a long, dark corridor of rock. Here, hundreds of feet beneath the earth's surface, rock formations bloom like exotic flowers. There's delicate cave coral; striated 'cave bacon'; long, fluted frozen waterfalls; and walls striped and swirled like taffy. The longest known cave system in the world, Mammoth has more than 400 miles (643.8km) of explored passages. It's all due to water drip-drip-dripping its way through the porous limestone for millions of years.

Native American remains have been found in the cave, leading archeologists to believe the first humans entered here about 4000 years ago. According to legend, the cave was rediscovered by settlers at the end of the 18th century, when a hunter chased a wounded bear right up to the cave entrance. Entrepreneurs soon realized Mammoth was full of saltpeter – which is used to make gunpowder – and began mining here during the War of 1812. Later, a doctor bought the cave and turned it into a tuberculosis hospital, believing the cave air would cure his patients. Some died, and the rest left; no one was cured. Noting the great acoustics, locals began holding Christmas singalongs here in 1883; the tradition continues today.

Tourists have been visiting since the 1810s, making this one of the oldest American tourist attractions. Early cave owners used their slaves as tour guides; one such guide, Stephen Bishop, became one of the first people to map the cave and name its features. The limestone hills in the Mammoth region are riddled with caverns; in the early 20th century, local farmers tried to lure tourists heading to Mammoth to their own caves, planting fake signs or claiming Mammoth was closed. The resulting skirmishes became known as 'the Cave Wars'. Today, there are numerous caves to visit in the area, but you can't miss Mammoth itself.

⬆ Throughout the year, park rangers lead subterranean tours of varying degrees of difficulty in Mammoth Caves.
➡ Green River.

Toolbox

When to go
While the outside temperature fluctuates, inside the cave it's a steady 54°F (11°C). Fall is the nicest season for hiking. Reserve cave tours ahead of time, especially in summer.

Getting there
Mammoth Cave is in central Kentucky. Louisville and Nashville, both with major airports, are both about two hours' drive away. The access town of Cave City has numerous motels and restaurants, but isn't much to look at. You'll need a car here.

Park in numbers

82.6
Area covered (sq miles)

1941
Year established

105
Depth of the cave's 'Bottomless Pit' (ft)

Stay here...

Mammoth Cave Hotel
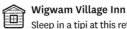
This 1960s brick hotel may not be pretty, but it's the most convenient base for exploring the cave and its surrounds. Right next to the visitor center, it offers basic-but-comfy rooms. Cottages are available during high season. There's a dining room and plenty of spots for picnicking. The cave's entrance is outside the door.

Rock Cabin Camping
Less than 10 minutes from the visitor center, these cool historic cabins were built from local stone in the late 1920s. Today they're kitted out with modern amenities.

Kids (and grown-up kids) will love roasting marshmallows under the stars on the fire pit. An adjacent campsite has tent and RV spots, with showers and toilets nearby.

Wigwam Village Inn
Sleep in a tipi at this retro-tastic Cave City inn, one of three surviving locations of the Wigwam Village chain from the 1920s and '30s. Don't expect luxury: rooms are as basic as they were when the place was built in 1937, and TVs don't feel much newer. But what you will get is a delightful slice of Great American Road Trip kitsch – and cool photo ops.

Do this!

Cave touring
At any time of year, there are a dozen different cave touring options at Mammoth. All are wonderful. The Historic Tour takes you through the old tuberculosis ward; the Violet City Tour is guided by lantern-light to recreate the experience of visiting the cave in the 1800s; and the Wild Cave Tour has you slithering on your belly through narrow passageways.

Horseback riding
Saddle up to roam 60 miles (97km) of horse trails north of the Green River. Local outfitters offer trail rides through the Mammoth Cave hills, traversing grasslands and sun-dappled oak and hickory forests. The

trails are particularly photogenic in autumn, when the leaves turn deep-gold and russet. The park even has a horse-friendly campground.

Canoeing & kayaking
The Green and Nolin Rivers wind through the park, offering opportunity for canoeing and kayaking; bring your own watercraft or book a trip with a local outfitter. You'll cruise through hardwood forests, passing sandbars, islands and bluffs. The waters teem with bass, crappie, bluegill and catfish, so bring a fishing pole if you're so inclined. Look up to see hawks, bald eagles, kingfishers and herons flapping their way through the blue Kentucky sky.

Hike this...

01 River Styx Spring Trail
Worth it for the name alone, this 0.4-mile (0.6km) trail passes through dense forest to where the subterranean River Styx leaves the cave and joins the Green River.

02 Mammoth Cave Railroad Trail
Following the old Mammoth Cave Railroad line, this flat 5-miler (8km) runs through hardwood forest. Ideal during fall, when the leaves put on a show.

03 Cedar Sink Trail
Descend into the valley to a neat limestone sinkhole surrounded by rocky outcroppings – if you're lucky, you'll spot some bats. It's 2 miles (3.2km) round-trip.

What to spot...

Even within the depths of Mammoth Cave, life abides. Far below the surface of the earth, creatures such as Kentucky cave shrimp, eyeless cave fish and blind cave beetles are perfectly suited to their subterranean surrounds. Above ground, the limestone hills, hemlock ravines and forest swamps support white-tailed deer, opossums, bobcats, coyote and bats, as well as a plethora of birds and fish. In spring, the valleys and ridges are carpeted in rue, bluebells, wood poppy and larkspur.

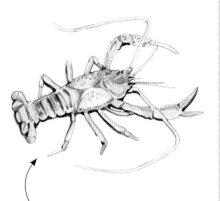

CAVE CRAYFISH These creepy crustaceans look like small, nearly translucent lobsters. They live in cave streams, though they can travel on land if need be.

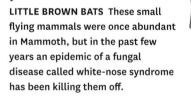

LITTLE BROWN BATS These small flying mammals were once abundant in Mammoth, but in the past few years an epidemic of a fungal disease called white-nose syndrome has been killing them off.

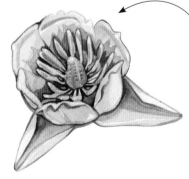

TULIP POPLAR Kentucky's state tree is a tall hardwood that blooms with yellow, tulip-shaped flowers in spring. Look for them in rich, well-drained soil.

Itineraries

Descend into cave history on the Domes and Dripstones Tour, hike the Mammoth Cave Railroad Trail or brave the Wild Cave Tour.

01
A day

Get the most cave in the shortest time period by doubling up on your tours. Park rangers say the Historic Tour and the Domes and Dripstones Tour are an ideal duo, as they cover very different territory. Start off early by descending into the darkness on the two-hour Historic Tour. See the cave through the eyes of a 19th-century visitor, learning about saltpeter mining and passing remnants of the old tuberculosis hospital (spooky!). Afterwards, enjoy a picnic lunch outside under the oaks before plunging back in with the Domes and Dripstones tour. This two-hour trip takes you through the most lavishly decorated parts of the cave – stalactites like icicles; spiky stalagmites; colorful pillars; intricate, frozen waterfalls. Emerge blinking in the afternoon sunlight, in time for a quick hike down to where the River Styx emerges from the cave, its milky jade waters flowing into the Green River. Cap off the day with spicy enchiladas and a margarita at El Mazatlan in Cave City.

02
Two days

On your first day, get the lay of the cave with the 75-minute Frozen Niagara Tour, so-called for the views of its frozen waterfall formation. Guides are full of facts – did you know that bands used Mammoth as an underground amphitheater for string and horn music until the early 20th century? After a picnic, take the 5-mile (8km) hike along the Mammoth Cave Railroad Trail, following the route that passengers used to ride into the park; you can still see Engine Number 4. Sleep in a stone cabin just outside the park at **Rock Cabin Camping**. In the morning, leave any claustrophobia behind and suit up for the 6-hour Wild Cave Tour. You'll descend nearly 300ft (91m) below ground, squeezing through passageways and dragging yourself on your belly through the muck (the park provides you with coveralls). Emerge and head straight for a Southern buffet of fried chicken and mashed potatoes at the park's Travertine Restaurant.

More than 30 miles (48km) of the Green and Nolin Rivers wend their way through the park.

41

CO

Mesa Verde National Park

In an arid corner of southern Colorado, these green mesas loom above the valley, with ancient dwellings etched into their cliffsides.

Mesa Verde is not your typical national park. Though it's a stunner, visitors don't come for its natural beauty, biodiversity or rare species. Instead, they flock to see an astonishing fragment of ancient America. Up until around the year 1300, Ancestral Puebloans inhabited this area and beyond for some 700 years. In that time, they created 600 cliff dwellings, among them homes, *kivas* (ceremonial centers) and storage bins set on alcoves slit into sheer rockface, often hundreds of feet above the valley floor. Ancestral Puebloans were no stranger to adventure.

In some cases, you can't just walk into the past at Mesa Verde. You scramble up ladders, scale rock and crawl through tunnels to enter these ancient homes. Even with helpful railings and rangers, it's exploration at its gritty best. Today there still isn't a full understanding of why the Ancestral Puebloans left this site some seven centuries ago. Browsing the rooms, puzzling over the relics and gazing out over the gawping views is the best way to enter into their long-ago lives.

From 1849 to 1850, a US Army lieutenant documented these spectacular ruins; some 25 years later a pair of cowboys herding stray cattle stumbled upon Cliff Palace, discovering its hundreds of rooms. They soon became guides, leading archaeologists into the site until a Coloradan campaigned for its preservation, leading Congress to enact the Antiquities Act in 1906.

Archeological sites are found throughout the canyons and mesas, perched on a high plateau south of Cortez and Mancos. While much of the park can be explored on your own, some key attractions allow only limited visitation, and others remain off-limits. While hiking takes a back seat, it's still worthwhile, if only to escape the crowds. It's also a great way to search for petroglyphs etched into the rock face.

⬆ Mesa Verde is a World Heritage site. Previous page: the Cliff Palace would have been an important ceremonial building.

Getty Images | Michael Snell; Kenneth Murray; Witold Skrypczak

Toolbox

⚙ **When to go**
The park is open year-round but ranger stations may be closed in the low season (mid-September to mid-May). There's camping from May to mid-October and accommodations from April through October. Summers are hot and winter offers several loops with snowshoe and cross-country skiing access.

🧭 **Getting there**
International flights serve Denver, Colorado, 370 miles (595km) away, with connections to Durango, 36 miles (58km) from the park. There is no public transportation here; rent a vehicle in either city.

Park in numbers

81
Area covered (sq miles)

8571
Highest point: Park Point (ft)

300–400
Number of occupants once living at Cliff Palace alone

Hike this...

01 Petroglyph Loop Trail
It's a challenge to spot all the mystical images on this 2.8-mile (4.5km), family-friendly loop, the only park trail with readily viewed rock art.

02 Spring House
Fit explorers should lace up for the all-day, ranger-led, 8-mile (12.9km) hiking tours to Spring House, a remote alcove that's the largest unexcavated cliff dwelling in the park. Fee required.

03 Spruce Canyon Loop Trail
Explore the shady canyon bottoms via this 2.1-mile (3.4km) loop; it begins at Spruce Tree House, the park's most accessible ruin.

⬆ Rock art, eight centuries old, adorns the cliff-side dwellings.
➡ Descending to the Balcony House at Chaplin Mesa, off the Cliff Palace Loop Rd.

Stay here...

Willowtail Springs

Slow yourself down to the pace of the pond's largemouth bass. Cabins with warm and exotic decor are snuggled into ponderosa forest. Highlights include clawfoot tubs, the owner's fabulous original art, a hot tub and a canoe hitched to the dock. It's also a wildlife sanctuary that releases raptors. For roamers, a little slice of heaven in Mancos.

Morefield Campground

Mesa Verde National Park's only camping option sits on the mesa top, with well-spaced sites on grassy grounds replete with grills and picnic tables. Nearby Morefield Village offers services, including a cafe and grocery store.

Jersey Jim Lookout Tower

From Jack Kerouac to Edward Abbey, some of America's best writers did stints in fire towers, so why shouldn't you? This former fire-lookout tower stands 55ft (17m) above a meadow at an elevation of 9800ft (2987m). Up to four adults can bunk down here, though it must be reserved well in advance. Open mid-May through mid-October. Outside of Mancos.

Do this!

Exploring Cliff Palace

The only way to see this grand engineering achievement with hundreds of rooms and dozens of *kivas* is to take the hour-long tour (fee required). However, it's well worth it. Ranger guides help illuminate the day-to-day experience of Ancestral Puebloans for visitors who follow in their footsteps seven hundred years later.

Exploring Balcony House

Indiana Jones, eat your heart out. To tour the 40 rooms of the Balcony House (one hour, fee required) you'll descend a 100ft (30m) ladder, crawl through a tunnel and negotiate even more ladders and stone steps. The adventure earns you outstanding views of Soda Canyon from Balcony House's large sandstone alcove. Tours are only available from late-April to mid-October.

Cross-country skiing & snowshoeing

In wintertime the crowds disperse and the sun comes out, leaving the cliff dwellings snowbound and sparkly with nary a tourist in sight. Cliff Palace Loop Rd closes to vehicle traffic, so strap on some snowshoes or cross-country skis to make the 6-mile (9.6km) loop, and look closely for rabbit tracks.

What to spot...

With great changes in elevation, Mesa Verde has unique geography along with diverse plant and animal life. Ancestral Puebloans made brilliant use of the park's seep springs and alcoves. There are 640 plant species, the most common being Gamble oaks, juniper, sagebrush and the edible serviceberry. In the park's mostly arid expanse, exuberant plant life lines the Mancos River corridor, attracting birdlife and black bears in berry season. Elk, mule deer and wild turkey frequent the campground.

MEXICAN SPOTTED OWL These owls prefer old-growth forests with high canopies, which are ideal for nesting. They are easily identified by their uniquely dark eyes.

PORCUPINE Arrayed in some 30,000 quills, these nocturnal herbivores are found in cottonwood trees; by day they rest in hollow trees and logs.

ABERT'S SQUIRREL With white tails and big, tufted ears, the small Abert's squirrel feasts on Ponderosa pine cones, dropping leftovers that are later enjoyed by mule deer.

Itineraries

Hike Petroglyph Loop Trail to Park Point for panorama magic, tour grand Cliff Palace or head for mountain biking mayhem at Phil's World.

➲ According to officials, wild horses are an unwelcome addition to Mesa Verde National Park.

01

A day

With Ancestral Puebloan sites scattered throughout the canyons and mesas of Mesa Verde, a day trip is a tall order, so give yourself an early start. Begin at the Chapin Mesa Museum, where prehistoric artefacts help put this group's 700-year habitation of Mesa Verde into context. Next up is Spruce Tree House, a sloping 0.5-mile (0.8 km) walk to an alcove structure dating from 1210. This is the only dwelling that visitors can walk through without a ranger-led tour and it's well worth checking out.

Bring an appetite to the elegant, award-winning Metate Room, where the innovative menu is inspired by Native American foods. Spend the afternoon hiking the Petroglyph Loop Trail or just exploring the views of the many other sites of Chapin Mesa, searching for the tell-tale alcoves. On your way out, stop at the fire lookout at Park Point; at 8571ft (2612m) it's the highest point in the park. Drink in the panorama of the San Juan and La Plata mountains, the sloping plateau, and the volcanic plug known as the Shiprock.

02

A weekend

Begin your first morning at the Mesa Verde Vistor and Research Center to obtain tickets for a ranger-led tour of the limited-access cliff dwellings. These are hot tickets, so aim to take the tour the following day. Continue on to Chapin Mesa, following the itinerary for the day trip. Make the most of your night in the park by attending one of the campfire programs at Morefield Campground. Start the second day in the park with the ticketed tour to Cliff Palace or Balcony House. While the grandeur of Cliff Palace cannot be beat, Balcony House is a blast for the intrepid – but not for agoraphobes or claustrophobes! Stop for lunch at the casual Far View Terrace Cafe, where oversized Navajo tacos are the house specialty. Pass the afternoon visiting peaceful Wetherill Mesa, the less-frequented western side of Mesa Verde. Stroll the mesa top Badger House Community and descend to the Step House; these sites from different eras offer clearer views on how the native culture developed.

03

Four days

Four days in Mesa Verde offers ample time to fully explore the park and bask in its surroundings. Follow the weekend itinerary for the first two days and consider a break from camping with a stay in nearby Cortez or Mancos. Cortez is convenient to Ute Mountain Tribal Park, where you can access fascinating sites from both Utes and Ancient Puebloans. Ute tribal members lead small-group tours with 4WD jeeps. If you opt for a half-day tour, stop in later at Guy Drew Vineyard to see a small, family-run winery.

On your last day, return to Mesa Verde for an all-day hike to Spring House, exploring remote sites along the way. (Remember to reserve this ranger-led tour in advance.) Or if you want a little more adrenaline, return to the Cortez area, where world-class mountain biking awaits at Phil's World, with 32 miles (51.5km) of singletrack rolling through piñon-juniper trees.

Satiate your appetite later at one of Cortez's downtown restaurants –our pick are the grass-fed burgers with tomato jam at Farm Bistro.

42

Mt Rainier National Park

Glacier-capped Mt Rainier, surrounded by waterfalls and meadows, may be among the snowiest places on earth but it's also one of the most sublime.

There you are, rounding a bend on a secluded alpine trail, when suddenly you glimpse brown fur in the bushes. You freeze. Is it a bear? OK, so it's probably just a marmot. If you're on a hike in Mt Rainier National Park, odds are good that you'll run across more than one wild creature along the way.

The mountain's name, surprisingly, has nothing to do with the weather: Rainier was named by the British Navy's Captain George Vancouver for his friend, Rear Admiral Peter Rainier, in 1792. The earliest documented ascent of Mt Rainier happened in 1870; the area was dedicated as a national park in 1899. Fifteen years later, the first cars came trundling along the road between Paradise and Longmire. As with many US national parks, Rainier benefited from the work of the Civilian Conservation Corps, which built and repaired most of its structures in the 1930s.

The park is a wilderness hiker's dream, with more than 260 miles (418.4km) of established trails. Rainier is the highest peak in the Cascade Range; since the 1960s, it has also served as a mountaineering training ground, especially for attempts on Mt Everest, thanks to its challenging terrain. It's an active volcano, formed some 500,000 years ago and then reduced by a few thousand feet in an eruption 5700 years ago. Since the 1800s, however, it's remained relatively calm.

Today Mt Rainier supports more than 35 sq miles (90.6 sq km) of glaciers spreading out from its summit. The glaciers move up to 3ft (0.9m) in a day, depending on weather. Emmons Glacier is easily seen from the viewpoint at Sunrise, the highest car-accessible point in the park. Nisqually Glacier and the Nisqually Icefall are even more accessible: use the Glacier View overlook on the road from Nisqually to Paradise.

Toolbox

When to go
Most roads in the park are closed in winter, except for the stretch between the Nisqually entrance and Paradise. Heavy snow sometimes closes the entrances; check online (www.nps.gov/mora) before you set out. Even in summer, when the temperature averages 70°F (21°C), plan to wear layers and always carry rain gear.

Getting there
Mt Rainier is in west-central Washington, about 87 miles (140km) from Seattle and 136 miles (219km) from Portland, Oregon. It's best reached by car as there's no public transportation to the park.

Park in numbers

369
Area covered (sq miles)

700
Thickness of Carbon Glacier (ft)

14,410
Height of Mt Rainier (ft)

Stay here...

Book well in advance for both of the historic lodges, and for campgrounds on summer weekends.

Paradise Inn
This beautiful and imposing building, listed on the National Register of Historic Places, was built in 1917 and has a stature worthy of its mountain. Rooms are basic (no phones or TVs; many have shared baths) but the huge lobby and comfy dining room both have massive fireplaces and killer views. Open from mid-May through early October.

National Park Inn
This historic 25-room inn in Longmire is open year-round and has something of a ski-lodge vibe (indeed you can also rent cross-country ski equipment and snowshoes here). There's a casual restaurant and lounge.

Cougar Rock Campground
Many of the sites at this lovely, wooded campground have views of the mountain; the outdoor amphitheater features ranger-led programs in the evenings. About half of the sites here are first-come, first-served. Closed in winter.

Do this!

Mountain climbing
Summiting Mt Rainier is one of those lifetime experiences you plan a whole vacation around. And it does take some planning: you'll need a permit to climb above 10,000ft (3048m), and of course you'll need the right training and equipment. If you'd rather not go it alone, there are several guide services available, most of which include training seminars.

Cycling
The steep, winding park roads around Mt Rainier make for thrilling, if rigorous, cycling. September and early October are best for this, with fall colors and reduced car traffic. Up for a challenge? Sign up for RAMROD (Ride Around Mt Rainier in One Day), organized each July by the Redmond Cycling Club.

Cross-country skiing
In winter, the town of Paradise becomes a base for snow sports – primarily cross-country skiing and snowshoeing, but there's also sledding and tubing in a designated play area. You can find trail maps and rental equipment in Longmire.

← Wildflowers at Mt Rainier.
→ From the Skyline Trail hikers can occasionally see as far as Mt Hood in Oregon.

See this...

01 Trail of Shadows
This family-friendly hike is a good way to see the highlights. It starts near the National Park Inn and takes you through the original Longmire settlement.

02 Nisqually Vista Trail
Starting in Paradise, this hike takes just under an hour, offering views of Mt Rainier and the Nisqually Glacier.

03 Skyline Trail
A challenging 5-mile (8km) hike, the Skyline starts at Paradise and follows a high ridge with a 1500ft (457m) elevation gain for views of Mt Adams and Mt St Helens.

What to spot...

Abundant wildlife inhabits Mt Rainier and the surrounding area, including adorable and hard-to-miss marmots, black bears, foxes, rabbits, ptarmigans and snowshoe hares (the latter two likely to be spotted in winter, when they're most active). Plant life includes alpine wildflowers, cedar, fir, hemlock and pine trees, mushrooms, heather and huckleberry shrubs and mountain bunchgrass. The park's elevation changes mean there are several ecosystems, resulting in unusually varied flora and fauna.

DOUGLAS FIR These magnificent conifers live all across the Pacific Northwest (it's the Oregon state tree). Fun fact: strictly speaking, it's not a fir tree – its scientific name means 'false hemlock.'

DOUGLAS SQUIRREL You'll have no trouble spotting these chirruping cuties. They hang out in forested areas all over the park, collecting seeds to eat, and having what must surely be fascinating conversations.

CASCADE RED FOX Small and bushy-tailed, this rare subspecies of red fox lives at the highest elevations in the Cascade mountain range.

Itineraries

Whether you hike the short Trail of the Shadows or the challenging Wonderland Trail, views of Mt Rainier and its glaciers won't fail to impress.

➡ Permits are not required for day hikes; for overnight wilderness camping you'll need to make reservations long in advance.

01

A day

Stop at a visitor center near the park entrance where you came in. Here you'll find a schedule of programs and talks for the day, including nature hikes and films, and you'll also be able to ask about weather, hiking conditions and wildlife (any recent bear sightings?) and get a map. A good place to start is the Longmire Museum; originally the park's headquarters, it still functions as a visitor center, but is also home to several exhibits on the area's natural history. From here, take the short and easy loop hike along the Trail of the Shadows for views of Mt Rainier and the mineral springs that first inspired development of the Longmire area. Be sure to explore the Longmire Historic District while you're here. Drive on to Paradise for refreshments and to scope out the gorgeous lodge. Got some time left? Hike the 1.2-mile (1.9km) round-trip Nisqually Vista Trail, which should take about 45 minutes; it starts from the lower parking lot at Paradise. It offers views of Nisqually Glacier and the slow-motion Nisqually Icefall.

02

A weekend

Take the first day's itinerary to get a feel for the area. Stay the night at the historic Paradise Inn (you'll need to reserve well ahead of time), enjoying its enormous stone fireplace and rough-hewn glory. In the morning, pack a lunch and make your way up the Skyline Trail, starting from the upper parking lot at Paradise. This fairly strenuous four-hour, 5-mile (8km) hike ascends the Alta Vista Ridge for excellent views of the surrounding glaciers and peaks, including Mt Adams and Mt St Helens. Be sure to check in at the visitor center first and make sure trail conditions are okay; it's a good idea to be flexible with your day-hike plans, as some trails may be closed and others busy, depending on time of year. After your hike, have dinner and spend the night at the National Park Inn, Rainier's other historic lodge (again, reserve well ahead); it's in Longmire, convenient for exiting the park at Nisqually the next morning.

03

10 to 14 days

With this much time, you can backpack the 93-mile (150km) Wonderland Trail circling Mt Rainier – and you should! Get backcountry permits in advance and make the usual preparations for a multi-day backpacking trip: plan your route with topographical maps, talk to rangers and be sure your hiking buddies are prepared, mentally and physically, for the duration and difficulty of the hike. Making the full loop requires careful planning and a skills assessment, particularly in choosing the distance between your camping spots. (Camping along the trail was limited to designated campgrounds at press time; check with rangers for the latest rules.) It's a challenging route and perhaps not ideal for brand-new backpackers: the ups and downs along the trail are fairly extreme, with elevations ranging from roughly 2300ft to 6400ft (701m to 1951m). Parts of the trail are snow-packed from October through at least June; meanwhile, you may find a lot of competition for campsites in July and August (the busiest months), especially on weekends.

Mt Rainier

43

North Cascades National Park

Dramatic and daunting, remote and challenging, this eerie wilderness in the Northwest attracts adrenalin-seekers like no other.

Getty Images | Mike Tittel

That only-person-on-earth feeling happens a lot in the North Cascades. Huge swaths of the landscape feel completely untouched, even though native peoples have lived in this area for thousands of years. The whole area somehow feels newly made, the glaciers on its jagged peaks creating streams and rivers before your eyes, the deeply carved valleys presenting you with gem-colored lakes. If what you're after is a sense of awe and a true appreciation for the land in this part of the world, you've come to the right place.

Established in 1968, the park is bisected by Ross Lake National Recreation Area. At the southern tip of the park is 50-mile-long (80.5km) Lake Chelan, most of which can only be reached on foot or by boat. The whole park complex, including the Ross and Chelan recreational areas, forms the core of more than 2 million acres (8094 sq km) of federally designated wilderness, the immense variety of which supports an unparalleled diversity of habitat. Among other things, it's a fantastic place to study an ecosystem in the raw and to monitor the effects of climate change.

The North Cascades is home to 312 glaciers, a third of all the glaciers in the lower 48 United States. All these glaciers and lakes feed into thousands of miles of rivers, providing great fishing and some epic waterfalls.

The subalpine region of the park historically was home to many Northwest Coast Indian settlements; archaeological digs have found 260 prehistoric sites, including homesteads, mines, and sheep farming settlements. On the cliffs around Lake Chelan there are ancient pictographs made with red ocher (see the replica panel at the visitor center in Newhalem). The study of archaeological sites here has led to new understanding in several areas of human activity across the centuries.

Toolbox

When to go
The park is open all year, but parts of the North Cascades Highway are closed in winter (usually mid-November to mid-April). The Park and Forest Information Center in Sedro-Woolley is open year-round. In July and August, wildfires may close roads and trails; check with ranger stations.

Getting there
The park complex is in northern Washington. State Hwy 20 (the North Cascades Hwy) provides the main access route through the park; the Golden West Visitor Center at the north end of Lake Chelan is accessible only by ferry or floatplane. Otherwise the park is best visited by car.

Park in numbers

1068
Area covered (sq miles)

9206
Highest point: Goode Mountain (ft)

400
Lowest point: Skagit River (ft)

Stay here...

Ross Lake Resort

Getting here really is half the fun: a night at this tranquil, isolated resort means a steep 2-mile (3.2km) hike from Hwy 20 down to a ferry dock. At the dock you'll find a mysterious telephone; pick it up to summon a water taxi, which will fetch you across the lake to the resort's string of floating wooden cabins. Once there you can also rent kayaks and rowboats for further exploring.

Stehekin Valley Ranch

You don't have much to worry about if you stay here: the ranch takes care of everything, from all your meals to transportation across the 50-mile (80.5km) Lake Chelan. On arrival, settle into a cabin with a private bath, or perhaps a more rustic tent-style cabin, and explore the surroundings by horseback. Haven't had enough of the lake? Opt for a guided kayak tour.

Colonial Creek Campground

Set in an old-growth forest at the edge of Diablo Lake, this campground is hard to beat. Kids and grown-ups alike will find the evening programs led by rangers both educational and entertaining, and during the day you can walk around the lake or choose from several other hiking trails that showcase the area's natural wonders.

Do this!

Boating

Take a cruise on the Lady of the Lake to the historic town of Stehekin, set at the headwaters of Lake Chelan. Catch the boat in the town of Chelan for either a day trip or a few days of backpacking. Gear up before you go: Stehekin is tiny and remote, reachable only by boat, hiking trail or floatplane.

Fishing

The Skagit River has trout, salmon and char. In Lake Chelan you can catch trout, kokanee and freshwater cod, while the Stehekin River is home to rainbow and cutthroat trout. You'll need to get a Washington state fishing license.

Learning

Get the kids hooked on nature with a fun and educational program organized through the Environmental Learning Center at the North Cascades Institute, an ecofriendly residential campus on Diablo Lake. Arrange for a day trip, long weekend or backcountry excursion with the family.

◀ The hike to Blue Lake is relatively short. Previous page: hiking on the Sahale Arm.

What to spot...

The wildly varying terrain of the North Cascades – from lowland forests to glacial peaks – supports a huge amount of biodiversity. The park boasts 75 mammal species and 200 types of birds, as well as plentiful fish. In terms of diversity, however, its plant life is where the park really shines: it has over 200,000 acres (809 sq km) of old-growth forest and more than 1600 different vascular plant species (no one seems to have counted all the fungi).

BALD EAGLE The national bird of the United States and sacred in many Native American cultures, the bald eagle is always thrilling to spot, even in places where it's relatively common.

BLACK-TAILED MULE DEER These are the most common hoofed animals native to the park.

CHINOOK SALMON
During fall, the Chinook and other salmon fight their way up the Skagit River to spawn. This is also your best time for seeing a bald eagle.

Hike this...

O1 River Loop Trail
One of several hikes near Newhalem, this easy, 1.8-mile (2.9km) loop starts at the visitor center and connects to the 'To Know a Tree' interpretive trail.

O2 Thornton Lake Trail
A fairly steep one-way 5-mile (8km) hike to a subalpine lake, this trail ascends through mature woods to alpine heather and huckleberry fields before reaching a high ridge.

O3 Bridge Creek Trail
This 12-mile (19.3km) stretch of the Pacific Crest Trail provides the easiest hiking route to Stehekin.

Itineraries

Hike the Diablo Lake Trail for exquisite waterfall and lake scenery, boat around Lake Chelan or do a little dusk fishing for maximum serenity.

◄ Trails in the park range from woodland walks to alpine ascents.
► Traversing the challenging North Ridge of Forbidden Peak.

01

A day

Cruise through the park on the North Cascades Hwy (State Hwy 20), starting from Marblemount along the Skagit River. Stop at the North Cascades National Park Visitor Center in Newhalem for a slew of information on the area; if you're lucky, you'll arrive in time for a ranger-led nature walk or presentation. If not, choose a self-guided hike from the many short trails that start at Newhalem, all of which make for scenic walks in the woods. Afterward, continue along Hwy 20 to Diablo Lake, where you'll find excellent picnic sites as well as more hiking; if time allows, take the Diablo Lake Trail, just over 7 miles (11.3km) round-trip, which climbs through old-growth forest and along dry creek beds to a steep gorge with impressive waterfalls, all the while featuring views of the turquoise lake below. If you're all hiked out, opt for some fishing in the lake, followed by an educational visit to the Environmental Learning Center, which offers programs and classes focusing on the ecosystem of the North Cascades. (Reverse this route if you're driving east to west.)

02

A weekend

Start your weekend just south of the park complex in the town of Chelan; load up on supplies here, park your car at the ferry dock, then hop on board the Lady of the Lake boat and head out onto beautiful Lake Chelan. The 50-mile (80.5km) boat ride to the tiny, historic settlement of Stehekin (the population is about 80 permanent residents) is an experience all its own.

Spend the night in Stehekin – you'll want to have booked accommodations well in advance – where the isolation and majesty of the surroundings combine to create an atmosphere you won't soon forget. **You might do some fishing at dusk, or just relax and enjoy the quiet. The next day, do a loop hike heading out from Stehekin (ask for recommendations at the Golden West Visitor Center first; fauna and flora includes woodpeckers and western red cedars) before catching the boat back to Chelan in the evening.**

03

A week

In a whole week, you have time to do both the previous itineraries and then some. Start with the Stehekin overnight trip, then head back onto Hwy 20 toward the Washington Pass Overlook. From here it's a short hop to join the Bridge Creek Trail, a segment of the famous Pacific Crest Trail. You could take this trail back to Stehekin, but there are also any number of round-trips or loop hikes that make for as much backpacking as you have time and energy to do; ask at a ranger station for recommendations. The backcountry campground at Bridge Creek is a good overnight stop; better yet, stay several nights here and spend some time day-hiking in all directions to get a sense of the variety of the landscape. After your hike, head back onto Hwy 20 and northwest to explore Diablo Lake and Newhalem. For your last day, take the short, steep hike up to Thornton Lake for a lofty picnic lunch overlooking the lake before exiting the park complex.

44

WA

Olympic National Park

It's often said, but this place feels like another world – or rather, three other worlds: mossy rainforest, lonely coastline, craggy peak.

Getty Images | Greg Vaughn

Each of this park's environments is so distinct that it really isn't much of a stretch to imagine that Hwy 101, which connects them, is some sort of interplanetary roadway. But in fact this otherworldly beauty is all right here in the same park – easily reached, no spaceship required.

The core of the park is Mt Olympus and its namesake Olympic mountain range. Flowing west from the mountain and into the Pacific Ocean is the Hoh River, surrounded by deep green rainforests full of huge trees draped in moss. And northwest of the river's mouth lie about 62 miles (99.8km) of the wildest coastal habitat left intact in the world.

Olympic National Park occupies the center of the remote, roughly triangular Olympic Peninsula and is adjacent to the reservations of several American Indian tribes: the Skokomish, Makah, Hoh, Quinault, Quileute, Jamestown S'Klallam, Port Gamble S'Klallam and Lower Elwha Klallam all have strong cultural ties to the land here. Traditions of the coastal tribes include the potlatch, an elaborate feast and social gathering. Most of the visitor centers in the park offer schedules of tribal cultural events and programs.

The Spanish explored this area in the 1770s, setting up a beachhead at Neah Bay in 1792. (It was abandoned after only a few months.) Pioneers of all sorts followed them here through the 1800s. The first pioneer settlement to be permanently established on the Olympic Peninsula was Port Townsend, in 1851.

A presidential tag team established the park: first, President Theodore Roosevelt decreed Mt Olympus a National Monument in 1909. Then in 1938, President Franklin

D Roosevelt signed the Olympic National Park into existence. Coastal wilderness was added to the park later, in 1953. The park is 95% wilderness and is officially protected from most development, including building, timber cutting, mining and hunting.

Getty Images | David Schultz

Toolbox

 When to go
Many areas of the park are unreachable in winter; most entrances are open all year, but roads may be closed due to weather. At high elevations, it can snow year-round. Summer is relatively warm and dry, but be prepared for rain and sub-70°F (21°C) temperatures. December and January see the most rain.

 Getting there
Olympic National Park is in northwestern Washington, about 90 miles (145km) west of Seattle. Access is via US Hwy 101. It's best reached by car. Clallam Transit (www.clallamtransit.com) has commuter bus routes between Port Angeles, Clallam Bay, Forks, Neah Bay and La Push.

Park in numbers

1442
Area covered (sq miles)

73
Length of wilderness coastline (miles)

300
Bird species

Stay here...

🏠 **Lake Quinault Lodge** Perched on the shore of Lake Quinault, this grand lodge blends a 1920s park vibe with Native American design elements. The dining room is named for Franklin D Roosevelt, who visited here in 1937. There are ranger talks, interpretive hikes and evening programs in summer, as well as boat tours and boat rentals.

🏠 **Kalaloch Lodge** This impressive coastal lodge has rooms, cabins and kitchenettes, all with private baths, and a restaurant-bar with stellar views. It's right at the edge of a marine wildlife sanctuary, so look for otters and various tidepool inhabitants. The lodge is 36 miles (58km) south of Forks along US 101.

⛺ **Kalaloch Campground** The only one of the park's 16 campgrounds that accepts reservations (the others are first-come, first-served), this forested area is situated high above the ocean on a bluff. Many of its sites have ocean views. It's open all year and has great access to coastal hiking trails.

Do this!

🎒 **Hiking** From the Hoh Visitor Center there are numerous self-guided hikes through the Hoh Rain Forest, or you can also join a ranger-led nature walk to learn even more about the area's unique features and natural history. Don't forget to bring your rain gear!

📖 **Learning** The Makah Museum in Neah Bay holds hundreds of artifacts from archeological research into a Makah village near Ozette that was partially buried in a mudslide around 1750. There are also guided tours and demonstrations of traditional weaving and carving practiced by native peoples.

〰️ **Soaking in hot springs** Cap off a hike or a long drive with some relaxing in Sol Duc's three mineral hot springs pools. You can also book a massage. Sol Duc Falls are an easy 3-mile (4.8km) hike from the hot springs resort (and if you're really in relaxation mode, you can drive two of those miles and only hike the last one).

← Olympic National Park receives a lot of rain, making it one of the wettest places in the US. Previous page: hiking past maple trees on the Hall of Mosses Trail in the Hoh Rain Forest.

What to spot...

The wildly different environments that make up the Olympic National Park – mountain, coast, temperate rainforest – result in equally diverse habitats and wildlife. Much of the coastline is a protected marine-life sanctuary: exploration of tidepools here is extremely rewarding. Bears, deer and elk roam from the lowlands to the alpine meadows of the Olympic mountain range, while the rainforests between mountains and coast teem with plant and animal life.

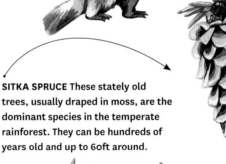

OLYMPIC MARMOT Found only on the Olympic Peninsula, these cat-size creatures are friendly and social. They eat mostly flowering plants and hibernate in winter.

SITKA SPRUCE These stately old trees, usually draped in moss, are the dominant species in the temperate rainforest. They can be hundreds of years old and up to 60ft around.

ROOSEVELT ELK The park is home to the largest wild group of Roosevelt elk in the US. They like to graze the forest floor in the temperate rainforests.

Hike this...

01 Hall of Mosses

This 0.8-mile (1.3km) family-friendly trail starts at the Hoh Visitor Center and wanders through thick rainforest, with moss-draped trees and a carpet of ferns. Keep an eye out for elk.

02 Ozette Lake to Sand Point

From the Ozette Visitor Center (off US 112), a 3-mile (4.8km) boardwalk path leads to the beach at Cape Alava; continue along the coastline to Sand Point for a 9.3-mile (15km) round-trip.

03 North Wilderness Beach Hike

The only way to access parts of the coastal wilderness, this 20-mile (32km) trail goes from Ozette Trailhead to Rialto Beach, taking two to three days.

Itineraries

Twilight fans head for Forks, but Hurricane Ridge's views will also make the blood rush. Hike Hoh River Trails or soak at Sol Duc Hot Springs.

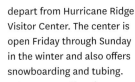

◄ A black-tailed deer on Cape Alava. Savoring Second Beach. ➤ Summer brings Indian Paintbrush flowers and lupines.

01
A day

With only a day to explore, start your visit at the Olympic National Park Visitor Center in Port Angeles. Behind the visitor center is an interpretive trail that makes a good appetizer for the park. From here, drive up the spur road to Hurricane Ridge (off Hwy 101). The views from this road are absolutely dizzying, and there's a gorgeous field of wildflowers sloping down from the top in spring and summer. If you're here in winter, ask about ranger-guided snowshoe and cross-country ski tours that depart from Hurricane Ridge Visitor Center. The center is open Friday through Sunday in the winter and also offers snowboarding and tubing.

In summer, if you're up for a little more driving (and possible vertigo), venture along the 8-mile (12.9km) gravel Obstruction Point Rd, which goes east from Hurricane Ridge, for awesome views of Mt Olympus. Trails in this subalpine area include the difficult but rewarding 14-mile (22km) Grand Valley loop, best attempted when you have more than one day.

02
Two days

Start as per day one, but when you return to the base of Hurricane Ridge, continue driving west on US Hwy 101. You'll pass Lake Crescent, which makes a good place for a picnic lunch. From here, head toward Sol Duc, which is just past the lake on a spur road bearing south. Settle into a cabin at the Sol Duc Hot Springs resort for the night; you can soak in the resort's powder-blue hot-spring pools. Start the next day with a short hike through old-growth forest to the Sol Duc Falls before heading back out.

03
A week

Follow the two-day itinerary, but after your Sol Duc hike, return to Hwy 101 and head west to Lake Ozette. (Keep in mind that driving between points on Olympic Peninsula often takes much longer than you might think. Be sure to refuel at every opportunity.) Stay the night at a lakeside lodge or campsite, then set out the next morning on the trail from Ozette Lake to Sand Point. Return to Ozette for another night, or push on northward to Neah Bay. The next day, spend some time at the Makah Museum in Neah Bay. Then it's back on the road, a roundabout route to Forks, where there are a handful of options for food and lodging, plus plenty of vampire lore (it's the setting for the *Twilight* series of books and films).

From Forks, head inland to the Hoh Rain Forest Visitor Center. Take a ranger-guided tour, or set out on your own into the dark and mysterious woods along the Hall of Mosses trail. If you have time, extend the hike by following the Hoh River Trail, which is 18 miles (29km) in total, as far as you like; there are waterfalls along the way.

Spend the night at the Hoh Campground. Next day, head back toward the coast, where Kalaloch Lodge and campground await. This is an ideal base for exploring the wild coastline, most of it accessible only by foot or boat. Kalaloch Ranger Station will have details and a schedule of walks and talks, or you can hike around on your own. There are also boat rentals and guided tours available. Spend the night here at the lodge or campground before meandering back toward your entry point the next day.

45

AZ

Petrified Forest National Park

Time travelers from the Triassic Period, petrified trees now rest comfortably on windswept grasslands flanked by brilliant badlands and intricate petroglyphs.

It takes a moment to comprehend the Crystal Forest. At first glance, the fossilized logs scattered across the landscape look like charred bales of hay. Or maybe they're embers left in the sand from a campfire built by giants. But a short walk on the Crystal Forest Trail reveals the true magic of the park's namesake treasures – each ancient tree hides a kaleidoscopic core of fiery reds, oranges and purples. Some even sparkle with crystals.

Rivers carried the trees to the floodplain here 225 million years ago. Silica-rich volcanic ash buried the trees before they could decompose. Groundwater dissolved the silica, which seeped into the logs and eventually crystallized into quartz. Iron, manganese and other colorful minerals joined the party. The 'forests' scattered across the southern reaches of the park began as log jams millions of years ago. Old Faithful, almost 10ft (3m) across, basks in the sun behind the Rainbow Forest Museum.

The rest of the park is a cabinet of curiosities writ large. Scenic overlooks and spur trails on the 28-mile (45km) scenic drive spotlight an amazing diversity of sights. At sunset, the Painted Desert, in the northern sector of the park, glows in a broad palette of colors. The Painted Desert Inn shares the region's history. Just south, a weathered jalopy memorializes Route 66, which bounced through the grasslands here in the mid-1900s. Ancestral Puebloans called the region home between AD 650 and the early 1400s – their eye-catching petroglyphs at Newspaper Rock suggest that social media is not a modern invention.

President Theodore Roosevelt established Petrified Forest National Monument in December of 1906, pursuant to the Antiquities Act, which had been created to protect Native American sites in the Southwest. The monument became a national park in 1962. Today, there is a breezy, unhurried vibe to the place. So ease off the pedal and relax – those rocks aren't going anywhere soon.

Toolbox

When to go
For wildflower viewing, the best time to visit is April and May, but the park can be windy in spring. Summer is high season. For the most pleasant weather and conditions, visit in fall.

Getting there
The park straddles the I-40 in northeastern Arizona. Flagstaff, Arizona, is 115 miles (185km) west; Albuquerque, New Mexico, is 204 miles (328km) east. Sky Harbor Airport in Phoenix is 260 miles (418km) southwest via I-40 and I-17. To prevent backtracking, westbound travelers should exit I-40 at exit 311; eastbound travelers should take exit 285 to Hwy 180 south.

Park in numbers

346
Area covered (sq miles)

650
Number of Newspaper Rock Petroglyphs

1250–1400
Human occupation of Puerco Pueblo (AD)

Stay here...

Homolovi State Park Campground
You'll be camping a short distance from Ancestral Hopi ruins at this state park, established in 1993. The setting? Scrubby grasslands with big-sky views. The campground is 50 miles (80km) west of the national park, which does not have a campground.

Wigwam Motel
To get your kicks on Route 66, drop your bags inside a concrete tipi at the beloved Wigwam Motel in Holbrook. Rooms are furnished with 1950s logpole furniture, and each tipi squeezes in a bathroom and a shower. Vintage cars in the parking lot add to the mid-century mood.

La Posada Hotel & Gardens
Art, history and architecture merge elegantly at La Posada, a grand hacienda in Winslow that originally opened in 1930. Designed by Mary Jane Colter, La Posada was the last of the grand railroad hotels commissioned by the Fred Harvey Company along the Santa Fe line.

Do this!

Cultural learning
Swirls. Footprints. Wild animals. Were Ancestral Puebloans leaving messages about local game? Were their shaman transcribing their visions? Or maybe the petroglyphs are no more than the doodles of a daydreamer. Make your own guesses from the catwalk overlooking the rocks at Newspaper Rock. For up-close views, check out the carvings beside the Puerco Pueblo Trail.

Historic touring
The Painted Desert Inn no longer hosts overnight guests, but it does welcome travelers interested in learning about the building's history and architecture. Hopi murals and exhibits spotlighting the Civilian Conservation Corps and Route 66 are highlights. Poke around the 1920s-era building on your own or join a ranger-led tour.

Cycling
The 28-mile (45km) Scenic Rd curves past the Painted Desert, then passes semi-arid grasslands, forests of petrified wood, Ancestral Puebloan ruins and crumbling badlands. Plan your trip for spring or fall, when traffic is lighter. Bike rentals are available in Flagstaff.

← A collared lizard warms itself on a fossilized log.
→ Rock art at the Newspaper Rock site, created by ancestral Puebloan people.

Hike this...

01 Blue Mesa
This steep, 1-mile (1.6km) loop drops into delicate badlands. The bentonite clay casts an otherworldly, blue-tinged spell.

02 Long Logs & Agate House
The largest collection of petrified trees in the park fronts a partially restored prehistoric pueblo. The hike is 2.6 miles (4.2km) round-trip.

03 Painted Desert Rim
The Painted Desert struts its stuff at sunset, when layered deposits of clay and sandstone put on a luminous show. An easy 0.5-mile (0.8km) trail between Tawa and Kachina Points provides a lofty view.

What to spot...

The lofty Colorado Plateau stretches across northern Arizona and parts of New Mexico, Colorado and Utah, a region collectively known as the Four Corners. Semi-arid native grasslands blanket the national park, which is dotted with mesas and badlands. Plants and animals here are a hardy breed, having adapted to an extreme range of temperatures. Early morning and dusk are best for wildlife viewing.

BLACK-TAILED JACKRABBIT
That pair of black-tipped ears – all 6in (15cm) of them – is to aid heat loss. These athletic hares can run up to 40mph (64km/h) and jump 20ft (6m).

PRONGHORN The fastest land animal in the country, these graceful antelopes can run about 60mph (97km/h). The backward-facing horns of male pronghorns can extend 12in (30cm).

GREATER SHORT-HORNED LIZARD
With a face only a mother could love, this flat and stocky lizard is noted for its spiky horns and pointy scales. When threatened, they may squirt blood from their eyes or poke at predators with their horns.

240

Itineraries

Take it easy with an Eagles tribute in Winslow, hit the Painted Desert for Hopi murals and sunsets or take a scenic drive to Crystal Forest.

← The Blue Mesa.
→ Fossilized trees from the Late Triassic period on the Long Logs Loop trail.

01

A day

As you drive past the ranger booth at the southern entrance, it feels like you're entering a prehistoric *Land of the Lost*. You won't see any dinosaurs lumbering about, but the giant petrified logs and the parched grasslands evoke a more dangerous age. The skeletons of giant lizards, stalking across the Rainbow Forest Museum, add to the menacing vibe. Join the ranger-led Triassic Talk, then walk the Giant Logs Trail.

From the museum, the 28-mile (45km) scenic road ribbons north, with pull-offs and spur trails along the way. The petrified trees scattered across the Crystal Forest were once part of an ancient log jam. Just north, on the Blue Mesa Loop Trail, the blue-tinged badlands are photographic fodder for your Instagram feed. On the Puerco Pueblo trail, a shaft of sunlight hits a spiral-shaped pictograph every year on June 21st, accurately marking the summer solstice.

Continuing north, the scenic drive rolls past I-40 into the northern section of the park, home to the Painted Desert badlands. Just beyond the highway, a rusted vintage car and an interpretative marker celebrate Route 66 – this is the only national park that's home to a stretch of the Mother Road. Enjoy a picnic lunch and views of the Painted Desert at Chinde Point Overlook.

Hopi murals are a highlight in the historic Painted Desert Inn. From here, take your pick of overlooks to watch the Painted Desert change colors as the sun drops on the horizon.

02

Two days

Breakfast at the Turquoise Room in Winslow's La Posada Hotel isn't for the timid: strawberry Belgian waffles, green-chile eggs, bread pudding slathered with prickly pear syrup – it's a decadent affair. After breakfast, take a few photos at Standin' on the Corner Park. This fun-loving spot celebrates the classic song 'Take it Easy' by The Eagles.

From here, it's an easy 50-mile (80.5km) drive to the southern entrance to the park. Check out the fossils and phytosaur diorama in the Rainbow Forest Museum.

The largest petrified log in the park, Old Faithful, sits a few steps away on the Giant Logs Trail. Follow the scenic drive north to the Crystal Forest. Crystals lurk in some of the petrified logs littering the forest's rocky plain. Sharp-eyed visitors may spot fossils embedded in the eroding badlands along the Blue Mesa Trail just north.

Ancestral Puebloans carved petroglyphs into the rocks at Newspaper Rock up to 2000 years ago – bring binoculars for optimal viewing. Enjoy a picnic at Chinde Point, then drive to Kachina Point to start an overnight backpack into the wilderness. Drop your tent at least 1 mile (1.6km) from the trailhead, then savor the backcountry solitude.

On day two, enjoy the sunrise then hike back to Kachina Point. Drive south to view the ruins of a 100-room pueblo on the Puerco Pueblo Trail. For one last look at petrified trees, walk the Long Logs Trail, which passes a lot of fossilized logs. For keepsakes, pull into Jim Gray's Petrified Wood Company, 1 mile (1.6km) south of Holbrook.

46

CA

Pinnacles National Park

Craggy volcanic peaks where endangered California condors fly shape the USA's newest national park, which feels almost like a secret.

Rocks jutting up toward the sky define Pinnacles' topography of peaks, canyons and caves. The park is all that remains of an ancient volcano born over 20 million years ago and far away, near the modern city of Los Angeles. Tectonic plate movement along California's earthquake-prone San Andreas Fault slowly dragged the volcano almost 200 miles (322km) north of its original location – incredibly, it keeps moving another 1in (2.5cm) every year. Over eons, wind and water eroded the volcano – which was once almost as tall as Mt St Helens – into the unusually shaped terrain you'll see today.

You might not expect such rich wildlife packed into a territory so small. Above the tangled chaparral that covers the valley floor and rolling hills, vertical cliffs and spires reach hundreds of feet into the air, making Pinnacles an ecological island. As you hike and climb among the jagged high peaks, where bears and wolves once prowled, you might be lucky enough to spot a California condor soaring overhead. The park is one of only a few release sites state-wide where captive-bred condors are set free into the wild, which is vital to species conservation and recovery efforts. Back down closer to earth, over a dozen kinds of bats roost in the park's unusual talus caves.

More than a century after President Theodore Roosevelt declared it a national monument, Pinnacles became the USA's youngest national park in 2013. It's also one of the smallest US national parks, and often overlooked because California superstars like Yosemite and Death Valley get more press. Yet finding this hidden spot is part of the fun. Pinnacles lies east of the agricultural Salinas Valley in rural Central California. It's a slow drive inland from US Hwy 101, which traces El Camino Real, the 18th-century road built by Spanish colonists between their Catholic missions, the first European settlements in what was then a province of Mexico.

Toolbox

When to go
A Mediterranean climate makes spring and fall ideal for visiting. Summers are exceedingly hot and humid, with daytime highs over 100°F (38°C). Winter temperatures may slip below freezing overnight.

Getting there
Pinnacles is just over two hours' drive southeast of San Francisco and SFO international airport. The park's east and west entrances are not connected by road – the only way to get between them is on foot. The main visitor facilities are on the park's east side.

Park in numbers

41.6
Area covered (sq miles)

3304
Highest elevation: Chalone Peak (ft)

238
Wild California condors left in the world

Stay here...

Pinnacles Campground
Near the park's east entrance, this family campground opens its outdoor swimming pool seasonally. Campsites are spacious and often partly shaded by oak trees, with a campers' general store just a short walk away. Watch out for wild turkeys strutting through your campsite in the morning!

Inn at the Pinnacles
Only a 10-minute drive from the park, this B&B inn is set among vineyards in Monterey County. Swim in the outdoor pool, sink into a deep-soaking tub in your suite, or grill dinner on the back patio. Rooms are simple, but some have gorgeous views of the surrounding countryside.

Joshua Inn Bed & Breakfast
About 30 miles (48.2km) northwest of the park in the town of Hollister, this lemon-yellow, turreted 1902 Queen Anne Victorian is an old-fashioned place, complete with a croquet set on the lawn, penny candies and themed rooms. The gourmet breakfast will fill you up.

Do this!

Rock climbing
Rock jocks scale walls and cliffs and tackle boulders alongside trails. Options range from top-roping for beginners to expert multi-pitch climbs. (Our favorite climbing route name? 'Tourist Trap.') Climbers should be aware of closures due to raptor nesting in sensitive areas from January through July.

Caving
Talus caves filled with jumbled rockfall are perfect for beginning spelunkers, because you can walk right up to them and step inside (bring a flashlight). Some caves are closed in late spring and summer, when bats roost inside. During the rest of the year, they are accessible to hikers via gentle trails that even kids can manage.

Nighttime exploring
Check the park's online calendar and make reservations to secure your spot on a moonlight or dark-sky hike, a nighttime cave exploration or a stargazing party with telescopes pointed into the Milky Way. These special, ranger-guided programs usually take place on weekends.

← Looking across the Pinnacles National Park to the High Peaks.
→ The lower entrance to Bear Gulch Cave.

Hike this...

01 High Peaks Trail
Make a thrilling, 5.3-mile (8.5km) ascent of the park's iconic rock formations on this steep, narrow trail, with steps and railings to help you.

02 Moses Spring & Rim Trail Loop
An easy, family-friendly, 2.2-mile (3.5km) hike passes through rocky scenery and heads out to Bear Gulch Cave.

03 Chalone Peak Trail
For eye-popping vistas, make a strenuous, 9-mile (14.5km) climb to the top of the park's tallest mountain, gaining over 2000ft (610m) in elevation.

What to spot...

From tiny ladybugs to enormous condors, a variety of wildlife thrives inside this isolated park. Birders will have a field day checking off various riparian, woodland and chaparral species, and even amateurs may be able to spot a raptor, such as a golden eagle or an American kestrel flying around the park's high cliffs. Inside Balconies and Bear Gulch Caves, you can glimpse more than half of all of the bat species found across California.

CALIFORNIA CONDOR Pulled back from the brink of extinction, North America's largest land bird spreads its wings almost 10ft (3m) wide and can fly over 150 miles (241.4km) in search of food.

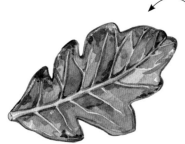

TOWNSEND'S BIG-EARED BAT Immediately recognizable by its extra-long ears, this brown bat roosts in the darkness of talus caves.

BLUE OAK Providing shelter and acorns for animals and shade for human campers, this woodland tree is just one of California's 20 majestic native oak species.

244

Itineraries

Hike the High Peaks loop, eyes peeled for California condors or be at one with the bats at Bear Gulch Caves.

 You can't miss the vivid blue of a Steller's jay.
→ Explore the volcanic spires of the Gabilan Mountains.

01

An afternoon

On your drive between Southern California's desert parks and the redwoods of Northern California, take the slower, scenic route up Hwy 101 along California's Central Coast, instead of the I-5 Fwy – then you'll have time for a quick detour to this peaceful park. On the park's west side, roll into Bear Gulch just in time to set out a picnic lunch underneath shady oak trees.

After stopping into the visitor center for a trail map, set out on foot to make a circuit of the High Peaks. As the trail grows ever narrower, climbing up steps carved into the stone, stop to spot myriad birds and for panoramic photos of the rocky pinnacles set against the mountains of the Coast Ranges beyond. Look out for rare California condors, which have a white spot on the underside of each of their black wings. As you loop down and around back to Bear Gulch, swing out to Bear Gulch Caves, where bats roost among the talus rocks.

02

A day

You can see and do a lot in just one day at this surprisingly small park. Start by driving across the valley flatlands to the park's east entrance. Stock up on drinks and snacks at the campers' general store, just inside the park. Keep driving west to Bear Gulch, where rangers at the visitor center can give you a free map and talk over all of your hiking options. But if you've only got one day, you'll want to do the High Peaks loop, hiking more than 5 miles (8km) up to the very tip-top of rocky precipices, then loping back downhill to Bear Gulch.

After lazing in the shade to have lunch and take a quick rest, follow a much easier hiking loop that leads to and through Bear Gulch Cave. Otherwise, rope up (with expert help if required) on one of Pinnacles' famous climbing routes, pitting your strength and agility against the sheer walls and oddly shaped rocks of this eroded ancient volcano.

03

Two days

Two days in the park gives you time to get out and explore places that most day-trippers miss. On day one, cruise from Hwy 101 over to the park's east side and pitch a tent at Pinnacles Campground, where you can swim in the outdoor pool if the weather is hot enough. Head west to Bear Gulch and hike out to its famous namesake cave, then hoof it up the High Peaks Trail, pausing to snap a photo of sunset over the valley. Head back to your campsite for s'mores and storytelling under the stars. On some weekends, especially during spring and summer, you may be able to join a ranger for an after-dark astronomy session or a moonlight hike before you turn in for the night. Devote all of day two to climbing Chalone Peak, the park's highest point, where panoramic views will make you forget the effort it took to get up there. Otherwise, pack up your tent and drive around to the park's west side, where you can take a short walk to Balconies Cave, which offers more chances to spy on the park's resident bat colonies.

47

CA

Redwood National & State Parks

In foggy forests among emerald fern groves, some of the world's tallest trees have been shooting skyward for 2000 years.

500px | Phillip Bindeman

I imagine how peaceful it is to walk among a forest of silent sentinels, these coast redwood trees over 60 times taller and hundreds of years older than you are. The stillness of the eternal watch they keep from high in the green canopy will slow your heartbeat, relax your pace and clear your mind. Despite its name, it's not just redwoods that this national park protects. It is also a safe haven for other threatened species, such as Chinook salmon that spawn in freshwater streams, Steller (northern) sea lions who haul out on coastal rocks, and California spotted owls, those great hunters who perch in the branches of mature conifers.

Tragically, only 4% of California's old-growth redwood forests have never been logged. Almost half of what remains lies inside this web of federal and state parks, extending from the edge of the Pacific Ocean to inland forests and prairies where elk graze, and along wild rivers where Native American tribes traditionally hunt and fish. In 1918, citizens united in the Save the Redwoods League to rescue these primeval forests from destruction by loggers. Their political activism was rewarded when Redwood National Park was established 50 years later, and again in the 1980s, when Unesco declared this region a World Heritage site and part of the California Coast Ranges Biosphere Reserve.

Redwood National Park and its three neighboring state parks – Prairie Creek Redwoods, Del Norte Coast Redwoods and Jedediah Smith Redwoods – together protect more than 200 sq miles (518 sq km) of land and almost 40 miles (64.4km) of rugged, undeveloped Pacific coastline. Bathed in a temperate rainforest climate,

the parks receive up to 140in (356cm) of rain every year. This cool moisture, along with rich forest-floor soil and the trees' ability to sprout new buds in burls, allows coast redwoods to reach lofty heights and venerable old age.

Getty Images | Patrick Orton

Toolbox

 **When to go**
The parks are open year-round. The sunniest weather arrives from May through October, when most visitor facilities are open. Winters can be cold and rainy.

 Getting there
San Francisco is the nearest major international airport. From there, it's more than a five-hour drive on Hwy 101 north to the national park's visitor center. Over the next 50 miles (80.5km), you'll pass three more state parks on the way north toward the Oregon border via Crescent City.

Park in numbers

217
Area covered (sq miles)

379.1
Height of Hyperion (ft)

45%
California's remaining old-growth redwoods protected here

Stay here...

🏕 Gold Bluffs Beach Campground

Just over two dozen sites wait at the end of a dirt road in Prairie Creek Redwoods State Park. Solitude, ocean views and nearby hiking trails feature in this coastal preserve, with soft sand only a short walk away. Reserve campsites in advance during summer.

🏕 Jedediah Smith Campground

This northernmost state park has the best drive-up campground for families, who picnic and swim in the Smith River. Pitch your tent in the shade of sweet-smelling spruce, juniper and fir trees – ah, bliss. Reservations are essential in the busy summer season.

🏠 Historic Requa Inn

On the banks of the Klamath River, not far from the ocean, this 1914 hotel beckons with glowing night-lights and a chef-run dining room. Old-fashioned rooms are tech-free (no TVs or phones, sorry) and have antique furnishings such as claw-foot tubs. Rent the cottage for a romantic weekend spent by the wood-burning fireplace.

Do this!

⚙ Scenic driving

If you're impressed by the scenery along Hwy 101, just you wait until you motor down the paved Newton B Drury Scenic Parkway, bordered by awe-inspiring stands of tall trees – or take bumpy Davison Rd out to Gold Bluffs Beach and backcountry Howland Hill Rd to the Stout Grove of old-growth redwoods.

🚲 Cycling

Most national and state parks don't allow mountain biking, but these parks do, along a few old logging roads and specially designated trails. Cycle among the ancient trees, out to coastal bluffs or around gentle prairies. A mixed terrain of easy, level loops and steep climbs keep things interesting.

🛶 Kayaking

In summer, paddle a kayak down the placid Smith River, the largest free-flowing river in California. Rentals are available in Orick. For ranger-guided kayak tours, sign up in person in advance at the Hiouchi Information Center, off Hwy 199 in Jedediah Smith Redwoods State Park.

 Jurassic giants: the redwood trees flourished in the cool, moist air here during the age of the dinosaur, 160 million years ago.

What to spot...

On the coast you'll find tidepools rich in marine life, such as the giant green anemone, and beaches where pinnipeds bark and bask. In misty forests, where the tallest trees grow, listen for owls hooting, then quietly watch Roosevelt elk graze in nearby prairies. As you hike along trails, be careful not to step on the yellow-colored banana slug, which wriggles along the rich, dirt-covered forest floor in search of its next meal.

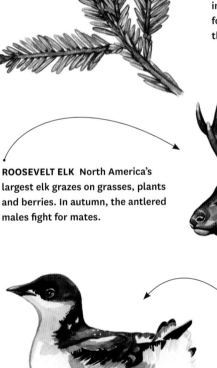

COAST REDWOOD *Sequoia sempervirens* isn't the largest or oldest tree in California, but it is indisputably the tallest. Redwood fossils have been found dating from the Jurassic period.

ROOSEVELT ELK North America's largest elk grazes on grasses, plants and berries. In autumn, the antlered males fight for mates.

MARBLED MURRELET Unusually, this North Pacific seabird with black-and-white plumage flies inland to lay its eggs, in nests high in the branches of old-growth conifers.

Hike this...

01 Lady Bird Johnson Grove Trail
Younger kids will delight in this short, 1-mile (1.6km) nature walk with educational signs that teach about the tall trees' ecology.

02 Fern Canyon Loop Trail
Birds serenade your 0.7-mile (1.1km) walk between mossy, fern-covered canyon walls, near Gold Bluffs Beach in Prairie Creek Redwoods State Park.

03 Damnation Creek Trail
Descend over 1000ft (305m) to a windswept beach where waves crash against the rocks in Del Norte Coast Redwoods State Park. The trail is 4.4 miles (7km).

Itineraries

Marvel at the redwoods on the Tall Trees Grove, hike the Jurassic-ly green Fern Canyon or drive the Newton B Drury Scenic Byway.

◄ Hiking Fern Canyon in Prairie Creek Redwoods State Park; the Prairie Creek coast, part of this group of parks.

01

A day

Driving north on Hwy 101 from the bayfront fishing town of Trinidad, the road curves toward the ocean and passes lagoons where birds flock and kayakers paddle. Stop at the national park's oceanfront Thomas H Kuchel Visitor Center to pick up information, to get a permit for visiting Tall Trees Grove and to stroll along the wild, windy beach. Just north of the tiny town of Orick, take the signed turn-off for Lady Bird Johnson Grove, where a beautifully bewitching nature trail circles old-growth redwood trees as songbirds flit overhead.

Drive further down the same side road and park by the trailhead for the hike to Tall Trees Grove, a memorable 5-mile (8km) round-trip that lets you gape in awe at some of earth's tallest trees, which grow almost as if in secret along Redwood Creek. After your hike, drive back to Hwy 101 and head a few miles north to Prairie Creek Redwoods State Park. Watch giant Roosevelt elk silently gather at dusk in Elk Prairie, then pitch your tent inside the park's forested campground.

02

Two days

After a campfire breakfast by the meadow, walk over to the Prairie Creek Redwoods State Park visitor center to get hiking advice from the rangers – and to tarry by the crackling fireplace to dry out any dampness that crept into your bones overnight. Hiking trails start outside the front door, ranging from easy nature walks to hardy treks out to the coast. Don't miss driving the park's Newton B Drury Scenic Byway, which winds for 10 miles (16km) between old-growth redwoods that rise like ancient gods on either side of a narrow ribbon of asphalt. Then backtrack south on Hwy 101 and take the turn-off for Davison Rd, a bumpy, partly paved route that leads to gorgeous Gold Bluffs Beach. Take a short nature walk through the unbelievably green Fern Canyon, where scenes from the movie *Jurassic Park 2* were filmed. Surrounded by such natural beauty, you may not want to leave the park just yet, and that's just fine. Luckily, Gold Bluffs Beach has some of the best campsites on California's redwood coast.

03

Three days

After sleeping soundly with the surf for your lullaby, pack up camp and drive back to Hwy 101 northbound. Cross over the Klamath River, a popular spot for fly-fishing, and pass ocean overlooks where you might be able to spot migratory gray whales in winter. Look carefully for the small roadside parking pull-off for the Damnation Creek Trail, which rushes headlong down through old-growth redwood forest inside Del Norte Redwoods State Park. The trail bottoms out at a rocky beach that you might have all to yourself. (Tip: time your hike to arrive at low tide, otherwise there's no beach!) Back in the car, keep driving north to Crescent City, with its mid-19th-century lighthouse and an endearing marine-mammal hospital you can visit. Outside town, turn onto backcountry Howland Hill Rd (which is dirt, but a 4WD usually isn't required), the back-door route to the impressive Stout Grove of old-growth redwoods inside Jedediah Smith Redwoods State Park. The park's wooded campsites alongside the Smith River are perfectly set up for family fun.

48

CO

Rocky Mountain National Park

Jagged peaks, eternally blanketed in glistening white snow, pierce the landscape of this alpine park, surrounded by thousands of acres of deep green virgin forest.

David Watts | 500px

In winter, when the crowds have gone and the park lies hushed beneath feet of freshly fallen snow, you glide through open fields on cross-country skies, icy winds pinking your cheeks. In this high-altitude wonderland it's just you and the elk, encircled by cloud-piercing mountaintops. In the heart of America, this is a world unto its own.

The names of the mountains, lakes and regions within the park speak to its wildness. The Never Summer Mountains. The Mummy Range. Wild Basin. Loch Vale. Explore them by foot through day hikes or overnight backpacking trips; ride through them on horses; fish for mountain trout in their gin-clear waters. You'll be rewarded by sweeping vistas as far as Wyoming, quiet moments of peace deep within fir and spruce forests, and thrilling glimpses at moose and bighorn sheep roaming the tundra. Come in winter, when the park is blanketed in silver snow; in spring, when wildflowers spangle the meadows; in summer, when the animals frolic; or in fall, with its amber glow.

Paleo-Indians have been passing through the region for more than 12,000 years, while the Ute and Arapaho inhabited the area more recently. From the mid-1800s, homesteaders began claiming land in the area for farming and cattle-ranching, followed closely by tourists. Irish nobleman Lord Dunraven tried to claim much of the land for himself using the Homestead Acts, but angry settlers put an end to that idea. The national park was signed into existence by Woodrow Wilson in 1915.

Longs Peak, the park's tallest mountain, is so iconic it appears on Colorado's state quarter; the 14,259ft (4346m) peak is named after 19th-century explorer Stephen

Harriman Long. A stone shelter on the popular Keyhole Route is a testament to the mountain's dangers: it's named after Agnes Vaille, a climber of the 1920s, who died (along with one of her rescuers) when she fell from the North Face.

 Climbing the Keyhole Route up Longs Peak requires technical expertise in summer and special equipment in winter.
Previous page: Bierstadt Lake; its hiking trail is ideal for families.

Toolbox

When to go
The park is most crowded in July and August, when wildflowers bloom and temperatures are comfortable. It's open year-round, but roads are often closed due to snow from mid-fall onwards.

Getting there
Denver, 90 minutes' drive away, has the nearest major airport. The park's access towns are Grand Lake to the west and Estes Park to the east; both have accommodations and restaurants. A shuttle serves parts of the park from May through October.

Park in numbers

415
Area covered (sq miles)

72
Number of peaks higher than 12,000ft

355
Miles of hiking trails

Stay here...

Longs Peak Campground
The park's accommodations are camping-only; if you want a roof, head to Estes Park or Grand Lake. This 26-site, tent-only campground is coveted by those making the early morning trek up Longs Peak. The scenery is stunning, but the air is thin – the campground is at 9400ft (2865m). Sites are all first-come, first-served.

Stanley Hotel
Stephen King spent a night at this grand Colonial Revival hotel, which inspired him to create the Overlook Hotel for *The Shining*. The Stanley embraces its creepy legacy – which includes a piano played by ghostly hands in the middle of the night – by offering daily ghost tours. Non-paranormal enthusiasts will be more interested in breakfasts served overlooking the Rockies and the cozy wood-and-bronze whiskey bar.

Mary's Lake Lodge
Western charm meets modern comforts at this pine lodge, set at the base of Rams Horn Mountain overlooking its namesake lake. There are rooms and private cabins, some with their own hot tubs. Enjoy a pint of Bighorn Brown Ale at the lodge tavern after a long day on the trails. In summer, laze in the pool.

Do this!

Scenic driving
The highest continuously paved road in America, the 48-mile (77km) Trail Ridge Rd passes through aspen and pine forests and crosses alpine meadows blanketed with fireweed and rosy paintbrush. Gaze across at peaks bluish-white with snow; the road's apex is above the tree line at 12,183ft (3713m). Look for elk, moose and bighorn sheep as you traverse between Estes Park and Grand Lake.

Snowshoeing
In winter, Rocky Mountain National Park becomes a wonderland of snow and ice, so strap on a clown-sized pair of snowshoes and float over feet of densely packed snow. The most popular snowshoe trails follow summer hiking paths but elk and mule deer are easier to spot against the endless white.

Mountain-climbing
In hiking lingo, a '14er' is a mountain higher than 14,000ft (4267m). There are 53 in Colorado, but only one within this park: Longs Peak. 'Bagging' Longs is a bucket-list item for many hikers: the view from the summit is otherworldly. The hike doesn't need any specialized climbing equipment (in summer, at least) but its ledges, rocky scrambles and thin air make it a serious challenge.

What to spot...

Much of the park is covered in iconic aspen, as well as evergreens, such as ponderosa pine and Douglas fir. Mosses cushion the dark forest floor, while open meadows sway with pale green grass. Large mammals – black bears, elk and moose – lumber through the trees, while cartoon-cute marmots and pikas frolic on rocky slopes. The rivers' clear waters are famed for their wealth of trout. Birds of prey, such as eagles, hawks and kestrels circle the wide blue sky.

BIGHORN SHEEP Look for these handsome creatures, the park's official symbol, around Sheep Lake in spring and early summer, and on the park's eastern side in winter.

QUAKING ASPEN These slender, white-barked trees grow at altitudes as high as 11,000ft (3353m). In fall, their fluttering (hence the name) leaves turn an extraordinary gold.

COLORADO BLUE COLUMBINE Colorado's state flower, these delicate buds are classically pale blue and white, though they can sometimes be yellow or pink. They bloom from June to August.

Hike this...

01 Lily Mountain
Not remotely up for a '14er'? This modest 1.5-mile (2.4km) climb offers panoramic views over Longs Peak, Estes Park and the Mummy Range.

02 Bear Lake
Families with kids dig this easy, paved, 0.6-mile (1km) nature trail, which circles the mountain-reflecting waters of Bear Lake and passes through shady fir forests.

03 Twin Sister's Peak
Just a notch easier than Longs, this 11,428ft (3483m) summit can be reached by a quad-burning climb through rocky slopes and meadows of alpine flowers.

Itineraries

Hike the Wild Basin, overnight in Stephen King's The Shining inspiration or mix with elk and moose at the Alpine Visitor Center.

 Crossing the rugged Big Thompson River.
 Cutthroat trout thrive in many of the park's rivers.

01
A day

Get a quick mountain high by crossing Rocky Mountain National Park in one day via vertiginous Trail Ridge Rd. Fuel up for your day with breakfast at Big Horn Restaurant in Estes Park, where locals linger over sturdy plates of bacon and eggs. Once you hit the road, your first stopping point should be Rainbow Curve Overlook, with valley views from 10,829ft (3301m) up. Further along, you'll almost feel like you can touch the clouds at Rock Cut Overlook, 12,110ft (3691m) above sea level.

The barren brown-and-gray landscape feels alien – and cold! Don't miss the Alpine Visitor Center, where elk and moose graze the alpine meadows far above the tree line; stop here for lunch at the homey cafeteria. At Milner Pass the road crosses the continental divide. A quick hike will take you to Poudre Lake, with deep blue waters surrounded by Douglas fir. Check out the Holzwarth Historic Site, a restored 1920s ranch, before descending to Grand Lake to conk out in a soft bed at Shadowcliff Lodge.

02
Two days

Get away from the crowds with a tour of the park's slightly quieter side. Instead of driving ultra-popular Trail Ridge Rd out of Estes Park, take the less traveled (and more dizzying) Old Fall River Rd. The speed limit is 15mph (24 km/h), and you'll see why – it's a steep drop off the narrow road to the granite chasms below. At the Alpine Visitor Center stop for a rather chilly picnic, watching pikas and marmots skitter across the rocks. From here, head down to Twin Sister's Peak for the calf-killing climb to 11,428ft (3483m), taking in unbroken views of Longs' snowy reaches. Back in Estes Park, crash in your plush bed at the creep-tastic Stanley Hotel, the inspiration for *The Shining*. The next day, hit the park's stunning Wild Basin area, where crowds give way to quiet trails through *Heidi*-like alpine meadows, ice-blue lakes and silvery waterfalls. Head back to Estes Park and treat yourself to a post-hike dinner of juice-dripping buffalo ribs at Smokin' Dave's BBQ and a pint of local brew. You've earned it.

03
A week

Spend day one acclimatizing to the thin air in Estes Park, the park's major access town, which has plenty of cute shops and restaurants to keep you occupied. On day two, drive Trail Ridge Rd as far as the Alpine Visitor Center, stopping at viewpoints to gawk at the dazzling white peaks of the Mummy Range. On day three, hike Lily Mountain, a fairly short climb to a summit overlooking the eternal snows of Longs Peak, with Estes Park in the distance. Reward yourself with an overstuffed burrito and a margarita (or three) at Ed's Cantina and Grill. Book a fly-fishing trip with Kirks Flyshop for day four; the experienced guides will lead you to the most stunning of clear mountain streams. On day five, hit the trail with a half-day horse ride: icy pinnacles and barren slopes look better on horseback. On day six drive Trail Ridge Rd to where it crosses the continental divide at Milner Pass, with the green Colorado River flowing through the distant valley. On day seven, explore the waters around charming Grand Lake, on the park's west side.

49
Saguaro National Park

The saguaro thrives in its namesake park, where sun-baked trails meander through a desert wonderland of prickly cacti and savvy wildlife.

If you're pedaling the Cactus Forest Loop Dr in late spring, keep a lookout for the elusive saguaro blossom. Taking the stage atop the upper trunk and arms of the saguaro cactus, this striking white bloom will survive less than 24 hours, just long enough for pollination and a few lucky photographers.

Established in 1933, Saguaro National Monument was the first federal monument created to protect a specific plant. President Bill Clinton confirmed this mission in 1994 when he signed a congressional bill creating Saguaro National Park. What's so special about this cactus? For starters, its habitat is limited to the Sonoran Desert, which stretches across southern Arizona, southeastern California and northern Mexico. Slow-growers, saguaros take 50 to 80 years to reach a height of 10ft (3m), so they're not quickly replaced. Saguaros are also iconic symbols of the American west. You don't mess with legends like these.

Beyond stats and mythology, there's something engagingly human about this cactus. With sturdy trunks and thick arms, saguaros look like protective sentinels. Their charges? The prickly pear cactus, the barrel cactus and the deceptively fuzzy teddy-bear cholla cactus – don't give that show-off a hug. Wildlife includes roadrunners, gila monsters and javelinas. Rock art, rock shelters and milling sites are reminders of the Hohokam people, who left the area 500 years ago. Other historic highlights include a 19th-century homestead and 1930s structures built by the Civilian Conservation Corps.

The park is divided into two distinct sections. Nature trails, petroglyphs and groves of saguaros grab the spotlight in the Tucson Mountain District, found on the western edge of Tucson. Thirty miles (48.3km) east, the Rincon Mountain District unfurls across six eco-zones, stretching from low-lying desert to the summits of mountains ranges. In the park, these mountain ranges are called 'sky islands.' Noted for their isolation and eco-system diversity, they rise starkly – and photogenically – from the desert floor.

Toolbox

When to go
The park is most inviting between October and April when temperatures hover in the 60s and 70s F (16 to 26°C). Depending on location and rainfall, spring wildflowers bloom from late February through early April; cactus blossoms appear in May and June. The temperature can be hot – over 100°F (38°C) – May through September.

Getting there
Both sections of the park border Tucson in southern Arizona. Speedway Blvd is the most convenient connector between the western Tucson Mountain District and the eastern Rincon Mountain District. The I-10 is the nearest interstate. You'll need a car.

Park in numbers

143
Area covered (sq miles)

78
Percentage designated wilderness

8666
Highest point (ft)

Stay here...

Gilbert Ray Campground
You can snooze beside saguaros standing guard at this county-run park, which is set just a short bike ride away from the Tucson Mountain District, the Arizona-Sonora Desert Museum and Old Tucson Studios.

Hotel Congress
History, rock and roll and good cheer collide at the convivial Hotel Congress, which doubles as the soul of Tucson. A little bit retro, a little bit wild, this was outlaw John Dillinger's final hideout in the 1930s. Today, this downtown hotel welcomes all comers with three bars, a restaurant, live music and no in-room TVs.

Arizona Inn
Open since 1930, this beloved inn celebrates the good life with stylish fun. Play croquet on the manicured lawn, read the newspaper beside your casita or sing along to piano tunes in the Audubon Bar. It's all very upper-crusty during afternoon high tea, when finger sandwiches and hot tea are served in the library.

Do this!

Horseback riding
As your horse clip-clops past the prickly pears, kicking up dust and pestering roadrunners, it feels like the Old West never disappeared – the only thing missing is Gene Autry and a cowboy song. Several outfitters and ranches lead trips in and around the Rincon Mountain District.

Bicycling
Wind in your hair, buttery pavement beneath your wheels, sky islands in your sightline and a devil's array of cacti keeping you firmly on the road. For cyclists, the 8-mile (13km) Cactus Forest Loop Dr is an invigorating introduction to the park. Scenic overlooks line the ride. For off-road cycling, the Cactus Forest Trail divides the loop and rolls past historic lime kilns.

Backpacking
Six lonely campgrounds dot the Saguaro Wilderness Area, which sprawls across the Rincon Mountain District. No motorized vehicles are allowed, and each campground is at least 6 miles (9.7km) from the trailhead. Your post-hike reward? Constellations and cacti without the crowds. A permit is required.

← The slow-growing saguaro cactus can live up to 200 years.
→ Close-up of an Engelmann prickly pear cactus.

Hike this...

01 Desert Discovery Trail
In the western district, this 0.5-mile (0.8km) interpretive loop spotlights Sonoran Desert flora, fauna and ecology. It's paved and wheelchair accessible.

02 Douglas Spring Trail
This 5.2-mile (8.4km) round-trip trail climbs from saguaros to desert grasslands in the Rincon Mountain foothills. Views include the Santa Catalina Mountains and a seasonal waterfall.

03 Tanque Verde Ridge Trail
Bring your hiking stick for this rugged and steep 18-mile (29km) round-trip in the eastern district. It climbs to Tucson Basin views and Tanque Verde Peak, which rises to 7040ft (2146m).

Getty Images | Witold Skrypczak; Danita Delimont

What to spot...

The Tucson Mountain District supports desert scrub and desert grassland communities. This lower-lying district, noted for its thick groves of saguaros, is home to desert dwellers like the desert tortoise and Gambel's quail. The loftier Rincon Mountain District holds six distinct ecosystems: desert scrub, desert grasslands, oak woodland, pine-oak woodland, pine forest and mixed conifer forest. Large mammals, including black bears and white-tailed deer, roam the higher elevations of the sky islands within the district.

SAGUARO CACTUS Average lifespan? 150 to 175 years. Filled with water, a saguaro (sah-wah-row) can weigh 6 tons (5443kg) and grow to a height of 50ft (15m). It's illegal to harm or move one, not to mention dangerous – a shooter was killed in 1993 when he blasted off the arm of a saguaro and it fell on him.

WESTERN DIAMOND-BACKED RATTLESNAKE A diamond pattern runs the length of this venomous pit viper, one of six species of rattlesnake in the park. Black-and-white bands border its rattle.

JAVELINA If it looks like a pig and rolls in mud like a pig, it must be...a peccary. Yep, these herd-traveling desert dwellers are members of the hoofed peccary family – they're not wild pigs. Javelinas are dark-haired, with poor eyesight and a strong sense of smell.

Itineraries

Get up close to saguaros and wildlife at the Arizona–Sonora Desert Museum, hike King Canyon Trail to Wasson Peak then picnic at sunset at Gates Pass Overlook.

⬅ A black-tailed jackrabbit.
➡ The saguaro cactus blooms in May.

01

Two days

With their upraised arms, the saguaros at the entrance to the Tucson Mountain District look ready to slap you a welcoming high-five – a temptation best avoided. Instead, get up-close with the cacti on the well-labeled Cactus Garden Trail beside the Red Hills Visitor Center. This short trail passes chollas, saguaros and prickly pears.

Roadrunners dart across your path as you motor to the Bajada Loop Dr, where saguaros bask in the sunlight. Enjoy a picnic at the Signal Hill Trailhead, then hike up the trail for ancient petroglyphs. For more desert exploring, follow the Hugh Norris Trail to ridge-top views of the cactus forest. End with a sunset panorama of the Sonoran Desert from Gates Pass Overlook to the east.

The next day, driving east toward the Rincon Mountain District from Tucson, modern hustle-bustle surrenders to the Old West. The mountains loom larger. A dusty horse trailer clangs past. And the road into the park? The Old Spanish Trail – even its name sets an adventurous mood.

Inside the Rincon Mountain Visitor Center, the movie *A Home in the Desert* spotlights desert wildlife. Interactive exhibits explore the desert's charms, but it's hard to resist the call of the Cactus Forest Loop Dr outside. This 8-mile (13km) drive swoops through a cacti wonderland. For closer views, hike the Mica View Loop Trail, stopping for lunch at the picnic area.

In the afternoon, catch the ranger program, then pick a final hike. For a taste of pioneer history, take the Freeman Homestead Trail. For sunset desert views, climb as far as you like on the Tanque Verde Ridge Trail.

02

Four days

For an engaging Sonoran Desert primer, spend your first morning exploring the excellent Arizona-Sonora Desert Museum. Listen for javelinas rustling in the underbrush, look for coyotes loping across the sand and take a few snapshots of the wild desert flora. From here, Kinney Rd leads south to Tiny's Saloon & Steakhouse, a roadhouse famous for its burgers. Next up? The Red Hills Visitor Center inside the Tucson Mountain District.

Catch the movie and join a ranger talk, then drive the scenic Bajada Loop Dr.

The next morning, sip your coffee beside a saguaro at Gilbert Ray Campground, then return to the western district for an early hike up the King Canyon Trail to the Hugh Norris Trail and 4687ft (1429m) Wasson Peak. It's 7 miles (11.2km) round-trip. Stop by the visitor center for an afternoon ranger talk. Ending the day with a sunset picnic at Gates Pass Overlook is always a good idea.

On day three, channel your inner cowpoke for a guided horseback tour into the foothills of the rugged Rincon Mountains. In the afternoon, pedal the 8-mile (13km) Cactus Forest Loop Dr. The fourth day ends with a bang. Or possibly pain. Lace up your boots and steel yourself for the steep Tanque Verde Ridge Trail, which crosses several ecosystems as it climbs to Tanque Verde Peak. It's 18 miles (29km) round-trip, so plan to camp at Juniper Basin campground.

50

CA

Sequoia National Park

Lose yourself in the Giant Forest, explore an underground marble cave or summit the USA's highest peak outside Alaska.

Sequoia

Serene in its magnificence, this southern Sierra Nevada park doesn't boast about its record-breaking natural attractions – though it should. The highest peak in the lower 48 states? Here Mt Whitney soars above the clouds on the eastern side of the range. The world's biggest tree? Crane your neck up at the Giant Forest's General Sherman Tree, which measures more than 100ft (30m) around its trunk and almost 275ft (84m) tall. California's longest cave? You'll find it here, too – in addition to alpine lakes that sparkle like precious gems, cascading rivers that feed roaring waterfalls and wildflower meadows where yellow-bellied mountain marmots whistle at hikers passing by.

In 1890, the same year Yosemite was declared a national park, Sequoia National Park was created by the US Congress to protect rare giant sequoia trees from further logging. The largest living things on earth, these trees grow only on the western slope of the Sierra Nevada mountains, where they can live for more than 2000 years. The first national park rangers sent to protect these gentle giants were African American regiments of 'buffalo soldiers' from the US Army Cavalry. The first waves of visitors didn't start arriving until the 1927 opening of the scenic Generals Highway, which still slowly switchbacks up from the foothills to the Giant Forest.

When spring wildflowers cover the hillsides at lower elevations inside the park, you can hike to waterfalls that gush through river canyons. During summer, higher-elevation trails wind through the Giant Forest and to the top of Moro Rock, where you can soak up panoramic views of snaggle-toothed peaks along the Great

Western Divide. Ambitious backpackers leave on high country trips from the remote Mineral King Valley, which is reached via a twisting road with over 700 hairpin turns (quite a workout behind the wheel!).

⬆ The giant sequoia can grow to the height of a 26-story building and live for 2000 years.
➡ Bullfrog Lake and the Sierra Nevada range.

Toolbox

When to go
Summer is the most popular time to visit. Spring brings wildflowers and waterfalls. Fall is less crowded, but still temperate. In winter, come play in the snow. Mineral King Valley is open only in summer and early fall.

Getting there
The park is a 3½-hour drive north of Los Angeles, which has a busy international airport. In summer only, buses to the Giant Forest depart from Visalia, in California's Central Valley. Seasonal, in-park shuttle buses are free.

Park in numbers

631
Area covered (sq miles)

52,500
Volume of General Sherman Tree (cu ft)

14,505
Height of Mt Whitney (ft), the park's highest mountain

Stay here...

Lodgepole Campground
You'll need to reserve well ahead to stay in the park's most popular campground, especially if you want a prime campsite next to the river. The seasonal park shuttle bus stops here, making it easy to head over to the Giant Forest or to Crescent Meadow for hiking and wildlife-spotting.

Bearpaw High Sierra Camp
This is an unforgettable overnight trip: hike 11 miles (17.7km) into the wilderness along a gorgeous trail to reach these canvas tent cabins. Rates include a hot breakfast and dinner, plus a boxed lunch to tote along with you on the trail the next day.

Wuksachi Lodge
The park's top-end lodging is not much more than a glorified, multi-story motel, but the woodsy setting near the Giant Forest is spectacular. The lodge's well-reviewed restaurant and a full calendar of activities for families are bonuses, as are steeply discounted room rates during the off-season.

Do this!

Caving
Carved by an underground river, 10,000-year-old Crystal Cave is full of stalactites, stalagmites, hanging curtains of milky-white marble and other bizarrely beautiful formations – all of which you can see on a family-friendly guided walking tour. Just watch out for bats and spiders! Diehard cavers can sign up for all-day spelunking adventures.

Swimming
When intense, mid-summer heat washes over the foothills, families flock to swimming holes near Potwisha and Hospital Rock. Later in summer, you can take a dip at Lodgepole Campground. Just make sure that the water levels in the park's rivers have dropped low enough to be safe; ask a park ranger if you're in doubt.

Skiing & snowshoeing
From Wuksachi Lodge, where you can also rent snowshoes and cross-country skis, rangers lead guided snowshoe treks into the Giant Forest. Backcountry skiers make the high-elevation trip to rustic Pear Lake ski hut, where you can bunk down overnight in the wilderness.

← Winter can bring snow and closed roads from November to April. Some low-level campgrounds remain open.

What to spot...

Possessing an incredible range of habitats, from the low-elevation foothills of the Sierra Nevada and to the rising peak of Mt Whitney, this park has a cornucopia of flora and fauna that will keep you busy with binoculars for days, weeks or years. Recently, Sierra Nevada bighorn sheep have been returned to their historic range here after being driven almost to extinction. The grizzly bear wasn't as lucky: it was eradicated from the park in the 1920s.

BLACK BEAR This lumbering ursine mammal weighs an average of 300lb (136kg) and eats voraciously whenever it's not hibernating during the colder, snowier months.

GIANT SEQUOIA These towering trees have bark stained deep red by tannin, which helps protect them from wildfires. Surprisingly, they also depend on fire for their seeds to sprout.

YELLOW-BELLIED MARMOT In high mountain meadows, this furry rodent perches atop rocky outcroppings, where it can quickly hide from predators.

Hike this...

01 General Sherman Tree
Take an easy, 1-mile (1.6km) walk through the Giant Forest to pay your respects to the largest living thing on earth.

02 Tokopah Falls Trail
Bring the kids on this pleasant, 3.5-mile (5.6km) riverside walk through a glacier-carved canyon, ending at a 1200ft-high (366m) waterfall, best viewed in spring.

03 Lakes Trail
Gear up for an epic, 12.5-mile (20km) day hike – or overnight backpacking trip – to a string of stunningly colored high-elevation lakes.

Itineraries

See the world's biggest tree at General Sherman Tree trailhead, tour Crystal Cave or take the hair-raising drive to Mineral King Valley.

◀ Rae Lakes Loop, a popular hike.
▶ There are 14 campgrounds in the park. Wilderness permits are required outside these sites.

01
A day

With just one day, you should head straight to the heart of the park: the enchanting Giant Forest. To get there on the historic Generals Hwy, it's a narrow, steep and winding 16-mile (25.7km) drive uphill, which curves more than a hundred times between the park's Foothills Visitor Center and the Giant Forest Museum, the best places to get oriented. Outside the museum, hop aboard the free seasonal shuttle bus north to the General Sherman Tree trailhead. After you inspect the world's biggest tree, get back on the shuttle to the museum; from there catch another shuttle to Moro Rock, where you can climb to the summit for panoramic views. Further along the same shuttle route is Crescent Meadow, where wildflowers bloom in early summer and black bears often ramble. Around sunset, get back on the bus and head north to the Wuksachi Lodge for a dinner, or even just a beer and flatbread pizza in the lounge. Sated, backtrack to Lodgepole Village and your forest campsite next to the Kaweah River.

02
Two days

Follow the day one itinerary then catch the shuttle bus or walk over to the Lodgepole Village market for a quick breakfast, then stop inside the visitor center to buy tickets for an afternoon tour of Crystal Cave. Return to Lodgepole Campground, then head out on the Tokopah Falls Trail, which rises gently through the forest to a cascade that runs down granite cliffs. Stare up at the enormous Watchtower rock formation, which looms high above the canyon floor. Have a picnic by the falls, then hike back to the campground. Pick up your car and take a winding drive down to Crystal Cave, where tour guides will take you behind the historic Spider Gate to wander among magical-looking stalactites, stalagmites and other abstract geological shapes.

Afterwards, drive down the Generals Hwy to the Foothills area of the park, where you can cool off with a dip in the Kaweah River in summer. Head outside the park to the town of Three Rivers to find lodging and a filling dinner.

03
Three days

Follow the two-day itinerary then stock up on food, drinks and gas for a scenic drive to Mineral King Valley. It can take two hours to drive just 25 miles (40km) from Three Rivers town to the valley, since the road makes almost 700 hair-raising turns and gains 7500ft (2286m) in elevation. The road passes by small waterfalls, picnic areas and old-fashioned cabins before finally petering out in a glacier-carved valley where miners once staked silver claims. All around you are skyscraping mountains, such as the 12,343ft-high (3762m) Sawtooth Peak. Wrap your car in a plastic tarp secured with rope to protect it from being chewed on by hungry marmots, then hit one of the steep hiking trails that leads up from the valley to alpine lakes. When you return to your car after such a hike, you might feel like staying the night at Cold Springs Campground. At least linger long enough in the valley to see the setting sun cast an alpenglow on the peaks.

51

Shenandoah National Park

There are scenic drives, and then there's Skyline Dr, the 105-mile (169km) road riding the spine of the ancient Blue Ridge Mountains.

Getty Images | OGphoto

To the west of Skyline Dr, the silver Shenandoah River glides through the lush valley far below. To the east, the green hills of the Virginia Piedmont roll gently towards the horizon. The slopes are frilled pink with rhododendron and mountain laurel, the roadside carpeted with blue-purple columbine and sweet ox-eye daisies. Watch closely (if you're not driving!) and you might just see a falcon circling overhead.

The origin of the name 'Shenandoah' is a bit of a mystery. It's almost certainly of Native American origin – some say it means 'river of high mountains,' 'silver waters,' or even the rather romantic 'daughter of the stars.' According to one legend, George Washington named the river and its valley after an Oneida chief who led native warriors in support of the colonists in the Revolutionary War. Whatever the truth is, this area looms large in Virginia's imagination.

Inhabited seasonally by native tribes, Shenandoah was permanently settled by Europeans in the 18th century. These settlers built farmsteads and mills and planted apple orchards along the slopes, and began logging the ancient forests. To create the park in the 1930s, the government had to resettle nearly 500 families; they then allowed the farmland and logged forests to regrow naturally – a novel idea at the time. Today, a few crumbling foundations and moss-choked cemeteries are all that remain of these early mountain communities.

Shenandoah runs north–south along a narrow stretch of the Blue Ridge Mountains. The peaks are mostly gentle, but a few will satisfy hardcore hikers. The former farmland has transformed into sylvan hollows where white-tailed deer graze and dark, ferny forests shot through with silvery mountain creeks and waterfalls. Only two hours or so from Washington, DC, Shenandoah is a favorite getaway of harried bureaucrats and other city-dwellers.

↑ Horse riders from Skyland Resort on the Limberlost Trail. Previous page: driving in the Shenandoah National Park.

Toolbox

When to go
The park's open year-round, but some facilities close in winter. The magical red-and-gold fall is the most popular season, with summer close behind.

Getting there
The park lies within the state of Virginia, running north–south down the Blue Ridge Mountains. Its north access town, Front Royal, is a two-hour drive from the airports of Washington, DC; its south entrance, Rockfish Gap, is about an hour from the college town of Charlottesville.

Park in numbers

311
Area covered (sq miles)

15
Park's width at its widest (miles)

1
Park's width at its narrowest (miles)

Stay here...

 Big Meadows Lodge
A classic National Parks charmer, this rambling stone-and-brown-wood lodge has a homey Great Room lined with couches and rocking chairs. On chilly nights guests pack in to play board games by the stone fireplace. Rooms are spartan but comfy; private cabins are worth the extra money, especially the ones with fireplaces. The grounds are home to hundreds of deer.

 Lewis Mountain Cabins
These rustic cabins are several steps up from a tent but still offer a back-to-nature vibe. Humble one- or two-bedroom units have private bathrooms. Roast your hotdogs in the fire pits outside – don't forget the marshmallows – or dine nearby at Big Meadows. A good choice for families, and those traveling with pets.

Big Meadows Campground
In wildlife-rich Big Meadows, this campground plays host to deer, wild turkeys and the odd bear. The 221 sites are tree-shaded and close to some of the park's finest hikes, including three waterfall trails. Some sites have views over the meadows, fringed with blackberry bushes; if you're lucky, you can pick some before the bears do. Its central location off Skyline Dr makes it a top choice.

Do this!

Scenic driving
The only road through the park, Skyline Dr skirts the peaks of the Blue Ridge for 105 miles (169km), passing enough scenic views for a lifetime (well, technically 75). To the west is the patchworked Shenandoah Valley; to the east are the green hills of the Virginia Piedmont. In spring, trillium, violets and bloodroot carpet the slopes, while in summer azaleas and mountain laurel put on a show.

Wildlife-watching
In the middle of the park, the tree-lined ridges open up to reveal a wide silver-green meadow. White-tailed deer munch away like warm-blooded lawnmowers; black bears forage for berries around the edge; chipmunks and squirrels run frantically up and down. Spread out a picnic and watch Mother Nature's show (but don't feed the bears!).

Vista-viewing
Shenandoah's highest point, 4050ft (1234m) Hawksbill is blanketed in balsam fir. Reach the summit via a trail from the parking area and climb the stone observation point. Look out for one of the park's peregrine falcons. Or just gaze down the emerald slopes into the cloud-filled valley below. The peaches-and-cream sunsets are particularly delightful.

What to spot...

As a forested oasis on the crest of the Blue Ridge Mountains, Shenandoah provides an important landing spot for migrating birds. It's also a year-round home to such bird species as red-tailed hawks, Carolina chickadees and barred owls. Some 50 types of mammal roam the pine, oak, hickory and poplar forests, notably black bear and white-tailed deer. Exposed rocky outcrops, protected valleys and deep woods are home to more than 1400 types of plants, from wildflowers to ferns to mosses.

CAROLINA CHICKADEE With gray bodies, black caps and big black eyes, these tiny birds are cartoon-cute. Listen for their call of chicka-dee-dee-dee, or look for them nesting in tree holes.

WHITE-TAILED DEER
You'll have no trouble spotting these increasingly un-shy mammals, who graze in meadows, stroll through campgrounds and dart in front of cars.

MOUNTAIN LAUREL In summer, these glossy green shrubs gush forth with foamy white-and-pink flowers. They often grow on steep, rocky slopes, and can be seen from Skyline Dr.

Hike this...

01 Dark Hollow Falls

Deceptively difficult for a short hike, the payoff from this 1.4-mile (2.3km) round-trip is the sight of 70ft (21m) of water flowing over ancient lava rock.

02 Fox Hollow

This 1.2-mile (1.9km) loop, which passes the crumbling remains of homesteads, is good for families and for bird-watching – you might spot a hairy woodpecker or a Carolina chickadee.

03 Old Rag Mountain

The park's most challenging hike, this 9-mile (14.5km) circuit involves several hairy scrambles on bare rock. Your reward? Stunning panoramic views for dozens of miles.

Itineraries

Get the binoculars ready for wildlife-watching at Big Meadows or Hawksbill Mountain for peregrine falcons. Horseback ride at Skyline Dr's highest point for wonderful views.

← Park wildlife includes deer and the Carolina chickadee.
→ Shenandoah scenery.

01

A day

Center yourself in the middle of the action at Big Meadows, where morning is prime wildlife-watching time. Park at the visitor center and set yourself up with your camera for an hour or two; it's like being on a mini safari in the middle of the American South. Take the short-but-steep trail to Dark Hollow Falls, where water cascades over mossy black volcanic rock into a clear pool; take the time to walk a little further to see some of the smaller falls of Hogcamp Branch. Refuel with lunch at Big Meadows Lodge – an overflowing sandwich or plate of fried chicken will hit the spot. Admire the classic 'parkitecture' of the Great Room, with massive windows overlooking the valley. Next, make your way up the Hawksbill Mountain summit, binoculars in tow for spotting the rare peregrine falcons that nest in the area. Drive north, stopping for stunning Shenandoah Valley views at the Crescent Rock and Pinnacle Peak overlooks before exiting the park via Thornton Gap.

02

Two days

'Do' Skyline Dr in its entirety, entering from the north at Front Royal on day one. Hit the Dickey Ridge Visitor Center for maps and exhibits before heading south. The first big overlook you'll get to is Gooney Run, named after the rapids that course through the valley. Forge onward to Range View Overlook, with views over craggy Stony Man Mountain, all the way to the bluish peaks of the Alleghenies. At Elkwallow Wayside, stock up on fruit and jerky and have a picnic lunch a few miles south at Pinnacle Peak's panoramic overlook. Finish the day at Big Meadows Lodge, challenging fellow travelers to board games in the Great Room as the night sky turns from blue to black outside. On day two, get up early for some wildlife-watching in the meadow, then head south as far as the trailhead to Blackrock Summit. Do the entire trail, including the spur, which leads to an enormous boulder field at the summit. Exit at Rockfish Gap for some hawk-spotting before heading onward to your final destination.

03

Four days

Spend day one in the cute access town of Front Royal, with some of the best (and cheapest) antiquing we've seen. Fuel up for your upcoming hike at Spelunker's, a well-loved local chain offering frozen custard and 'cavern burgers.' On day two, enter the park from the north, taking in the luscious overlooks of the chartreuse-and-yellow Shenandoah Valley and the rolling hills of the Virginia Piedmont. Book an afternoon horseback ride at Skyland Lodge, a classic stone-and-wood national parks lodge at Skyline Dr's highest point. After riding through forests of oak and poplar, dine on river trout and other hearty staples at the Pollock Dining Room before retiring to your room. In the morning of day three, exit the park to the west to visit Luray Caverns, a vast, dripping cave best known for its 'Great Stalacpipe Organ,' which taps stalactites with rubber mallets to play a melody. Head back into the park and spend the night at Big Meadows, rising for a day of waterfall hikes and wildlife-watching on the south stretch of Skyline Dr.

52

ND

Theodore Roosevelt National Park

For Roosevelt, this was 'a land of vast, silent spaces, of lonely rivers, and of plains where the wild game stared at the passing horsemen.' Little has changed.

Populated by thousands of animals – and very few people – Theodore Roosevelt National Park is spread across three sites in the unforgiving wilderness of North Dakota's badlands. The South Unit, North Unit and Elkhorn Lodge are delicately laced together by three threads: the Little Missouri River, Maah Daah Hey Trail and the memory of a man who helped shape the entire national parks system.

In 1883, seven years after Custer passed through, en route to his infamous engagement with Sitting Bull's Sioux warriors, a young Theodore Roosevelt came to North Dakota's badlands to hunt.

While here, he discovered a powerful love for the land. This passion informed his attitude towards conservation when he became president, and during his time in the White House he would go on to protect 230 million acres (930,777 sq km) of American wilderness. Under Roosevelt, five new national parks were created and the Antiquities Act was passed, enabling presidents to protect national monuments – many of which would later become parks.

The Oval Office was where he did his best work, but Roosevelt was most at home in the badlands backcountry, where he operated two ranches. The region turned from hunting ground to healing ground

when his wife and his mother died within hours of each other on Valentine's Day, 1884, and he sought sanctuary in the womb of the wilderness.

After Roosevelt himself died in 1919, three years after the National Park Service was established, the region was explored as a possible park site. By 1935 the Roosevelt Recreation Demonstration Area had been established; 11 years later it became the Theodore Roosevelt National Wildlife Refuge. President Truman created the Theodore Roosevelt National Memorial Park in 1947 – the only National Memorial Park ever established – and in 1978 it was reclassified as Theodore Roosevelt National Park.

Toolbox

When to go
The park is open year-round, but most hikers and campers take advantage of the long summer days. Winter commonly sees road closures. Wildflowers erupt into life in late spring and early fall.

Getting there
The park is spread across three separate units in the badlands of western North Dakota. The South Unit entrance is near Medora, reached via I-94. The North Unit is 70 miles away (113km), up I-85, en route to Watford City. Elkhorn Ranch is roughly midway between them; it's best accessed via the South Unit.

Park in numbers

110
Area covered (sq miles)

2855
Height of Buck Hill, the highest point (ft)

70
Optimum size of the park's wild horse population

Stay here...

Cottonwood & Juniper Campgrounds
Picture this: you wake to a badlands' birdlife ballad – and then, upon looking through the tent door, discover you're sharing a campground with a couple of bison. It's enough to make you feel like Teddy Roosevelt himself...and this scenario is a distinct possibility in the park's established campgrounds: Cottonwood in the South Unit and Juniper in the North Unit. Both sites occupy spots alongside the Little Missouri River, and both offer grills and picnic tables. Juniper is more serene, partly because the North Unit is less visited, but also because there's no traffic noise.

Backcountry camping
It's possible to camp in the backcountry for free with a Backcountry Permit. Horseback riders can camp in the backcountry, or stay at Roundup Group Horse Campground in the South Unit.

Lodgings
As befits its adventurous image, Theodore Roosevelt National Park has no permanent accommodations. You'll find inns and motels in nearby Medora.

Do this!

Wildlife-viewing
Following in Roosevelt's footsteps, people still come here to hunt animals – although cameras have now replaced rifles. The park boasts many mammals, including mountain lion, bison, feral horses, elk, bighorn sheep, white-tailed and mule deer, and prairie dogs.

Maah Daah Hey Trail
This classic trail, 140 miles (225km) in its entirety, links all three units of the park. It can be hiked or ridden, but unfortunately guided horseback trips are not currently being offered. Mountain bikers can enjoy one of the country's top-rated off-road cycle trails between the parks, which goes past Elkhorn (but bikes aren't allowed on any trails inside the South and North Units).

Canoeing & kayaking
An adventurous way of linking the park's three sections in summer is by taking a float trip down the Little Missouri River. It's 107.5 miles (173km) from Medora (near the South Unit) to Long X Bridge on US Hwy 85 (near the North Unit). A gentle paddle will take around five days (unless the water is low, when portages may be required).

← Wild horses won't drag you away from Theodore Roosevelt National Park.

→ The River Bend Overlook in the North Unit.

Hike this...

01 Wind Canyon Trail
A quick, 0.4-mile (0.6km) stroll along a wind-sculpted canyon in the South Unit rewards a half-hour's effort with fantastic views over the Little Missouri River – a great sunset-watching spot.

02 Buckhorn
A full-day, 11.4-mile (18.3km) North Unit escapade across a range of terrain, from deep canyons to high open prairies, that offers a treat of wildlife encounters, including a prairie dog town.

03 Jones/Talkington/Paddock Loop
For a real overnight badlands backcountry adventure, try this 23.4-mile (37.7km) South Unit epic on for size. It combines the upper and lower Talkington and Paddock trails.

What to spot...

The diversity of its ecosystem is one of the park's biggest drawcards. Besides big-ticket, crowd-pleasing mammals, such as mountain lion and bison, the park has 186 species of bird, including golden eagles, ruby-throated hummingbirds, sharp-tailed grouse, wild turkeys, belted kingfishers and several species of owl. Some are permanent, others migratory. Remember that bison and feral horses can be dangerous – take care during backcountry encounters. The venomous prairie rattlesnake is particularly active during warmer months.

PORCUPINE Charismatic badlands residents, porcupines can often be seen alongside the park's roads at nighttime, and during daylight hours in trees and bushes feeding on twigs.

FERAL HORSE Found only in the South Unit (and often seen by people exploring the Scenic Loop Dr), the park's feral horses are descendants of domestic stock.

PASQUEFLOWER In April, this is typically the first flower to burst into bloom: its appearance is seen as an announcement that spring has arrived in the badlands.

Itineraries

Explore the Scenic Loop Dr, watch bison, longhorn steers and prairie dogs on Little Missouri National Grassland or hike through junipers into Painted Canyon.

◀ Head to the North Unit to find these cannonball concretions.
▶ Bison cross the Little Missouri River.

01
A day

Stopping in at the South Unit's Medora visitor center, learn about the park's history, and the life and legacy of the man it's named for, before exploring the preserved Maltese Cross Cabin – Roosevelt's first residence here and a building that's survived a series of remarkable journeys. Then it's time to experience the wilderness and wildlife that so inspired the president-to-be with a counter-clockwise spin around the 36-mile (58km) Scenic Loop Dr, keeping your eyes peeled for prairie dogs and bison as you go.

Punctuate the drive with short hikes to get a proper taste of the park, starting with a stroll along the Ridgeline Walk, armed with a brochure about the region's ecology. A little further around is the short, steep climb to the park's highest accessible point, Buck Hill.

With the sun sinking fast, pick a place to watch it set – from the highpoint at the end of the Boicourt Overlook Trail, with its vista across the badlands, or from the Wind Canyon Trail, where views extend over the Little Missouri River.

02
Two days

After a day exploring the South Unit, watch the setting sun turn the badlands crimson, then head to Cottonwood Campground. Above your tent, the Milky Way spills across the sky, a spectacular mess of stars.

Wake early and drive 70 miles (113km) to the park's North Unit. Rolling along the 14-mile (22.5km) drive to the Oxbow Overlook, it puzzles you that more people don't explore this part of the park. Behemoth bison feed on the lawns of the Little Missouri National Grassland, and there's a small herd of longhorn steers, a living history exhibit maintained in memory of the days when these magnificent animals were driven along the Long X Trail by cowboys – a lifestyle that captivated Roosevelt.

To continue the wildlife theme, hike a short section of the Buckhorn Trail to a prairie dog town to observe a community of these garrulous rodents.

Return to the car: the Oxbow Overlook awaits, and it's a fitting finale, delivering fine views of the colorful river.

03
Four or more days

With more time, explore the park's North Unit first, spending a night at the Juniper Campground and doing a day-hike along the whole Buckhorn Trail.

En route to the South Unit, stop to explore Painted Canyon, where a nature walk takes you through rock layers and junipers into the canyon itself – the perfect place for a picnic lunch. To investigate some of the park's less trodden trails, dedicate a day to doing the Petrified Forest Loop. This stunning hike loops around the northwest corner of the South Unit, threading through ancient petrified forests and raw badlands wilderness before returning along a section of the Maah Daah Hey Trail.

Round your trip off with an adventure to the undeveloped site of Roosevelt's Elkhorn Ranch, found in a remote area of the park 35 miles (56km) north of Medora. This refuge, the third unit of the park, was the conservationist president's true badlands home – and it's not hard to see why he fell in love with it.

53

VI

Virgin Islands National Park

These 15,000 acres of jade-green mountains, sugar-white sands and reef-studded turquoise seas make for one of America's most breathtaking parks.

Dive in to the crystal-clear, blood-warm waters of the Caribbean Sea, gently kicking your flippers as you glide over reefs, rocks and gardens of swaying seagrass. Gaze down at bright elkhorn, pillar and mountainous star coral, all increasingly rare in the world today, due to warming oceans. To your right, a spotted eagle ray with a wingspan longer than you flies through the ocean like a strange bird. To your left, a green sea-turtle – born when the US was still fighting WWI – nibbles experimentally on a rock. Everywhere around you, fish in all the colors of a Crayola box flit hither and thither.

Some 40% of Virgin Islands National Park is underwater, so snorkeling, swimming, diving, and boating are crucial to experiencing its beauty. The above-water parts of the park ain't bad either, with mountains tumbling dramatically towards the sea, and miles of pale-sand beaches and hidden coves.

Native Carib and Arawak people lived on these islands before the arrival of Columbus, leaving behind petroglyphs and other artifacts. Danish settlers arrived here in the 1600s, planting sugar and cotton with the labor of enslaved Africans. In 1733, 150 St John slaves revolted against their masters, one of the first slave rebellions in the Americas. Danish officials begged for help from the French in nearby Martinique,

who sent a militia to put down the rebellion; many slaves committed suicide rather than be recaptured. Slavery would not be abolished in the Danish West Indies for more than a century.

Denmark sold the Danish West Indies to the United States in 1917. On a Caribbean cruise, Standard Oil heir (and UFO enthusiast) Laurance Rockefeller fell in love with the area. He acquired 5000 acres (20 sq km) of land, which he donated to the federal government. The park was established in 1956.

⬆ Warm waters make sea kayaking a great way to explore.
➡ Mangroves are an important island habitat.

Toolbox

When to go
The weather is generally lovely year-round, but June through November is hurricane season. Accommodations are most expensive December through April.

Getting there
The park covers 60% of the island of St John and nearly all of nearby Hassel Island. To get to St John, fly into St Thomas, cross the island via car or taxi, and take the ferry. You'll want a car to explore. Cruz Bay, on the west side, is the main settlement.

Park in numbers

23
Area covered (sq miles)

1 million
Number of visitors per year

302
Species of fish in the park's waters

Stay here...

Cinnamon Bay Campground
Cinnamon Bay is the only campground within the park's boundaries. Open your tent flap and step directly onto the white sand of Cinnamon Bay Beach. Amenities abound, including a watersports center. There are also rustic cabins, as well as canvas safari tents with beds.

Caneel Bay Resort
On a 170-acre (69 hectares) peninsula within the park's borders, this luxury resort and its seven pristine beaches attract celebrities and other schmancy types – the property was once owned by the Rockefeller family as part of its resort chain. Borrow a complimentary set of fins and snorkel the flamboyant reef off Honeymoon Beach or rent a jeep to explore the park's back roads.

Concordia Eco Resort
South of Coral Bay, Concordia offers a hybrid of camping and resort. Wood-framed 'eco-tents' (more like cabins) perch amid vegetation on the hillside overlooking Salt Pond Bay, each with its own kitchen, deck and composting toilet. Guests gather at the pool, breakfast on fruit in the cafe, do yoga in the pavilion and watch family flicks during movie nights. The beach is a 15-minute hike away.

Do this!

Snorkeling
Put on fins and a mask and submerge yourself in a psychedelic wonderland. The ocean floors of Honeymoon Bay and Hawksnest Bay sprout delicate elkhorn coral and dance with iridescent fish. At popular Trunk Bay, an 'underwater trail' has submerged plaques explaining the wildlife you're seeing. It's crowded, but good for beginners. Maho Bay's swaying seagrass makes for prime sea-turtle spotting.

Fishing
For many, a day spent casting into the park's gin-clear waters is the best part of the trip. Depending on the time of year, the quarry includes yellowfin, tiger grouper, blue runner and bonito. Tarpon and bonefish are catch-and-release only, but the rest can be taken back to be grilled with lime over a fire.

Beach-going
The best thing about Virgin Islands National Park is that you don't have to do anything more than snooze on a beach and get up occasionally to cool down in the sparkling surf. Cinnamon Bay has a mile-long (1.6km) stretch of sand and a neat trail to the ruins of an old sugar factory. Popular Trunk Bay has lifeguards, showers and a snack bar.

See this...

01 Reef Bay Trail
This strenuous 2-miler (3.2km) goes straight down a steep mountain, passing pre-Columbian petroglyphs, plantation ruins and wild limes on the way to a rocky beach.

02 Francis Bay Boardwalk
This family-friendly elevated 0.5-mile (0.8km) walkway follows the edge of a salt pond and passes through bird-filled mangrove forests, ending in a lovely crescent-shaped beach.

03 Cinnamon Bay Trail
Follow the old Danish plantation road for 1 mile (1.6km) through the jungle, passing old sugar factory ruins and stopping at an overlook for dazzling ocean views.

What to spot...

With emerald mountains plunging towards the shoreline, Virgin Islands has a dramatic variety of ecosystems. Subtropical forests, salt ponds, cactus scrubland and mangroves are alive with birds like smooth-billed ani, iridescent warblers and tiny hummingbirds. In the park's vast underwater precincts, living reefs teem with tropical fish and dolphins, and sea turtles stop by for a bite. At twilight, bats – the island's only native mammals – swoop and dive in the purple sky.

MANGROVES These tangle-branched shoreline trees live in brackish water, their underwater roots serving as nurseries for all manner of fish, sharks and algae.

BANANAQUIT These small, yellow-bellied birds are ubiquitous throughout the Virgin Islands (they even show up on the state seal), flitting from flowers to branches to shrubs.

GREEN SEA TURTLE The largest of the hard-shelled turtles, these mammoths can grow to 500lb (227kg). Maho Bay is known as a good turtle-spotting location.

Getty Images | Porterfield - Chickering; Wolfgang Kaehler, Alamy | Marc Muench

Itineraries

Snorkelers will love Trunk Bay's Underwater Trail, Maho Bay or Coral Bay. On land, hike the Reef Bay Trail or bird-watch at Francis Bay.

◄ Make time to play on Trunk Bay.
➤ Snorkelers search for fish among the coral formations.

01

Two days

Park yourself at Cinnamon Bay Campground, the loveliest place you've ever pitched a tent. From here, explore your surroundings: hike through the deep, wet forest to the spooky ruins of a sugar plantation, swim to the tiny island in the middle of the bay's azure waters and lounge in the powdery sand. If you're feeling ambitious in the afternoon, head west to Trunk Bay, where the Underwater Trail is a top choice for newbie snorkelers. For dinner, head to Cruz Bay to sample local specialties, such as curried goat, creole chicken and roti (a savory pancake) at De' Coal Pot. The next day, wake for an early swim before setting off on a day cruise. Look out for dolphins and sea turtles as you sail the clear water, anchoring in quiet coves for splashing and snorkeling. Watch the sun set a furious orange as you head back to port. That night, treat yourself to dinner at Turtle Bay Estate House at the Caneel Bay Resort, where the likes of fennel-infused snapper and mango panna cotta are served on white tablecloths.

02

Six days

On day one, take a scenic drive along North Shore Rd, stopping for a dip at different beaches along the way: Hawksnest Bay, Trunk Bay and Cinnamon Bay. Day two, snorkel Maho Bay, keeping your eyes open for sea turtles, octopi and angel fish. Walk the short trail around nearby Francis Bay, a top bird-watching area. On day three, hike the Reef Bay Trail, exploring ancient petroglyphs and old sugar plantation ruins along the way. Have dinner in Cruz Bay; its west-facing location offers superb sunsets. Take a yacht tour on day four or do a scuba trip, scouring the depths for rays and nurse sharks. On day five, head to Coral Bay, where you can hike the Ram Head Trail and snorkel the east side's best snorkel spots. Have lunch at The Tourist Trap in Concordia (if you can find it), a seasonal roadside shack slinging blackened-fish sandwiches and lobster rolls. On day six, book a guided kayak tour along the island's coastline, where rainbow-colored fish swim under your boat as you paddle.

54

MN

Voyageurs National Park

Once a thoroughfare for French fur traders, who traveled thousands of miles each summer, America's youngest national park is a watery playland for boaters in search of big fish.

I f only these rocks could talk. That thought inevitably crosses one's mind while standing on exposed two-billion-year-old granite – that's half the age of the planet Earth – looking out over the yawning expanse of 24,000-acre (97 sq km) Lake Kabetogama. In total, Voyageur National Park encompasses four massive, linked lakes that stretch 56 miles (90km) long. The Ojibwe Indians have lived in this region for centuries and were crucial trading partners with the French Voyageurs traveling from Montreal in search of 'soft gold' – the beaver pelts that kept all of Europe in hats until the mid-1800s. Prospectors found actual gold on Little America Island in 1893, and in the early 1900s timber barons logged the entire region. A few of the old-growth white pines remain, reminding visitors just how majestic the forest here once was.

Established only 40 years ago, Voyageurs National Park is 39% water. Below its surface swim trophy walleye, northern pike and smallmouth bass. Above water, bald eagles stalk prey from the top of stately pines and loons trill haunting cries from one lake to the next. Unlike Minnesota's Boundary Waters Canoe Area Wilderness, which is directly east, motorized boats are allowed in Voyageurs, which makes the park more accessible to families, and folks who may not want to heft a canoe from lake to lake. While the four big lakes – Rainy, Kabetogama, Namakan, and Sand Point – are the main draw, the 75,000-acre (304 sq km) Kabetogama Peninsula wilderness is dotted with chains of smaller lakes.

The park is a different world in the winter. Ski, snowshoe or snowmobile the vast white expanse, or try the – underrated! – sport of ice fishing. Northern Minnesota often records the lowest temperatures in the Lower 48, but the payoff is the sight of a solitary wolf running across a frozen lake, the dancing emerald pulse of the Northern Lights or a fresh walleye dinner in January.

⬆ All the park's campsites are only accessible by watercraft but canoes and rowboats can be rented.

Stay here...

⌂ Kettle Falls Hotel

This historic hotel at the junction of Rainy and Namakan Lakes, built by a timber baron in 1910, was the epicenter of bootlegging during Prohibition. Less than 0.5-mile (0.8km) from the Canadian border and 15 miles (24km) from the closest road, the only way in is by boat or float plane. Choose from an antique-filled hotel room or a villa that sleeps up to eight people.

⌂ Woodenfrog State Forest Campground

Carved out of the boreal forest on Lake Kabetogama's shore, each of the 60 sites at this primitive campground feel luxuriously private. There's a beautiful strip of beach for all and easy access to the lake, which makes this a budget-friendly jumping off point for adventures in the park. Rent a canoe, fishing or pontoon boat at Grandview Resort.

⌂ Voyagaire Lodge & Houseboats

Family-owned Voyagaire is on Crane Lake's south shore (not officially in the park). The restaurant deck overlooks a massive lawn where kids can play until their food – specialties include a perfect walleye sandwich – is ready. The resort also rents houseboats that sleep from two to 12 people.

Do this!

Fishing

A Minnesota rite of passage, walleye are exciting to catch because they are so unpredictable. They swim deeper in the hottest months and feed right before sunrise or after sunset, but they also show up in unusual places. Better than catching a walleye is eating one, especially lightly grilled with butter, spritzed with lemon and sprinkled with salt, pepper and garlic.

Canoeing

There's nothing as peaceful as paddling through a freshwater lake, listening to the wind whistle through the white pines. Paddle quietly enough and you'll become part of the scene, in which a mama duck may be shepherding her ducklings, a loon is trilling its cross-lake call to a wayward mate, or a moose is crashing through the underbrush on the shoreline to reach its favorite watering hole. The woods are at once silent and alive.

Cross-country skiing & snowshoeing

Most years from late November to April, the park is a silent expanse of white. It may seem frozen and lifeless, but the park is actually magical at this time of year – packs of timber wolves sprint across the frozen lakes, 20lb northern pike lurk under the ice, and snowy owls take flight.

What to spot...

Dense with birch, aspen, spruce, and pine, this northern boreal forest is alive with wild critters, including moose, bear, wolves, fox, white-tailed deer, and beaver. Most don't announce their presence, but the more time you spend in these woods, the more signs of wildlife you'll see everywhere – domed beaver dams rise out of swampy lakes, eagles' nests balance atop dead trees, and pine needles from the lowest branches of balsam fir trees have mysteriously disappeared, the handiwork of hungry moose.

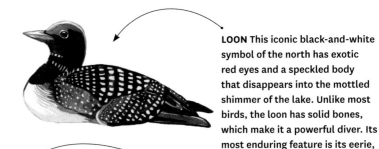

LOON This iconic black-and-white symbol of the north has exotic red eyes and a speckled body that disappears into the mottled shimmer of the lake. Unlike most birds, the loon has solid bones, which make it a powerful diver. Its most enduring feature is its eerie, unmistakable call.

BEAVER Hunted almost to extinction by the mid-1800s for the fur that supplied most of the fashionable hats in Europe, the beaver has bounced back. These fascinating herbivores spend the winter under the ice, feeding on tree branches they stored up over the winter.

BALD EAGLE This once-endangered symbol of the USA has flourished under its protective status. It's still a thrill to see this massive, white-and-gray raptor perched at the top of a white pine, silently stalking its prey.

Hike this...

01 Cruiser Lake Trail
This 9.5-mile (15.3km) hike, accessible via boat from Rainy or Kabetogama Lake, allows you to get deep into the interior wetlands – where you may see moose.

02 Beast Lake Trail
The 2.5-mile (4km) trail off Namakan Lake starts with a steep climb, but it mellows on the ridgetop, which has views to the shimmering water below.

03 Blind Ash Bay
The 3-mile (4.8km) trail starts at the Ash River Visitor Center and traverses a steep grade to an overlook of Kabetogama Lake before plunging back into the pines.

Toolbox

When to go
The park is officially open year-round, but only one of three visitor centers, Rainy Lake, is open in the winter. To beat the heat, the mosquitoes and the crowds, visit in September. For the best walleye fishing visit in the spring or fall.

Getting there
Just south of the Canadian border in Minnesota, Voyageurs is 273 miles (439km) directly north of state capital Minneapolis, roughly a five-hour drive. All three visitor centers are easily accessible off US Hwy 53.

Park in numbers

341
Area covered (sq miles)

550
Total length of shoreline (miles)

500
Number of islands

Itineraries

Canoe your way down War Club, Quill and Loiten Lakes; hike the Cruiser Lake Trail or rent a houseboat for an extended trip.

◄ Fall colors around Rainy and Kabetogama lakes; a wintery scene.
➡ A white-tail doe and fawn at Lake Kabetogama.

01

A day

Far removed from the interstate and fast-food America, Voyageurs is a destination park that requires a few days and a good boat to properly see it. But there are many travelers who pass through on their way to a private cabin at one of the hundreds of nearby lakes in northern Minnesota and Canada. For the fastest, most comprehensive sense of the park's history and its watery expanse, visit the historic Ash River Visitor Center, housed in a log cabin built in 1935 (replete with a stuffed loon and bald eagle, so large up close that they're a little creepy). Get the lay of the land from the knowledgeable rangers, then launch your own boat to tool around the archipelagos of Lake Kabetogama for a day. If you don't have your own boat, call in advance to reserve a spot paddling in a 26ft (8m) 'North Canoe,' a replica of the massive boats the Voyageurs paddled in the 1700s. Or for a panoramic view of Lake Kabetogama from land, hike 0.5 miles (0.8km) to the high point of 3-mile (4.8km) Blind Ash Bay Trail.

02

Four days

Experience the best of both worlds – the big water of Lake Kabetogama and the smaller inland lakes on Kabetogama Peninsula. Grab a key at any of the three visitor centers to access a boat from the park's supply of inland-lake canoes. Camp at Woodenfrog State Forest Campground and get an early start the next morning before the waves get big. Paddle your own boat or a rental northeast to the trailhead of Locator Lake Trail; stash the boat and portage the gear 1.9 miles (3km) into Locator Lake, where you'll find more of the park's canoes. Paddle across the lake to the campsite and spend the next two days exploring the daisy chain of War Club, Quill and Loiten Lakes (all of which have their own park canoes, so no portaging is necessary). The thrill of canoeing here is that the weather can change quickly, forcing even skilled campers to stay on their toes. Whether paddling on a mirror-calm lake, surfing 3ft (1m) swells or emergency bivvying through a thunderstorm, every day is unique.

03

Six days

Since almost half of the park is water, skip land-based accommodations and opt for a houseboat, especially if your priority is fishing, sunning and finding secluded swimming holes. The freedom of puttering in any direction at any time of day is addictive. But the quality of rental houseboats varies greatly across the four lakes, so do some homework before paying a hefty deposit. (The fleet at Voyagaire is one of the best.) Starting at the southern end of Crane Lake, there's 56 miles (90km) of park to explore. Putter through Sand Point Lake to the Kettle Falls Historic District on the north end of Namakan, or stop off to hike the 9.5-mile (15.3km) Cruiser Lake Trail that starts at the head of Ash Bay on Kabetogama. Park rules require that the boat be moored at night, but maritime maps mark all of the well-spaced and secluded overnight camping sites. A fishing boat with a motor comes with every houseboat, so anyone on board can check the lunar tables and sneak away during peak fishing hours.

55

SD

Wind Cave National Park

In the Black Hills of South Dakota, beneath prairie-roaming bison and backpackers, an apparently endless cave mysteriously breathes, whispering secrets from a hidden world.

and out of the cave – but the effect is spellbinding.

The site has been sacred to the Sioux Nation Lakota for centuries, but in 1881 it caught the attention of two wandering white men, Tom and Jesse Bingham – apparently by knocking Tom's hat off with a dramatic exhalation. In 1890, the South Dakota Mining Company paid Jesse D McDonald to search the caves for potential bounty. He discovered no tangible treasure – but McDonald sensed he'd found something almost as lucrative as minerals.

With his family – notably his son, Alvin, who methodically mapped the caves – and a partner, McDonald began running candlelit tours of the cave. Within a few years, however, Alvin had died and the partnership with 'Honest John' Stabler turned sour, resulting in a court case about who owned the rights to the site. It was decided that neither party did, and in 1903 the region joined a clutch of unique wilderness areas to be protected by President Theodore Roosevelt, becoming one of the world's earliest national parks, and the first one focused on a cave.

But what few visitors expect from Wind Cave National Park, even now, is how much there is to see and do beyond the cave. Animals range across the park, including hundreds of bison, and there are 30 miles (48km) of hiking trails.

The subterranean universe of Wind Cave is an otherworldly place, where 132 miles (212km) – and counting – of explored passages eventually give way to black holes that disappear still further into the shadows, leading to as-yet-unknown depths. The seemingly infinite catacombs feature impossibly intricate 'boxwork' formations, 60- to 100-million-year-old honeycomb-like calcite formations that are seen almost nowhere else on the planet.

And yes, it's true. The cave does breathe. In and out, like a slumbering dragon. The scientific explanation is prosaic – it's the barometric pressure equalizing inside

↑ The Wind Cave bison herd, one of the nation's most important in terms of genes, was restored more than 100 years ago.
→ A resident red-headed woodpecker.

Toolbox

When to go
The cave and visitor center are open year-round, and the underground temperature remains a steady 53°F (12°C). Hiking is best enjoyed May to September, while wildflowers are a colorful attraction in spring.

Getting there
Wind Cave is in South Dakota's Black Hills, between Hot Springs and Rapid City, less than an hour's drive from Mt Rushmore. From Rapid City, the scenic route is via Needles Highway, through Custer State Park to the park's north entrance. Large RVs and trailers go via Hot Springs. Driving through the park is free, but there's no public transportation.

Park in numbers

52.9
Area covered (sq miles)

651
Depth to which the caves have been explored (ft)

400–450
Number of bison

Stay here...

Camping
Pitch your tent on a proper prairie, on the flanks of the Black Hills and at the edge of the forest, and let the wildlife come to you. Tent and RV sites are available at the park's mystifyingly quiet Elk Mountain Campground, which is open year-round and features fire pits, drinking water and flush restrooms (the latter in the summer months only). Deer are common visitors, there's an informative evening ranger program and the night sky here is spectacular.

Backcountry camping
In the northwest part of the park hikers can strike out along routes, including the Centennial Trail, and spend a night under the stars on the prairie. Primitive camping is free, but a Backcountry Permit form must be completed in the visitor center.

Wind Cave Cabin
Lying back in the six-person hot tub, watching the star-spangled sky twinkle into life between the treetops, that great heaving, breathing cave seems a long way distant – yet this lodge, nestled high in the southern Black Hills above Hot Springs, is right on the periphery of the park.

Do this!

Caving
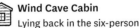
Naturally, it's the Wind Cave that pulls people in, and myriad tours allow visitors to explore many of the passages that have been mapped thus far. An interesting option is the Natural Entrance Cave Tour, where you can see the small hole that led to the original discovery of the cave. Beyond the standard Garden of Eden and slightly longer Fairgrounds tours, it's also possible to do some more-involved candlelit and crawling tours.

Wildlife-spotting
Beyond the cave, the park's impressive wildlife is a major attraction. Hundreds of bison roam freely across the small park – alongside pronghorn, mule deer, and prairie dogs – and visitors very commonly encounter these animals. Elk, who occupy the forests, can be heard bugling during fall.

Horseback riding
With 33,851 acres (137 sq km) of open prairie and forest, Wind Cave is ideal for exploring on horseback. Riders need to get a (free) permit, and avoid maintained trails and campgrounds. Guided trail rides are also available in adjoining Custer State Park.

Hike this...

Getty Images | Stephen Krasemann; Visions of America

01 Rankin Ridge Nature Trail
At the end of a scenic drive, this easy, 1-mile (1.6km) loop features 14 interpretive stops. You can't climb the tower, but the trail boasts good views of the Black Hills.

02 Wind Cave Canyon Trail
A scenic, 1.8-mile (2.9km) round-trip route renowned for bird-spotting opportunities – scan limestone cliffs for great horned owls and listen for red-headed and Lewis woodpeckers hammering away in dead trees.

03 Centennial Trail
A 6-mile (9.7km) section of this epic, 111-mile (178.6km) Black Hills trail takes hikers across prairies, through forests and along Beaver Creek. Arrange a car drop, or loop back along Highland Creek Trail.

What to spot...

The park sits on a riparian seam where the mixed-grass prairie of the Great Plains runs into the ponderosa pine forest of the Black Hills, and this wonderful mix of terrain accommodates an eclectic range of wildlife. Several mammalian species hunted to near-extinction in the 19th century, including bison, have been successfully reintroduced. Bird species range from prairie falcons and meadowlarks to forest-dwelling nuthatches, owls, woodpeckers and wild turkeys.

BLACK-FOOTED FERRET Reintroduced to Wind Cave in 2007, these beautiful and rare animals help control the park's population of prairie dogs in the absence of apex predators, such as wolves.

PRAIRIE DOG Possibly the park's most popular characters, these sociable, rabbit-sized rodents build 'towns,' with dedicated sleeping quarters and toilets. They earned their 'dog' tag thanks to their canine-like bark.

PURPLE CONEFLOWER Each spring, wildflowers set the park's mixed-grass prairies ablaze. Besides looking pretty, the purple coneflower has been used by Native Americans here for centuries for its painkilling and curative properties.

Itineraries

Hike Lookout Point Trail to Beaver Creek for wildlife watching, then choose between the Garden of Eden Tour or, for spelunkers, the Wind Cave Crawling Tour.

◄ The park's pronghorn antelope feed on grasses and sagebrush.
► Blacktail prairie dogs are part of the squirrel family.

01

An afternoon

The visitor center's staff, exhibits and video displays do an awesome job of explaining the park's attractions – from its ultra-intriguing underworld to the richness of the prairie life on the surface. If you can only spend an afternoon exploring, get a taste for the park by purchasing a standard tour ticket for the cave. The Garden of Eden Tour is the least strenuous of the options, and lasts for only an hour, but during the 0.3-mile (0.5km) subterranean stroll you still get to see some of the exquisite cave formations that Wind Cave is famous for, including boxwork, cave popcorn and flowstone. Back above ground, you have time to explore the 1.2-mile (1.9km) Elk Mountain nature trail before taking a spin along the scenic drive, spotting bison and enjoying views of the Black Hills as you go. Reach Rankin Ridge with enough daylight left to check out the 1-mile (1.6km) nature trail before heading north on Highway 87, leaving the park behind…for now.

02

A day

With a full day at your disposal get an early start, and set off on a 4.5-mile (7.2km) wake-up walk along Lookout Point Trail, returning on Centennial Trail. Beginning in the morning means you avoid the worst of the heat, and it also gives you a slightly better chance of seeing wildlife. The trail takes you across the undulations of the prairie and over Lookout Point to finish at Beaver Creek. Head back to the crossroad with Centennial Trail and follow that back to the trailhead. Explore the rest of the scenic drive, but keep one eye on your watch, because this afternoon you've booked a cave tour with a difference. The Candlelight Tour promises to take you back in time, to the end of the 19th century, when young Alvin McDonald was painstakingly making notes as he wandered around the unmapped underground wilderness into utterly unknown subterranean territory. It's a two-hour adventure that takes place in one of the less-trodden corners of the cave, and you can't wait.

03

Three or more days

The only way to really slip into Alvin McDonald's shoes is to sign up for the most extreme and exciting of the excursions into the park's catacombs: the Wind Cave Crawling Tour. As the name implies, this will see you do some proper spelunking (under supervision of experts, of course). The tour takes place well away from the busier areas of the cave, and takes four hours in total. When you emerge, blinking, back into the sunlight, have a picnic in the area by the visitor center.

After exploring the nature walks around the center, it's time to go and bag a good pitch at the first-come-first-serve Elk Mountain Campground. Once you've seen the sun go down, lie on your sleeping mat and watch the sky come alive with a billion and one stars.

On the second day, break camp and begin another adventure, taking on a section of the Highland Creek Trail, spending a night out in the backcountry and then returning south on day three along the Centennial Trail.

56

AK

Wrangell-St Elias National Park

America's largest national park offers uncharted adventures among the peaks, rivers and glaciers of one of the world's last great frontiers.

4Corners | Bernd Römmelt

K icking off expeditions into this nearly impenetrable wilderness is a challenge. But with the right skills, a healthy budget and a good helping of courage, a journey through this vast, 13.2-million-acre park – that's an area six times the size of Yellowstone – can deliver unprecedented solitude, adventure and chart-topping views unlike any other.

This park is so big, so grand, so wild that you'll find hyperbole and superlatives on every corner. Not only is it the largest national park in the US, but if you combine its area with neighboring parks (Glacier Bay National Park and Preserve; Kluane National Park and Preserve; and the Tatshenshini-Alsek Provincial Wilderness Park in Canada), you have the world's largest international protected wilderness. Nine of the 16 highest peaks in the US are found here, including towering Mt St Elias, the second highest in the US. It's also home to any number of glaciers that win big on awe factors. The Nabesna Glacier is 80 miles (129km) long, making it the longest non-polar valley glacier in the world, while the Malaspina Glacier is larger than the state of Rhode Island. You can top it all off with turn-of-the-20th-century mining towns; the sinuous Copper River, which is chock-full of salmon; an active volcano; and roaming herds of caribou.

Mostly covered in glaciers, ice and rocky mountaintops, the park has a fascinating geological past from its location at the corner of four major mountain ranges – the Wrangells to the north; the Chugach, on the southwest coast; the coastal St Elias Mountains, which rise from the Gulf of Alaska; and the eastern edge of the Alaska Range, which defines the park's northern border. All of this geological grandeur hides treasure beneath: between 1911 and 1938, mines in this region extracted huge amounts of gold and copper.

⬆ Braided river channels.
➡ Glaciers cover a quarter of the park. Previous page: Kennicott and Root glaciers.

Getty images | Frans Lanting

Toolbox

When to go
You can visit the park year round, but most people go from June to August. Visit at the edges of this high season and you may not find anybody staffing the visitor center or hotels.

Getting there
The McCarthy and Nabesna Rds take you to the edge of the wilderness, where you'll find a few old mining towns, lodges and short hikes. If you have the budget, hire a bush plane to drop you for remote hiking, climbing and paddling.

Park in numbers

20,625
Area covered (sq miles)

18,008
Height of Mt St Elias (ft)

1500
Weight of the largest grizzly bears (lb)

Stay here...

Ultima Thule Lodge
This remote lodge on the Chitina River offers unexpected luxury from the middle of the bush. The wood-hewn cabins give you the pampering you need before heading out on wild adventures in the park. Your room rate includes a guide, bush plane service, equipment and gourmet meals from the organic garden.

Ma Johnson's Hotel
Back in the mining heyday, McCarthy was the party and brothel district for wrung-out miners looking for some release after months working the Kennecott Mines. Ma Johnson's preserves the relics from this era, with small rooms featuring antiques and other rustic touches. The real treat here is sitting on the front porch, with the cool Alaskan air fanning you as you plan your next day's adventure.

Kennicott Glacier Lodge
With glacier views from some of the rooms, this restored mining building blends modern comforts with old-style charms. It's your best spot for accessing easy day hikes.

Do this!

Flightseeing
The scale and grandeur of this park only makes sense from the air. Head out for a once-in-a-lifetime flightseeing tour to see the mountaintops, glacier valleys, snowfields, rivers and untrammeled wilderness that make this one of the most iconic and dramatic mountain landscapes on earth. Add a stop in the bush for some unbelievable backwoods hikes

Rafting
Take a full-day float on the Kennicott, Nizina and Chitina Rivers, with a return flight to McCarthy on a bush plane. The run through the steep-walled Nizina Canyon is a real highlight. Not far from here, the Copper River Delta offers spectacular birding and some easy canoeing.

Glacier hiking
Traveling on a glacier is an otherworldly experience that's both transformative and just a bit scary – these moving, living frozen flows are masterworks of nature. Head out with crampons and axes for nearby day hikes on the Root Glacier, or find some vertical ice on an afternoon ice-climbing adventure.

September sees rich fall colors arrive on the alpine tundra of Wrangell-St Elias National Park.

What to spot...

Given the park's unique range – from snowcapped peaks and glaciers to spruce forests and bogs – there's an interesting combination of plant and animal life to be seen here. Stop for a while to scan the horizon and you might just spot Dall Sheep, or look near willow bogs for moose. Along the salmon streams you'll find plenty of birds, and even a few large mammals, such as grizzly and black bear, mountain goats and caribou. The park also has two herds of transplanted bison.

BALD EAGLE Soaring overhead like a beacon of freedom, these elegant birds of prey love being by the riversides, where you'll find plenty of other avian species.

CARIBOU These stately ungulates reach up to 400lb (180kg). There are 32 herds in the state of Alaska, with 950,000 animals. Unlike other deer, both sexes grow antlers.

SALMON A critical food source for Alaska Natives, bears and hungry fishers, salmon run these rivers. In a few remote villages, you might even find fish wheels used to catch them.

Hike this...

01 Root Glacier Trail
Head out from Kennicott on this classic 8-mile (13km) round-trip that takes you to the glimmering blue-and-white wonderworld of the Root Glacier.

02 Bonanza Mile Trail
From Kennicott, this steep trail ascends 3800ft (1158m) in a 9-mile (14.5km) round-trip that takes you to an amazing viewpoint – where you can see the confluence of the Root and Kennicott Glaciers.

03 Skookum Volcano Trail From the Nabesna Road, head up this 2.5-mile (4km) trail to explore an eroded volcanic system. You end the trip on an alpine pass where Dall sheep are often sighted.

Itineraries

Hike Root Glacier and Bonanza Mine Trails, paddle the rivers, ice-climb the glaciers or have a bush plane drop you into remote escapism.

◄ Ice climbing on Root Glacier, for the experienced only.
► The railroad bridge to Kennecott mill town; inside Kennecott Glacier.

01

Three days

There are two rough roads that lead into the park. The McCarthy Rd is the most popular and takes you through excellent hiking territory, past the Kuskulana River, with its towering bridge, and on to the Kennicott River, where you cross a footbridge to access wild-haired McCarthy; stop here for the night or take a shuttle on to Kennecott, where you'll find the majority of park services.

Spend your second day getting acquainted with the park, taking day hikes on the Root Glacier and Bonanza Mine Trails, and a fun history tour of the town. If you're not tuckered out, check out an evening park ranger program at the Copper River Princess Wilderness Lodge or head to McCarthy for some bluegrass stomp sessions.

On day three, take on a little more adventure with a paddle on nearby rivers or an ice-climbing glacier adventure. On your return, stop in the small village of Chitina for salmon fishing and bird-watching, before heading back to daily life.

02

Seven days

If time and money aren't an issue, this dream itinerary should get you going. Start with a drive along the remote Nebesna Rd. Stop in at the Slana Ranger Station for some tips on local hikes, then continue to Kendesnii Campground for a night or two of chilled-out camping, with day trips along the nearby Caribou Creek Trail and Skookum Volcano Trail. Return to the main road and head to the southern entrance at McCarthy. From here, you may consider three nights in the remote Ultima Thule Lodge, or

spring for a bush plane to take you to one of the remote corners of the park. There are 14 backcountry cabins in the park: most are rustic log-cabin affairs left over from the mining and trapping days; some sit idyllically on lakes and are easily accessed by bush plane. If you have time to spare, consider taking on a skiing or climbing expedition on one of the vertiginous peaks found here. End your trip with a paddle on nearby rivers or a flight down to Cordova for sea-kayaking.

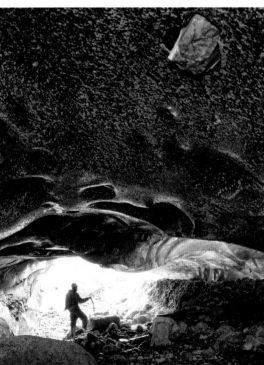

57

WY

Yellowstone National Park

Yellowstone looms large in the public's imagination, the name people are most likely to associate with 'national park' – the very symbol of the American West.

Few who haven't visited Yellowstone know how weird it is. Weird in a good way – a fantastic way – but weird nonetheless. This isn't all scenic mountains and wildflower meadows. This is fields of burbling mud like something out of *Curse of the Swamp Creature*. This is cracks in the earth that belch steam and howl like the mouth of hell. This is pastel-blue hot springs that will boil an adult alive in three seconds flat. This is geysers that erupt without warning, sending sulfurous water hundreds of feet in the air. And sure, there are also scenic mountains and wildflower meadows – and a pretty darn photogenic canyon, some grand glacial lakes and magnificent old park lodges, all raw logs and antlers and three-story stone fireplaces. But first and foremost, Yellowstone is about its geothermal features, in all their bizarre glory.

Yellowstone sits atop an active caldera, the remains of a supervolcano that last erupted 650,000 years ago. Volcanic activity beneath the caldera gives rise to more than 10,000 geothermal features within the park, from geysers to pools of bubbling mud to fumeroles (cracks in the ground that release steam) to hot springs. Wandering through Geyser Country, the area of the park with the most impressive geothermal features, is like visiting another planet. Time things right, and you can see half a dozen geysers erupt within a few hours.

Yellowstone was inhabited by Native Americans for some 11,000 years before trapper John Colter, the first European-American to see it, reported it in 1807 as a place of 'fire and brimstone.' President Ulysses S Grant signed Yellowstone into existence in 1872, making it the world's first national park. Most visitors arrived here by

rail until the mid-1900s, when it became a magnet for a new breed of car tourists. Today, more than 3 million visitors hit the park each year. To visit Yellowstone is to cross a major item off many people's bucket list.

⬆ A hot spring in the West Thumb Geyser Basin.
➡ A gray wolf in Yellowstone.
Previous page: Grand Prismatic Spring in the Midway Geyser Basin.

Toolbox

When to go
As Yellowstone's roads can become massively crowded in July and August, the most pleasant times to visit are early spring to early summer and late summer to early fall. You'll still have warm enough weather, but far fewer traffic jams.

Getting there
Some 96% of Yellowstone is within the state of Wyoming, in its far northwest corner. There are small airports near the park at Jackson Hole, Cody and West Yellowstone, but Denver and Salt Lake City, both about a day's drive away, are the nearest major facilities.

Park in numbers

3468
Area covered (sq miles)

300
Height of highest geyser, Steamboat (ft)

674–839
Number of grizzly bears

Stay here...

Lake Yellowstone Hotel
Built in 1891, this Colonial Revival building evokes the elegance of a slower age of travel. Play along and nestle into one of the sunroom's armchairs with a novel; have a cocktail in the lounge as a pianist plays; dine on fresh trout and bison tenderloin. Rooms are renovated to modern standards. Rustic cabins are an option for the budget-minded.

Old Faithful Inn
An example of 'Parkitecture,' this 327-room lodge is a log palace. The open three-story lobby is all glossy wood and candelabras; day-trippers sit around the stone fireplace. It's been a popular choice since it was built in 1903 – fortunately, rooms have been updated since then, with simple, plaid furnishings and wooden desks.

Roosevelt Lodge
Raw wood and stone give this lodge an Old West feel. Horses in a nearby corral, stagecoach adventures and an Old West Dinner Cookout complete the picture. Unsurprisingly, this is a popular choice for families with kids. The Frontier Cabins are simple but comfortable, while the Roughrider Cabins, heated by woodstoves, are for the adventurous.

Do this!

Geyser-watching
Old Faithful is not Yellowstone's biggest geyser. It's simply faithful. Erupting every 90 minutes, it's one of six that park officials offer eruption time predictions for. Get them early and you can catch Old Faithful exhale 3700 to 8400 gallons (14,000 to 31,800L), then hit the boardwalk path to watch neighbors, such as Riverside and Daisy, in action.

Boating & floating
Vast, blue and very deep, Yellowstone Lake is the biggest lake in America above 7000ft (2134m). Skip across its waters in a rented sailboat or explore its bays and channels in a canoe. For a grand adventure, paddle the Lewis River Channel between Lewis Lake and Shoshone Lake. Or take the relaxed route by floating down the Yellowstone River in a raft.

Hiking
A slash of pink and orange stone, the 1000ft-deep (305m) Grand Canyon of the Yellowstone cleaves the land for some 20 miles (32km). At its northeast end, the jade-green Yellowstone River crashes over Upper Falls and Lower Falls before raging southwest. Sure, you can admire the canyon from the rim, taking pictures at lookouts such as Artist Point – but why not get closer? Hike Uncle Tom's Trail, with steel ladders running down to the viewing deck of Lower Falls.

What to spot...

The sheer number and variety of large mammals have given Yellowstone the reputation as a sort of safari park; you'll see what we mean when you wind up in a 50-car jam behind a grizzly. But almost every part of the park is unbelievably rich in flora and fauna, from the songbird-filled lodgepole pines and slopes of fiery-tipped Wyoming paintbrush to mountain goats scrambling up rocky outcrops. There are some 1300 species of native plants, including dozens of rainbow-hued wildflowers.

GRIZZLY BEAR In summer, the iconic bears can be most easily spotted in the meadows between Tower-Roosevelt and Canyon, and in the Hayden and Lamar Valleys. Lock up your food!

BISON Yellowstone has nearly 5000 bison, who have lived here since prehistoric times. Look for them in the Hayden and Lamar Valleys.

GRAY WOLF Killed off by ranchers in the early 1900s, wolves were reintroduced in 1995; there are now about 100 in the park. Lamar Valley is your best bet to see them.

Hike this...

O1 Fairy Falls
For a birds-eye view of psychedelic Grand Prismatic Spring, hike this popular trail for 1 mile (1.6km), then cut left up a faint track leading up the slope.

O2 Mt Washburn
Peak-baggers can't miss this 10,243ft (3122m) summit, with 360-degree views over Yellowstone Lake and the Hayden Valley – all the way to the Beartooth Range. Leave early to beat crowds. A hard 5 miles (8km).

O3 Elephant Back Mountain
This family-friendly, 3.5-mile (5.6km) loop offers killer views over Yellowstone Lake and beyond. The summit is a popular picnic spot.

Itineraries

Follow the geyser trail from Old Faithful to Norris Geyser Basin for eruption suspense; hike Yellowstone's Grand Canyon; or kayak, swim or fish in Yellowstone Lake.

◄ Fairy Falls; Old Faithful Geyser.
► Pure-bred Yellowstone bison.
Previous page: the Lower Falls of Yellowstone River.

01
Two days

You can drive the entirety of the figure-eight shaped Grand Loop Rd in two very packed days, seeing most of the park's most iconic sights. Start off early at West Thumb, hitting Old Faithful and the rest of the geyser trail at the first daylight eruption times. Proceed to Grand Prismatic Spring to gawp at the neon blues and reds, then head north towards Norris, where the Norris Geyser Basin is home to some of the coolest, loudest, most colorful thermal features in the park. Nearby are the Artist

Paint Pots, so called for their colorful hues of mud. Grab some fortification at Canyon Village, then end the day watching osprey fly over Yellowstone Lake. The next morning, drive straight to Grand Canyon of the Yellowstone and watch the early sun play across the pastel rockface. Continuing northwest, take in the falls around Tower Junction, than hit the sulfur-smelling terraces at Mammoth. Dine on bison meatballs at the classy Mammoth Hot Springs Dining Room while elk graze on the hotel lawn outside.

02
Four days

Do everything in the two-day itinerary, but take your time with it. Plan on saving the Grand Canyon of the Yellowstone for the third day, so you can spend several hours hiking around the rim or down Uncle Tom's Trail. Spend the afternoon of the third day around Lake Yellowstone, which is a fly fisher's paradise, with endless edges to explore by kayak or canoe. Dine at Lake Yellowstone Hotel Dining Room (reservations necessary), a grand old establishment where duck risotto and Montana lamb is

served on white tablecloths.

Pick at least one full day-hike for the fourth day – Mt Washburn is always popular or, for fewer crowds, try the 16-mile (26km) loop through Pelican Valley, where the rolling hills are carpeted with wildflowers, and grizzlies amble through the meadows looking for berries. If you don't have to leave early on the fifth morning, do some dawn wildlife-watching before heading home – staying near the Lamar or Hayden Valleys will make this easier.

03
A week

On day one, start things off with a bang at Old Faithful, timing your visit to see other geysers, such as Daisy and Riverside, go off. You can easily spend half a day or more wandering the boardwalk trails, taking in the cerulean, turquoise and jade waters of the hot springs. Don't miss lunch at the stunning rustic dining room in Old Faithful Inn. One day two, try kayaking on Yellowstone Lake or fish for cutthroat trout in its navy waters. On day three, hike Uncle Tom's Trail in the Grand Canyon

of the Yellowstone, coming daringly close to the thundering Lower Falls. On day four, get up very early for the best wildlife-spotting ops in the Lamar Valley. One day five, pack lunch and plenty of water and head out early to summit Mt Washburn, one of the park's most iconic hikes. On day six, hit some of the geothermal features on the south Great Loop, including Grand Prismatic Spring and Norris Geyser Basin. On the seventh day, take in the terraces at Mammoth before heading home.

58

CA

Yosemite National Park

Celebrate a glacier-carved landscape of granite peaks, wildflower meadows and alpine lakes in one of the USA's oldest national parks.

Yosemite

Entering Yosemite Valley, the panoramas from roadside Tunnel View make everyone gasp. Standing above the lush green valley floor, carpeted with meadows and a meandering river, you'll view a scene that's been 10 million years in the making. On the right, Bridalveil Fall gushes over cliffs, while above it hang the pointed Cathedral Rocks. On the left, El Capitán towers more than 3000ft (914.4m) above the valley floor – it's the largest granite monolith in the world, issuing a siren's call to rock climbers. Far off in the distance is the curved tooth of the polished granite Half Dome, the park's most famous landmark. Yet all this is only the beginning of Yosemite's natural wonders.

The Sierra Nevada mountains – what naturalist John Muir anointed as 'the Range of Light' – are California's backbone. As recently as 10,000 years ago, during the last ice age, glaciers were still hard at work shaping these mountain peaks, alpine lakes, granite domes and river canyons and valleys. Yosemite's showstopping landscapes are matched by its wealth of wildlife. Spot a black bear sauntering beside the trail below Glacier Point. Capture a portrait of summer wildflowers at Tuolumne Meadows. Ogle giant sequoia trees that have been growing in Mariposa Grove for almost two millennia.

Yosemite is a park for all seasons. When snowmelt in the Sierra Nevada high country makes rivers swell, waterfalls in the valley spring to life. When summer warms the grassy meadows, lakes and high-mountain passes, hikers and backpackers set out on overnight trips while families swim and cycle around the valley. In fall, rock climbers can still be spotted hanging off granite walls

and boulders. Even winter is a beautiful time to visit, especially after a snowstorm – when you can snowshoe or cross-country ski through fresh powder to icy waterfalls or hushed groves of giant sequoia trees.

⬆ Rafting down the Merced River.
➡ Mist Trail. Previous page: Yosemite Valley from Tunnel View, with Bridalveil Falls, El Capitan and Half Dome in the distance.

Getty Images | Lorne Resnick, Alamy | Gabbro

Toolbox

When to go
Yosemite Valley is open year-round. High-elevation Tioga Rd to Tuolumne Meadows and Glacier Point Rd both close after the first major snowfall in fall; they don't reopen until the following year in late spring or early summer.

Getting there
East of California's Central Valley, Yosemite is a three-hour drive from San Francisco, which has a major international airport. Amtrak trains stop in Merced, from where buses connect to the park. Free shuttle buses circle Yosemite Valley year-round.

Park in numbers

1190
Area covered (sq miles)

1890
Year the park was established

2425
Height of Yosemite Falls (ft)

Stay here...

Majestic Yosemite Hotel
Designed by famed park architect Gilbert Stanley Underwood in the 1920s, this elegant stone and wood hotel in Yosemite Valley has hosted everyone from Queen Elizabeth II to Steve Jobs. If you're there in winter, curl up with a hot toddy by the roaring fireplace in the Great Lounge.

Half Dome Village
Offering a family summer-camp atmosphere (but open year-round), this collection of canvas-and-wood tent-cabins beneath Glacier Point has been a Yosemite Valley fixture since 1899. Swim outside in the pool when the weather is hot; in wintertime you can opt for ice skating on an outdoor rink.

Big Trees Lodge
Step back into Victorian times at this national historic landmark, located in the southern area of the park not far from the Mariposa Grove of giant sequoias. Built in 1876, the white, multi-story hotel has wraparound verandas, cocktails and evening entertainment. Civilized vacation resort activities include golf and tennis.

Do this!

Rock climbing
Yosemite Valley is a wellspring of modern rock climbing in the US. Yves Chouinard (founder of the Patagonia brand) and Royal Robbins were among the first to tackle these granite slabs. Today you'll find big-wall climbers hanging out at Camp 4 near El Capitan in Yosemite Valley from spring through fall, and at high-elevation Tuolumne Meadows, with its many granite domes and bouldering opportunities, during summer.

Swimming
Splash in the Merced River on a hot summer's day, or brave the icier waters of alpine lakes, such as Tenaya Lake (off Tioga Rd near Tuolumne Meadows), which has a sandy, crescent-shaped beach.

Skiing & snoeshowing
Yosemite Ski and Snowboard Area is California's oldest ski resort. Beginners can learn to swoosh downhill on skis or a snowboard here, while cross-country enthusiasts can ski along Glacier Point Rd to a wilderness hut overlooking the valley. For snowshoeing, go tramping around the valley or to groves of giant sequoias.

⬅ There are dozens of routes up El Capitan, some taking two or three weeks to complete.

What to spot...

Yosemite was designated a World Heritage site in 1984, partly because of its rich natural resources. An astonishing variety of wildlife ranges across more than 1000 sq miles (2590 sq km) of wilderness and along two nationally recognized 'Wild and Scenic Rivers,' the Tuolumne and the Merced. Over a thousand plant species thrive here, as do more than 400 vertebrate animals in varied life zones, from chaparral-covered foothills to stream-fed alpine meadows to glaciers high above the tree line.

SIERRA NEVADA BIGHORN SHEEP
This endangered horned animal with a white rump-patch grazes craggy peaks and alpine meadows, where it is rarely seen by humans.

BLACK BEAR Faster and usually bigger than you are, black bears can eat up to 20,000 calories a day while preparing for their winter hibernation.

WESTERN TANAGER The male of this forest bird species is easily spotted – look for its bright-red head, yellow breast and black wings.

Hike this...

01 Mist Trail
It's a thrilling, 1.6- to 5.4-mile (2.6 to 8.7km) climb up slippery stone steps from Yosemite Valley to the top of Vernal and Nevada Falls.

02 May Lake & Mt Hoffman
Take a gentle forest walk to an alpine lake, followed by a peak ascent for panoramic views. The trail is 2.5 to 6 miles (4 to 9.6km).

03 Half Dome
Epic, all-day 14-mile (22.5km) hike and climb to the top of the park's most famous granite dome; advance permits required (by lottery).

Itineraries

See Yosemite Falls, the tallest waterfall in North America, watch the sun set from Glacier Point or laze by Tenaya Lake.

← Reaching Nevada Falls via the Mist Trail; hiking to Yosemite Falls.
→ A black-tail deer with fawn.

01
A day

The road into Yosemite Valley winds beneath trees beside the Merced River, where early morning fog may linger. Stop the car and get out for the short stroll to Bridalveil Fall, a monumental cliffside cascade. Further east, leave your car behind in a day-use parking lot and hop on the free shuttle bus to Yosemite Village. Peruse fine-art prints at the Ansel Adams Gallery and the free history, ecology and art exhibits inside the visitor center and museum. After grabbing a trail lunch from Degnan's

Deli, get back on the shuttle bus for a ride to the Happy Isles stop. Head to the Mist Trail and start climbing the stone staircase to the top of not one, but two waterfalls where rainbows shimmer in the spray.

After hiking back to the trailhead, catch the shuttle bus to Yosemite Falls, a triple-tiered beauty that's the tallest waterfall in North America. As the sun sets, walk over to the Lodge at Yosemite Falls and the cozy Mountain Room restaurant and lounge for dinner and drinks.

02
Two days

After waking up at your campsite underneath pine trees in Yosemite Valley, take an early morning walk out to Mirror Lake, which perfectly reflects Half Dome in its still waters during spring. Afterward, have a picnic lunch in El Capitán Meadow while watching rock climbers scaling the granite monolith. In the afternoon, drive up Glacier Point Rd, stopping to scramble up Sentinel Dome before arriving at the famous viewpoint. From Glacier Point, you can look straight out at the hooked shape of

Half Dome and down over dramatic Nevada and Vernal Falls. Stay to watch the sun set, then head back down to the valley. Reserve a table in advance for dinner in the grand dining room of the Majestic Yosemite Hotel, or else content yourself with drinks and small bites in the hotel's convivial lounge, where the piano tinkles with old-fashioned melodies from the early 20th century.

Before going back to camp, take a stroll in the moonlight by the Merced River, crossing over the historic Stoneman Bridge.

03
Three days

Follow the two-day itinerary then, on day three, take a scenic drive up the Tioga Rd, which follows an old pioneer wagon trail and an even earlier Native American footpath. Your final destination is Tuolumne Meadows, fed by streams and blushing with wildflowers in early summer. En route, stop at high-elevation Olmsted Point to get a different perspective on the Yosemite Valley – you'll recognize Half Dome in the distance. From the vista point, free seasonal shuttle buses head east to Tuolumne Meadows, where

you can hike up granite domes and picnic by the river. After lunch, head back to Tenaya Lake and laze by the beach all afternoon or take a chilly swim. If you're eager to stretch your legs, instead take a short hike to smaller May Lake, where you can scramble up Mt Hoffman, set at the geographical center of the park, for impressive 360-degree views.

When the sun goes down, if you're reluctant to leave all this high Sierra beauty, pitch a tent or rent a canvas tent cabin at Tuolumne Meadows on your last night.

59

UT

Zion National Park

Narnia, Mordor, Westeros... Zion? With its castle-like walls, weeping rocks and shadowy narrows, Zion Canyon beckons like a valley of enchantment in an epic storybook.

Your adventure begins on the Zion–Mt Carmel Hwy as it twists through groves of golden sandstone. Gripping the wheel more tightly, you wonder about the 1.1-mile (1.8km) tunnel ahead, a Depression-era marvel that jackhammers through a sandstone wall. And whoosh – you're suddenly inside its inky darkness. Arched galleries flash past, offering a whip-fast glimpse of the red rock grandeur to come. Back in the brightness, the road plummets through six tight switchbacks, squeezed close by red rock walls.

The heart of the park is Zion Canyon, a verdant valley flanked by sheer walls of Navajo Sandstone. These red rock cliffs, soaring more than 1000ft (305m) feet overhead, began as sand dunes more than 200 million years ago. After a turbulent period of geological uplift, the Virgin River and its tributaries began carving the canyon and its narrows. Today, the riparian landscape attracts wildlife galore – as well as beauty-seeking tourists. To reduce congestion, the park prohibits cars on the canyon floor from mid-March through October and on weekends in November; park shuttles stop at nine sights and trailheads. The Kolob Canyons section of the park, home to a high-elevation scenic drive, is 40 miles (64.4km) northwest.

Southern Paiute Indians roamed these lands before the arrival of Mormon settlers in the mid-1800s. Mukuntuweap National Monument, which was named after the Southern Paiute word for 'straight canyon,' was created in 1909. The name was changed to Zion National Monument in 1918 – 'Zion' being a biblical term for a place of refuge or sanctuary – and the national park was established the following year. Today, with

its skinny slot canyons and vertigo-inducing cliffs, the park is a prime spot for outdoor adventure: canyoneering and wild hiking, from the Narrows to Angels Landing, bring the adrenaline junkies. But the allure of the park is also writ small. The low-key spots – a weeping rock, hanging gardens, hidden ponds – may impress you as much as the red rock.

Getty Images | Michele Falzone

Toolbox

When to go
High season is May through September, but temperatures commonly soar to 100°F (38°C) while visitors clog the canyon floor. May brings both wildflowers and bugs. Fall is cooler and ideal for hiking.

Getting there
Zion Canyon borders the town of Springdale in southwestern Utah. The park can be reached from the west or east on Hwy 9 (called the Zion–Mt Carmel Highway between Zion Canyon and the east park entrance station). Las Vegas is 160 miles (257.5km) southwest via Hwy 9 and I-15. Kolob Canyons is 30 miles (48.3km) northeast of St George, Utah, off the I-15.

Park in numbers

229
Area covered (sq miles)

75
Species of mammals

6521
Height of Observation Point (ft)

Stay here...

🏠 Zion Lodge
The wide and grassy front lawn here is a gorgeous place to daydream. Crisp blue skies, crimson cliffs and a homespun brown lodge frame this inspiring spot. Rooms in the lodge and its cabins channel the Old West with a bit of style – and no TVs. Overnight guests are permitted to drive into the canyon to park at the lodge.

⛺ South Campground & Watchman Campground
A dip in the adjacent Virgin River is a pleasant way to cool off before settling into your camp chair. Once settled, cottonwoods provide the shade while sandstone cliffs offer the view. Both campgrounds are within walking distance of the Zion Canyon Visitor Center.

🏠 Under the Eaves Inn
The details close the deal at this quaint 1930s bungalow, with a clawfoot tub in the suite, arts-and-crafts style in the living room, and Adirondack chairs in the garden. Seven rooms are scattered across the main house, a cabin and a cottage.

Do this!

Canyoneering
Rappelling into a narrow slot canyon is just one part of a canyoneering adventure in Zion – expect to do some wading, scrambling, swimming, hiking and problem-solving ('Just how do we escape this diabolical maze?'). The names of Zion's most famous slot canyons evoke their individual charms: the Narrows and the Subway.

🚲 Cycling
Pull on your 'Life is Good' T-shirt for a morning pedal on the Zion Canyon Scenic Drive. This 7-mile (11.3km) strip of easy pavement runs alongside the Virgin River as it unfurls beneath iconic big rocks, from the Court of Patriarchs to Angels Landing. No cars are allowed in high season.

🔭 Bird-watching
As you scan the skies from your perch atop Angels Landing, keep watch for California condors soaring gracefully between the sandstone monoliths – their 9½-ft (3m) wingspan is something amazing to behold. But California condors are just the start: the bird list at Zion includes 288 species.

← Hiking The Narrows inside Zion Canyon. Previous page: the Virgin River flows through the park.

What to spot...

Elevation at Zion stretches from 3666ft (1117m) at Coal Pits Wash to 8726ft (2660m) at Horse Ranch Mountain. Four ecosystems exist between these extremes: desert, riparian, piñon-juniper and conifer woodland. Within these pockets of life are more than 1000 species of plants. Among the mammals you might spot are mule deer, bighorn sheep and rock squirrels. A further 29 reptile species and almost 300 bird species seek food and shelter here too.

CALIFORNIA CONDOR These enormous scavengers, which date from prehistoric times, have a 9½-ft (3m) wingspan. They almost became extinct in the 1980s, but a successful breeding-and-release program has boosted their numbers.

ARIZONA TOAD This plump brownish toad looks for love in shaded, high-elevation tributaries of the Virgin River. The male mating call is a 6-second, high-pitched trill.

PIÑON PINE Famous for their crooked trunks and nutritious edible nuts, piñons grow on dry and rocky sites at high elevations, often near juniper trees. Slow growers, they can take 80 years to reach 10ft (3m).

Hike this...

01 The Narrows
Iconic and challenging, this 16-mile (25.8km) one-way hike squeezes through wet and skinny canyons along the Virgin River's North Fork.

02 Angels Landing
Possibly America's best day hike, this 5.4-mile (8.6km) round-trip trail hugs a cliff, climbs tight switchbacks and crosses a thin ridge flanked by sheer drops. The reward? An epic view of Zion Canyon.

03 Emerald Pools
Streams of water tumble into tiered pools on this 5-mile (8km) round-trip climb into Zion Canyon's greenery.

Itineraries

Summit Angels Landing for sheer canyon views; hike the Narrows; go canyoneering; or admire red rock grandeur on Kolob Canyon Rd.

⬅ Inside a slot canyon; walking up Walter's Wiggles.
➡ Bighorn sheep are at home high on a bluff.

01
A day

Baby, it's a busy day. Hop the Springdale shuttle to the Zion Canyon Visitor Center. From here, the visitor shuttle rolls into the canyon, where splashes of riparian greenery soften the majestic red walls. Your stop? The Grotto, the starting point for the Angels Landing Trail.

Cross the Virgin River and look up...up...up. Hmm, just where have those angels got to? Let your adrenalin carry you up a steep cliff wall, then relax with a romp through Refrigerator Canyon. The burn will return on Walter's Wiggles, but you can catch your breath at Scouts Lookout. End your hike here or, if you dare, teeter across a ridge with a scramble up Hogsback Ridge. The reward is the 5790ft-high (1765m) summit of Angels Landing. It's a fine picnicking spot.

For a taste of the Narrows, ride the shuttle to the Temple of Sinawava stop at the end of the route. From here, follow the Riverside Walk 1 mile (1.6km) upstream, then splash into the mouth of the dragon, otherwise known as the Narrows. End this wild day with a hearty meal in Springdale.

02
Two days

Swoop into the park on the exhilarating Zion–Mt Carmel Hwy and stop by the Zion Canyon Visitor Center for the 'Ride Along with a Ranger' tour, an entertaining 90-minute introduction to the park, which includes a few stops not on the regular route. Enjoy lunch at the Zion Canyon Lodge, then explore the canyon by bike or by horseback. Dig into carne asada tacos at the Whiptail Grill in Springdale for dinner, then return to the park for an evening ranger talk about wildlife, history or the starry skies.

The next morning, fuel up with coffee and crepes at Meme's Café in Springdale, then tick more adventures off your life list. Test your fear of heights on the Angels Landing Trail; huff and puff up to expansive park views on the Observation Point Trail, which tops out at 6521ft (1988m); or rappel into a sandstone slot canyon (canyoneering outfitters in Springdale can kit you out with the proper gear). Post-adventure, celebrate with a rib-eye and a Utah-brewed Polygamy Porter at Bit & Spur Restaurant & Saloon.

03
Four days

Begin the morning with green-chile-and-chorizo omelet at Oscar's Cafe. You'll burn off this meal on tomorrow's adventure: the 16-mile (25.8km) trek through the Narrows. After breakfast, stop by the Zion Canyon Visitor Center for questions about weather, campsites and required permits. Loosen your muscles with an easy afternoon hike to the lush Emerald Pools, followed by an afternoon ranger talk or a scenic drive on the Zion–Mt Carmel Hwy.

In the morning, the trail from Chamberlain Ranch to the Narrows leads to a wonderland of towering canyon walls, tight passages and hanging gardens, not to mention splashing and wading aplenty. Find your reserved riverside campsite and enjoy your night in the wild. On day three, emerge just north of the terminus of the Riverside Walk and explore more of the canyon (if your legs allow). Spend your last day on a stunning red rock drive on Kolob Canyons Rd, with sweeping views of cliffs, mountains and finger canyons to wow you.

Index

First Edition

Published in August 2016

by Lonely Planet Global Limited

ABN 36 005 607 983

www.lonelyplanet.com

ISBN 978 1 7603 4064 3

© Lonely Planet 2016

Printed in China

10 9 8 7 6 5 4 3 2

Managing Director, Publishing Piers Pickard

Associate Publisher & Commissioning Editor Robin Barton

Art Direction Daniel Di Paolo

Layout Johanna Lundberg

Editors Karyn Noble, Ali Lemer

Index Tasmin Waby

Wildlife illustrations Holly Exley

Spot illustrations Jacob Rhoades

Cartographer Wayne Murphy

Pre-press Production Graham Parsons

Print Production Larissa Frost, Nigel Longuet

Written by: Amy Balfour, Becky Ohlsen, Carolyn McCarthy, Emily Matchar, Greg Benchwich, Patrick Kinsella, Regis St Louis, Sara Benson, Stephanie Pearson

LONELY PLANET OFFICES

AUSTRALIA

The Malt Store, Level 3, 551 Swanston St, Carlton, Victoria 3053 T: 03 8379 8000

USA

150 Linden St, Oakland, CA 94607 T: 510 250 6400

IRELAND

Unit E, Digital Court, The Digital Hub, Rainsford St, Dublin 8

UNITED KINGDOM

240 Blackfriars Rd, London SE1 8NW T: 020 3771 5100

STAY IN TOUCH

lonelyplanet.com/contact

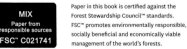

MIX
Paper from responsible sources
FSC™ C021741

Paper in this book is certified against the Forest Stewardship Council™ standards. FSC™ promotes environmentally responsible, socially beneficial and economically viable management of the world's forests.